5/10

THE
STUDENT-ATHLETE'S COLLEGE RECRUITMENT GUIDE

THE
STUDENT-ATHLETE'S
COLLEGE RECRUITMENT
GUIDE

ASHLEY B. BENJAMIN, M.D.
MICHAEL CAUTHEN
PATRICK DONNELLY

Ferguson Publishing
An imprint of Infobase Publishing

The Student-Athlete's College Recruitment Guide

Ferguson
An imprint of Infobase Publishing
132 West 31st Street
New York NY 10001

Library of Congress Cataloging-in-Publication Data

Benjamin, Ashley B.
  The student-athlete's college recruitment guide / Ashley B. Benjamin, Michael Cauthen, Patrick Donnelly. — 1st ed.
      p. cm.
  Includes index.
  ISBN-13: 978-0-8160-7662-8 (hardcover : alk. paper)
  ISBN-10: 0-8160-7662-6 (hardcover : alk. paper)
  1. College athletes—Recruiting—United States I. Cauthen, Michael. II. Donnelly, Patrick, 1956– III. Title.
  GV350.5.B46 2009
  796.04'3—dc22
                              2008047689

Ferguson books are available at special discounts when purchased in bulk quantities for businesses, associations, institutions, or sales promotions. Please call our Special Sales Department in New York at (212) 967-8800 or (800) 322-8755.

You can find Ferguson on the World Wide Web at
http://www.fergpubco.com

Text design adapted by Kerry Casey
Cover design by Takeshi Takahashi

Printed in the United States of America

MP FOF 10 9 8 7 6 5 4 3 2 1

This book is printed on acid-free paper and contains 30 percent post consumer recycled content.

Contents

Acknowledgments

Ashley B. Benjamin: To my son, Armand, who teaches me to live every minute, and my daughter, Melayna, who reminds me to smell the roses along the way.

Completion of this book, almost 20 years after the idea first took hold, has been a very rewarding experience. This could not have been accomplished without my coauthors, role modeling from my coaches, feedback from our editors, or support from family and friends.

First, thanks to Michael Cauthen, whose coaching expertise, critical insights regarding many of our topics, and sustained enthusiasm has been invaluable. During discussions, Michael and I realized that a talented sports journalist as a coauthor could provide a greater breadth of sports coverage, as well as access to some of the most successful and ethical coaches, both necessary components for this book to reach its objectives. I am very grateful to Patrick Donnelly, whose inside knowledge coupled with his unique angles on many aspects of the recruiting process really added a professional touch.

This book in many ways describes how ethical coaches should act. Being coached by or coaching with the following coaches allowed me to personally conceptualize what good coaching is all about. Thanks to Roger Bowen, Tom Dowling, Herbert Foster, Randall Pfeiffer, Brian Renshaw, Steve Sublett, Robert Timmons, and Frank Zubovich for role modeling the belief that coaches have the capacity to educate in a very unique way.

As much as we believed we had an idea worthy of publication, it was editors James Chambers and Jennifer Way who really gave this project hope, direction, clarification, and an emphasis on ensuring that our words conveyed the facts to the reader in a profoundly meaningful way. Their flexibility and hard work has helped us create a better product than we envisioned possible.

I want to thank my wife, Mahshid Mosallaei-Benjamin, without whose support, acting as a soundboard on the cultural and medical aspects sections, and personal sacrifice, this book could not have been accomplished. A theme that is noted throughout the book—that the learning process and ethics are not only complementary but heavily intertwined—has been instilled in me by my parents, Bezaleel S. and Nora Benjamin. I also appreciate my sister, Jennifer Jenks, and brother-in-law, John Jenks, who utilized their journalism backgrounds to help keep my writing honest and precise. In addition, fellow writer and friend Kenneth Crawford played a key role in helping me weather all the ups and downs during the last two decades of the writing process, as well as provided insights regarding many aspects of the book.

Too numerous to mention are the many family and friends whose support and interest have been sustaining. Finally, I sincerely thank all the coaches, athletes, and other individuals whose willingness to share their many personal stories has provided the reader with a true inside look at the college recruiting process.

Michael Cauthen: I would like to thank, most of all, my co-author, Dr. Ashley Benjamin. It was his vision that began this project, nearly two decades ago. His dogged persistence, great organizational skills, foresight, and discipline ultimately guided this book to its completion. But had I not been under the tutelage of former Ohio State University track and field coach Mamie Rollins, between 1985 and 1988, Ashley and I would have never met. I would never have had the wonderful opportunity to collaborate on a book with our coauthor, and my newly found friend, Patrick Donnelly. I also need to pay homage, therefore, to those sports mentors who have initiated and facilitated my rich and fruitful association with the scholastic sports community.

I began my career in collegiate competition at Alfred University, some 33 years ago. I was coached there by the now retired and outstanding coach of track and field and cross-country, Clifford DuBreuill. My first experience as a coach was made possible, in the early 1980s, by Lane Custer, the boy's head track and cross-country coach of West Lafayette High School in Indiana. Under both mentors, I learned what it was like to mold the talents and competitive aspirations of young student-athletes into championship form.

My greatest mentor in the sports realm, however, was the late director of the USA TAC coaches' training program, and the former head of Purdue University's women's track and field and cross-country programs, Fred Wilt. Coach Wilt was a two-time Olympian, winner of seven cross-country titles, and author of the *Encyclopedia of Track and Field*. But more than anything, he was an extraordinary teacher. As his assistant coach (1983–1985), I learned the fundamentals of every track and field event and how to teach a student-athlete each discipline from scratch.

My mother, Odaris Cauthen, my father, Jewel Cauthen, and my fiancée, Janice Gaymon, have been great sources of strength and inspiration. My father passed away, unfortunately, this summer, and I would like to dedicate my portion of this book to his memory. I also gained a new fountain of pride and joy last winter when my daughter, Savannah, came into the world.

I sincerely hope that readers find that I and my coauthors have provided, in this book, information that may have half as great an impact on their lives as these figures have had on mine.

Patrick Donnelly: This project would not have passed the conceptual stage without the persistence and vision of my colleague, Dr. Ashley Benjamin, who has carried more than his share of the load since day one. I also thank Michael Cauthen for his invaluable insights and contributions, and editors James Chambers and Jennifer Way for their support and guidance.

Great thanks to all of the coaches who generously shared their time and wisdom in the interviews for this book, and a special thanks to all of the coaches along the way who have taught me so many important lessons: Paul Bowar, for endless batting practice on hot summer days; Jim Senske, for showing me that your contributions don't have to come between the white lines; Brad Schaper, for reminding me of the power of passion and enthusiasm; and Dennis Denning, for daring to be great.

Finally, many thanks to my parents, Tom and Mary Donnelly, for always believing in me; to my daughters, Fiona and Nora, for keeping my life fun and my challenges in perspective; and to my wife, Kris, for her unconditional love and support.

Introduction

Thinking about playing college sports? As an athlete, who would not want an opportunity at the college limelight: Possible championships, television appearances, and—realistic or not—fleeting thoughts of a shot at the Olympics or even playing professionally?

Maybe you are a parent, coach, or mentor, and envision your athlete playing college sports. Sounds good if some or all of that tuition was paid for by athletics. Thus far, athletics has probably been a very big part of your lives. Considering all the money, time, and sacrifice that you have invested to develop your athlete's talents, a college scholarship would be a nice payoff. In addition, you may view sports as a venue for teaching concepts such as teamwork, perseverance, winning with humility, and losing with grace. Despite all the workouts, driving, tournaments, and games, there may be a part of you that wants your athlete's career to continue. But is this really the best thing for him or her?

At the major universities, sports such as football and basketball are about big business, advertising, semi-professional training, and entertainment. Indeed, a few stellar college athletes with hopes of a professional sports career receive notoriety in the daily and national newspapers. For these athletes, academics usually take a back seat. Most college athletes, however—especially in non-revenue sports—are in college for the education as well as the experience of college athletics. Do not delude yourselves: college will be a full-time job.

In many cases, the coach or the program may be upstanding but the overall situation may not be right for you and your athlete. This "goodness of fit" may involve athletic and/or non-athletic factors. We believe most coaches are quite scrupulous and also want a good fit. But coaches realize that some athletes are going to be unhappy, become ineligible, transfer, or quit. This is simply the cost of doing business. In order to provide this insiders' view, many athletes, coaches, and others involved with college sports requested anonymity. This was surprising, as some of the individuals could not be directly affected based on their comments. This reflects the often very secretive nature and intense loyalty that is part of college athletics.

This three-part guidebook will ensure that you know how to spot red flags during the recruiting process. After reading this book, you will understand the pertinent issues. You will also know not only *who* to ask but also *how* to ask the specific questions you need answered to make an informed decision. Sections on the technical aspects of recruiting, the assessment of values of the athletic organization, and opinions from coaching gurus from numerous sports will prepare you for the recruiting process ahead.

Section I

Section I covers the technical aspects of recruitment. However, before we get to the technical aspects, we first help you answer the most important question that should *not* be taken for granted: *Is it worth your time and effort to play college athletics?* Many excellent high school athletes elect not to participate in college athletics. However, if you choose to participate, we want to help you cement this decision, as the commitment is significant.

For athletes who decide to compete at the college level, we discuss the many factors such as location and academics that can influence your decision. Next, we explain the different levels of competition ranging from NCAA Division I to Junior College. You will also understand the competitive variation even among the divisions.

The actual recruiting process is exhilarating and frustrating. One of the most misunderstood aspects of recruiting is selling yourself. Yes, the ideal is when coaches come to you, but don't wait: Be proactive! This section shows you how to play the recruiting game.

Next, we talk about the business aspects of athletics. The best way to maximize your scholarship opportunities is to understand your value to a program and appreciate the program's and college's financial constraints. Too many athletes are unaware of these factors.

Making the final decision on a program can be an extremely arduous experience. We can't do it for you, of course, but we do provide some composite athlete case scenarios to illustrate some of the issues you might face and help you select an appropriate course of action.

Do not underestimate the positive or negative impact that individual counselors, coaches, or professors can have during the recruiting process. Learn how these individuals can influence your opportunities.

Section I ends with a discussion of two critical recruiting factors: budgets and "spiels." Too many athletes are unwittingly manipulated by slick spiels, thinking, *"They must want me more since they contacted me first and more often than others did."* The other false assumption is *"The coaches are so nice on the phone; this is how they are all the time."* Once you understand these two factors, you will have the ability to make a more informed decision.

Section II

Section II begins with a discussion on the topic of values. Many of you play sports or have encouraged your athlete to play sports because of the values that can be learned from competition. Many of these values are minimized at the college level, where winning and money are too often the top priority. We identify the distorted values that are often seen in collegiate athletics. Next, we identify some values that can help ensure a positive experience. Awareness of what you want to avoid as well as what you hope to experience will allow for better decisions or at least better-informed decisions.

The next three chapters focus on gender, racial, religious, and cultural issues. More women are playing intercollegiate athletics than ever before; you need to know the unique emotional, medical, and psychosocial factors that are important to your health. Factors pertaining to racial backgrounds are discussed, as well. Did you know that some coaches recruit differently based on an athlete's race? Furthermore, racial stereotypes can affect relationships with your coaches, which can affect your athletic experience. America's "melting pot" nature is reflected in the diversity of cultural, ethnic, religious, and regional backgrounds of its college athletes. Learn from athletes who hold different religious views or have cultural values that are different from yours. Playing for coaches or with players who are intolerant of your background can be agonizing, as well as a very lonely experience.

This is a natural lead-in to the next chapter, regarding athletes who play sports while participating in a college exchange program. If you want to be among the thousands of athletes from around the world who attend college in the United States on an athletic scholarship, this is the *only* book that focuses on issues in college sports from this perspective. After reading this chapter, you will know what to ask by e-mail or telephone, as you most likely will make a decision without ever meeting the coaches or teammates, or knowing the geography. On the flip side, American college athletes are more likely than ever to compete with international athletes. We will discuss how to assess the stereotype that often, coaches who rely on recruiting international talent might be more managers than coaches.

Also addressed in this section are issues such as disability, sexual orientation, and homeschooling. College athletic institutions tend to be conservative settings where there can be discomfort with those who are different. We discuss situations student-athletes who fall into these categories might face, as well as how to handle these topics during the recruiting process.

Finally, research in sports medicine, sociology, and psychology has grown significantly in the last few decades. Safe training and competing is based on research breakthroughs in several of these fields. Ignorance of such topics as how to deal with a concussion or how to prevent hazing can truly be a matter of life and death. To paraphrase the principal tenet of the medical field: *Above all, a coach should do no harm.* In simple terms, we bring you up to speed on some common potential medical issues, and discuss how to ensure that these are minimized during practice and competition.

Section III

Section III covers the recruiting and interview process. The chapters in this section contain invaluable information from coaches who not only have had very successful careers but who are also regarded as having maintained the highest ethical standards. We interviewed coaching greats who are in or near retirement—coaches able to provide the inside story from looking back over their own coaching and recruiting experiences. Conversations with an athletic director and strength coach are also featured here, as these individuals have a considerable impact on the integrity and safety of any program.

Appendixes

Appendix A discusses proposed student-athlete rights, which have been adapted from retired coach Robert Timmons' *The NCAA: Who Protects Student Athletes? A Proposal for a Student Athletes' Bill of Rights*. Coach Timmons has fought for the rights of student-athletes for over 40 years.

Appendix B is an expansion of a previously published contribution by Dr. Benjamin, which discusses suggested changes to college athletics with the focus of taking the business out of athletics and bringing back integrity by reemphasizing academics.

What This Book Is Not

Information that can be easily found on the Internet or details that can change from year to year are not covered in this book. These include aids for improving athletic and academic performance, specific NCAA, NAIA, or NJCAA procedures and rules, college reference data, and how to reach the professional ranks. Many of these topics are books in themselves and inappropriate to cover in a compressed manner. Beware of books that claim to cut through all the NCAA or NAIA or NJCAA rules. Why? Because many of these rules regarding recruiting bylaws or academic standards change from year to year. These types of books get outdated quickly. We provide specific Internet references to access the divisional rules and academic standards.

Reference information about colleges, athletic programs, coaches, win-loss records, and statistics are available on each university's Web site. Unfortunately, programs can be discontinued and coaches can leave. Check the specific college's Web site for these details.

Summary

We hope that a positive collegiate athletic experience and love for sport will help you maintain a positive image of maintaining a continued healthy lifestyle. Our hope is that the practical insights provided in this book give you the opportunity to complete your academic goals while fulfilling your athletic dreams or potential.

Finally, we focus on the student-athlete, hoping to find a program that maintains academic balance and athletic perspective. We do not focus on future professional athletic careers. However, if this is your goal, we believe you still need this book. With your talents, unethical coaches see you as a ticket to championships and might not look out for your best physical and academic well-being. Keep in mind that your odds of having a meaningful professional career are very poor. Our advice? Be smart, don't be used: prepare for a pro career, but also progress toward a meaningful degree.

SECTION I

Recruiting: The Technical Aspects

1

Why Play?

It seems like a silly question, but former university president James Appleberry, Ph.D. doesn't think so. He said, "The first question every athlete should ask themselves is 'Why I am doing this?' One day, no one is going to care about your athletic skills. Learn what you need to know for the rest of your life!" Thinking through this question may potentially save you time, energy, and expense. Many fine high school athletes realize that competing at the college level is not for them. Here are some considerations in determining whether intercollegiate athletics is really best for you.

Maybe you "love to play the game" or you "love to compete." Our view is that that is not enough to sustain and motivate you through the rigors of four years of college sports. Even at the least competitive divisions and schools, athletics is a full-time endeavor. Academics and social activities take secondary roles, especially during the season.

Want to play or compete? Consider club sports, local city leagues, or intramurals. Edmond Racquet Club comanager Dwight Nuckolls gives an example of a program that allows non-varsity tennis players to actually compete against players from other schools without the oversight, control, or extensive hours that are involved in interscholastic competitive tennis.

For some high school students, a desire to focus solely on academics or a complete lack of interest in academics (i.e., no true interest in attending college), and a lack of motivation to train and compete at a sustained high level year-round are reasons enough to forego college athletic competition. Lack of dependence on an athletic scholarship to pay for tuition also gives you the option to not compete or to simply walk on. We cover the advantages and disadvantages of scholarship versus walk-on status in the upcoming chapters.

On the other hand, scholarship opportunities and access to more prestigious colleges and a desire to play college sports and maximize your athletic potential, which includes preparation for a professional career, are valid reasons to play. Family expectations can also be a strong factor.

Academics

College athletics is often focused on advertising and winning. Athletics serves as a strong community outreach and alumni rallying point. At larger universities, winning in high-profile revenue sports such as football or basketball almost guarantees increased revenues for the athletic department and a possible increase in enrollment for the college. As former NAIA college vice president and chief operating officer Alfred Branch explained, "Sports are the front porch to a university." The local community provides a fan base that often has no academic connection to the university. Supporting a winning team fosters community pride. Even with non-revenue sports or small college sports, competing well is of a primary importance. Donna Carroll, a president of a Division III university that switched from the NAIA, concurred. She said, "Athletics provides a balance with academics, provides a sense of team and school spirit, along with discipline, camaraderie, and student collaboration. It can improve the individual experience and sense of belonging to the campus."

Schools promote graduation rates and play up awards, which recognize combined athletic and academic accomplishments. Don't be fooled. The bottom line is that your academic endeavors are truly up to you. NAIA soccer player Megan Blake said, "I went to college for the academics with athletics as an extra bonus. But when you get up at 4:30 A.M. to go to practice, are in class all day, followed by a game, well, it gets crazy." More of Blakes's story is presented in the "Desire to Play" section of this chapter.

Former all-state track-and-field long sprinter and middle distance runner Jason Young opted to eventually forgo college athletics as well. The challenge of balancing his academic load, symphony participation, and work-study with his track practice resulted in some soul-searching after his first year at a prestigious Ivy League school. He said, "I didn't want to give up track as we set the 1,600 meter freshman relay record. However, I had so many opportunities that I had to set priorities, otherwise, I realized I would be a champion of none." Young did not compete after his first year.

You often hear about the Rhodes Scholar with a 3.95 grade point average (GPA) who is also an All-American, but these student-athletes are very rare. College athletes from every division and every sport contend that their GPAs would be higher if they didn't have a year-round commitment to athletics. This brings us to the caveat: *Only you* can weigh the benefits of athletics versus the possible decrements in your academics. Only you know how much you can handle in taking on the student-athlete balance.

The opposite might also be true. Maybe you really have no interest in college. If your plan is to play professionally, see the "Maximizing Potential" section in this chapter. However, if you prefer non-academic vocations, which do not require a college degree, be honest with yourself. Coaches often assume that if you are talented enough to compete in college athletics, then you also must want to go to college to pursue a degree. Dr. Benjamin recounts the dilemma of a former high school All-American middle distance runner who began his college career at a storied Division I track program. This athlete was there to run. However, when he got injured, he was unable to compete and felt emotionally burned out, and he began questioning if college was best for him. A year later, he transferred to a local junior college program and then finally quit school. This brings us to a second caveat: Simply attending college because you possess athletic talent or because of family pressure can be a recipe for disaster. There are times when everyone wants to quit, but the importance of getting a degree keeps a lot of students going.

Scholarship Opportunities

The American university system is unique in that it allows you to capitalize on your athletic talents. Scholarship opportunities and access to highly selective schools are great reasons to consider college sports. In fact, for many athletes, acquiring an athletic scholarship may be the only way to go to college. For example, former Division I college football player Paul Duren said, "I couldn't afford to go to college without a scholarship. I knew football could be my ticket."

Be aware of how you match up academically to your peers, warns Chris Lazzarino, a former sports journalist. He said, "My

> ## Ask yourself the following questions:
>
> 1. Do I really want a college degree? Do I enjoy learning? Do I really want to go to college for academics?
>
>   Students who attend college to "party," join social organizations, or access the social scene are likely to drop out in their first year. It's important to consider why you want to go to college. If getting a degree isn't at the top of that list, you should reconsider your options.
>
> 2. Am I willing to accept a lower GPA as a result of my commitment to athletics?
>
>   If your plan is to pursue a specialized graduate program such as astrophysics, your GPA and test performances in college become of premium importance. This rigorous academic plan can be tough to balance with college athletics. On the other hand, many employers and graduate programs search for well-rounded candidates. Jabari Wamble, a former Division I All-American track sprinter who currently serves as the Assistant Attorney General of a Midwestern state, certainly agrees. He says, "College athletes are perceived as team players, battle tested, and willing to work hard. While doing interviews before and after law school, my athletic history would come up as a positive experience."

dad was a second-generation Italian and neither of his parents went to college. Because of his football skills as a defensive lineman, he got into an Ivy League school but transferred, as he did not have the academic background or foundation to succeed at such an institution. He transferred to another respectable but less academically rigorous program and earned a degree. I am convinced that he was able to attend college because he received an athletic scholarship."

This vignette also points out the danger of blindly accepting the notion that coaches at prestigious universities fully consider your grades and academic preparation when they recruit you. In the next chapters we help you gauge your prospective level of success at a university and look past the hard-sell approach some university athletic programs employ. This brings us to a third caveat: If you are fortunate to get some or all of your education paid for, get a degree! You will not regret it.

Desire to Play

You may want your sport to remain as much fun as it was in high school. "College football is nothing like high school football. It is hard work and it is 365 days a year," says Duren. High school principal Mark Landrith says that during the 17 years that he has witnessed athletes return and talk about their college experiences, even with all the glamour, "It is not as fun. It really is a job."

If you think the above applies only to Division I or sports like football or basketball, guess again! Regarding her NAIA soccer experiences, Blake said, "I wish I [had known] how much work college soccer was going to be. In high school, the off-season time was my own. In college, I was playing all year-round, lifting weights, and traveling." She stuck it out her freshman year because she attended an expensive private college on a nearly full-ride soccer scholarship and because of this, could not quit playing for the team. In essence, she felt trapped even though she liked the school and program. At the end of the year, she transferred to a less expensive school closer to home and chose to not continue her collegiate career. Currently, she is finishing her senior year in college and coaching high school girl's soccer. Looking back, she said, "I had no idea how intense it [a smaller division program] would be." Many athletes like Blake realize that they do not want athletics to dictate their college experiences and in many cases, athletics certainly can and will.

Her experience highlights the trade-off. This is especially true if you are on an athletic scholarship, which means that the coach and program can dictate your schedule. Your time is not your own and noncompliance or partial compliance can result in the termination of your scholarship. We discuss this issue in more detail in Chapter 5, "Scholarship Negotiation."

Simple burnout can also be an important factor. All-State soccer player Melissa Iseman began playing soccer when she was five years old. She described going to high school and then club soccer practice, with weekends replete with tournaments. Despite numerous contacts from college coaches, she decided as a junior that she would not play in college because "I was burned out. I wanted a normal life." Now a junior at a major university, she has no regrets as she plays intramural soccer, which is a part of an active college life.

Maximizing Potential

The opportunity to realize your athletic potential might be one of the strongest reasons to compete in college. Mark Thompson, a former high school All-American runner, had a burning desire to see how fast he could go. He chose a university partly based on the prestigious track program because "I wanted a place to reach my potential."

College sports may represent your best opportunity to achieve your athletic goals, especially if the professional ranks are not in your future plans. If this is your intent, you should first clarify your specific athletic goals. An NJCAA assistant men's basketball coach says, "Do you want an opportunity to play on a team that wins, or to play on a team that is capable of winning championships?"

As an aside, let's talk briefly about the professional ranks. Your odds of a professional career are less than 1 percent. Couple this with the average professional athletic career lasting less than four years, and you realize that your chances of a glamour-filled professional career are slim. Former baseball player Paul Rogers, who played in the Toronto Blue Jays organization, said, "Although I do not regret my decision to go right to the minor leagues after high school, I do think that the college experience may have helped maturity-wise." He got close to his aspiration of a major league opportunity, playing for six years in the minor leagues. The limelight of the pros might be exciting, but if you cannot wait, consider the option of playing professionally and going to college. Michael Turek describes how this might be done. Turek said,

"My son, Travis (Turek), plays professionally in the minor leagues for the Cleveland Indians but continues to take college courses in the off-season. In fact, they are supportive of this and actually help financially toward his classes." Do not underestimate the difficulty of playing in the pros when it comes to non-revenue college sports. Brad Wilhite, a former college golfer who has been around golf all his life, says, "For golf, it's probably less than 1 percent as only 5 to 10 players make it per year."

For the serious student who has athletic talent, the American university system can be beneficial. This, however, is unfortunate if you have no academic interests. You are caught up in the reality that professional sports use the university athletic system as their semi-professional leagues. This is discussed in more detail in Appendix B. A more practical option might be the semi-professional leagues created by the pros. For example, the NBA now has a developmental league in which athletes make a minimum salary but get an opportunity to showcase their skills without having to worry about academics. Some sports such as tennis, baseball, and golf have a semiprofessional system, which also allow you to hone your athletic skills and earn some money. Many players quit these semiprofessional leagues, however, because they do not have the finances to continue on these tours.

Remember Lazzarino's father, who used his football skills to attend college? He was a lower round draft pick and decided against taking a shot at professional football. With a family to feed, he fell back on his education and attained a law degree and had a successful career as a school superintendent in education.

Family

Your family, support system, and community contribute to your athletic success. They may also feel a great deal of pride and satisfaction in your performance, but this can be a double-edged sword. Sometimes, the ones who care the most about you may also be the most disappointed if you do not continue athletics at the college level. There may also be feelings of vicarious living or the positive feelings associated with your athletic success that they do not want to give up. There may also be financial or scholarship motivations for their wanting you to play. It is fine when parents and athlete are equally committed to the athletic process. When there is pressure to play, however, or to attend a specific college, or play for a specific program or coach, there can be problems.

Parents and mentors need to be honest with themselves. Do you think your child is possibly playing to please you? What messages are you giving to your athlete regarding the importance of continuing at the college level? How disappointed would you be if he or she didn't compete?

The possibility of not playing college sports may be something that none of you even thought about. Don't be surprised if these discussions bring up a lot of emotions. Remember that athletics has been a big part of all of your lives.

Transfer to Compete

There is another option for you if you just have to get college athletics out of your system: Consider a brief transfer to a college program that fits your competitive level. This is exactly what co-author Dr. Benjamin did:

> I just could not pass up going to a great journalism school, [but] I knew that I was not a Division I caliber runner. So, I took one semester off and competed at a local NAIA college to satisfy my dream of competing at the college level. The new coach needed athletes to complement the current team. I still graduated from the journalism school of my choice. It was a great experience.

If the transfer option for a semester or even a year strikes your fancy, search for a program that might be rebuilding or could use some extra athletes to complete the roster. As discussed in the next chapter, walk-ons contribute to a lot of programs, especially in Division III and NAIA. Most coaches would prefer to train you for at least a year or two, but if you find a program where you can be competitive, it can be a win-win situation. However, be up front with your intentions if you plan on leaving that program before you graduate.

Summary

- Consider all options to satisfy a desire to continue playing your sport.
- College sports will become your first priority if you want to stay competitive.
- Athletic scholarships can open up great opportunities. However, you will not be in control.
- Playing professionally is very rare. Maximizing potential may be a more realistic goal.
- Get an education while in the process.

2

Considering a University

Selecting a college or university is one of the most important and challenging decisions you will ever have to make. It is a choice that will affect the rest of your life. You are not alone: over 2 million people go through this process annually.

A general standard is to choose the best college that provides a good academic fit and is affordable for you. In this chapter we outline the academic factors you should take into consideration, as well as location, family, and institutional factors. Financial factors are covered in Chapter 5.

Academics

Academics is truly a broad topic. Two questions can help you get started on finding the best academic fit for you: First, has your high school academic background been sufficient to ensure a successful college experience? Second, what does the university you are considering offer?

Personal Academic Background

Consider these factors when analyzing your academic background:

- Are you an outstanding student? Did you work hard to achieve good grades or did the good grades come to you easily?
- Do you perform well on standardized tests? Do your test scores match your grades? For example, if you are a 3.90 student, do your ACT or SAT scores also rank in the top percentiles?
- Are you willing to work hard in college? It seems like a silly question, but universities vary significantly regarding academic rigor. Competing and maintaining grades

are difficult enough. If you simply want "a degree" with minimal effort, then choose a less rigorous college.

- Are your parents or mentors well educated, or will you be the first college graduate in your family? Although seemingly unimportant, family mentoring can make a difference in succeeding in college. Retired high school coach Steve Sublett said, "Sometimes, even though the athlete was bright, if I did not think they had the family background to succeed, I would recommend a less academically competitive and possibly smaller college." Regarding another athlete from a large family without the financial means to attend college without financial aid, his sole goal was to help "match him to get the best financial package where he would experience academic success."

University Factors

Consider these three main factors when weighing different colleges:

- Overall prestige or reputation of the college. If you are unsure regarding a particular major, a university with a solid reputation should suit you fine. Later, we discuss how to match your academic performance with an equivalent college to enhance your chances to succeed.
- Specific reputation of the program. One of the advantages of having many choices is that if you have a unique interest such as marine biology, there are many programs that might be outstanding regardless of the overall reputation of the university. If you have narrowed down your major, give this factor more weight than the specific reputation of the university, if all other factors are equal.
- Specific professor or research track. Staying with the marine biology example, if you have a specific interest in the language of dolphins, then seek out the professors and research programs that are studying this topic. If your passion for study is so well defined, use this as the key criteria.

All three factors can occur within one university setting. However, sometimes a large university that is considered average overall may have an outstanding program or an expert in a specific area or topic that fits with your career ambitions. This is especially true if you have specific graduate school aspirations. It is also important to consider colleges in your home state, which can often be an advantage both in terms of selection process and cost.

Determining the school that best suits your needs is no easy task. However, there is no shortage of published material on the relative ranking of colleges and universities, primarily in terms of academic quality or in terms of the best value for the cost. A few prestigious schools annually rank among the highest in academics. On the other hand, many other schools rank highly in relation to cost or value. Major periodicals, like *US News and World Report* and *Kiplinger's Personal Finance*, and test prep companies such as *The Princeton Review* rate American universities every year. These guides allow you to compare schools on a number of factors, including average test scores, GPAs, cost, cultural and racial diversity, and ease of acceptance. Some include personal comments from former or current students.

Highly Prestigious Universities and Colleges

While what makes a school "prestigious" is subjective, a list of the most academically rigorous and highly regarded schools in the United States usually includes the following:

- The Ivy League. This well-known group of Division I schools boast large endowments and centuries of tradition. They do not offer athletic scholarships.
- A group of East Coast private liberal arts colleges dubbed the "Little Ivy" and collectively in the NECAC. These schools are the Division III version of the Ivy. They are very competitive both academically and athletically, boast small professor-to-student ratios, and have very large endowments.
- A host of academically competitive but very expensive private liberal arts colleges. These universities, typically in Division III or NAIA, are based throughout the country and are very selective in terms of test scores and GPAs. As with the Little Ivy, they have smaller professor-to-student ratios
- The military academies. Perennially ranked among the most rigorous and difficult to get into, as leadership,

discipline, and willingness to heed to authority are premium for getting in.

- A number of highly prestigious large public and private universities. These universities often have large endowments and research funding. Universities from this group are typically spread among the majority of the large conferences. These universities tend to cater to a vast range of students. They tend to use graduate students to teach large introductory classes, and competitive honors programs for the brighter and academically motivated students.

In general, these universities have low acceptance rates and also take their athletics very seriously. The Ivy League, Little Ivy, Division III institutions, and the military academies do not give athletic scholarships per se. However, being an athlete does increase your chances for admission. This is because all of these programs also want to boast competitive athletic programs. Therefore, an athlete—despite having slightly lower average test scores or GPA—has an advantage, as coaches often have a certain amount of slots assigned for athletes.

Young, an Ivy League graduate who conducts alumni interviews with prospective students, admits that, "Nine out of ten students that I interview will not get in. The truth is everybody who attends an Ivy League school is from that top band of high school students. They are super solid and multitalented students who are driven to be successful." As he points out, this "incredibly stimulating" academic environment is not for everybody.

Little Ivy graduate and field hockey goalie SM[1*] concurred. She stated that attending "was a great experience, although very expensive" as she is still repaying her loans. She added that her school, which has one of the top alumni contributions, had "great resources in terms of training, equipment, and playing fields" compared to other smaller division colleges. She felt that this sort of institution would only be best for the academically qualified student who was highly motivated both academically and athletically.

---

1 * Some interviewees have asked to remain anonymous so that they may speak more freely. Their names have been changed to initials unrelated to their identities.

Geography

Geography may be underestimated as a factor, but it can be important in choosing the right college for you. Consider the following:

- How do you feel about the typical climate of the school you'll attend? Dr. Benjamin recalls one former high school All-American from the Southwest who attended a Midwestern institution and "hated the snow and the cold." Factors such as the amount of rain, average temperatures, proximity to beaches and mountains, or amount of sunlight all can affect how you feel, especially if your academics and athletics are not going as well as you would like.
- Do you prefer a rural, suburban, or urban campus? If you are used to one extreme or the other, it can initially be quite a shock. Issues like traffic, commuting time, or access to big city amenities versus the space in the countryside can affect your decisions about where to attend.
- What is the campus and surrounding area like? Are you comfortable with the setting? This is especially important if you are an international student, a minority, or a student with different than average needs. These topics are discussed further in Section II.

Family

Many families are actively involved in both the academic and athletic lives of student-athletes. The presence of extended family (i.e., aunts, uncles, grandparents, cousins, or godparents) often satisfies the student-athlete's need for a familial safety net. Thus, this consideration might weigh heavily in choosing a college.

- Do you want to be within a convenient travel distance from your immediate family?
- Are you close with your family? Do you want to stay near home, no matter what? As Duren stated, "I wanted to be close enough so my family could see me play on a regular basis."
- Do you envision getting away from home as a growth or maturity experience? In this case, you might want to establish a significant distance from them. What constitutes "distance" is unique to each family, however.

Coach Cauthen said:

> I remember a mother and father of one female ath-
> lete routinely drove 10 hours, across several states, to
> attend home competitions; they often followed the team
> to relatively distant away meets as well. This offered
> great comfort to their daughter—and ultimately to
> teammates and coaches as well—as they became an
> integral part of the fan support and emotional support
> network of the program.

Institutional Factors

Consider the following factors about the colleges you are thinking about attending:

- Financial issues. Consider what you and your family can
  afford. This may be a limiting issue, and many athletes
  end up chasing the money because this is the only way
  to attend college. Corbin Cawin, a basketball player,
  recalls how he attended an expensive NAIA college in
  the Northwest and, a few weeks into the semester, an
  audit performed by the university showed that his family contribution should be more than initially expected.
  "I remember getting a letter one day from the registrar's
  office stating that I owed an additional $6,000. The
  school's policy was to only grant up to $8,000 dollars for
  a maximal athletic award. I had to transfer at the semester as I could not afford the additional expenses."
- Will you be comfortable at a small school with a couple
  thousand (or fewer) students or with a large school with
  tens of thousands of students? Even smaller schools can
  have large classes, and big schools, especially within
  their honors programs, can have smaller classes.
- Would you prefer a unisex campus or a coed university?
  Some female students feel more comfortable in a female-
  only college; this factor is covered in greater detail in
  Chapter 4 of Section II.
- Do you belong to a religious, cultural, or ethnic group
  with which you strongly identify? Weigh the importance
  of being around others who share these similar characteristics. Some athletes who minimize the importance

of this consideration often end up feeling lonely and isolated.

- Are there any specific social or college clubs or opportunities that you seek? This could range from desiring an active Greek system or just the opposite. Other examples might include specific clubs or organizations that meet cultural, political, charitable, athletic, or other needs.
- How important is a safe college environment to you? This is a much larger concern after the rare but tragic events over the last few years. Inquire about campus safety, prevention, and preparedness regarding any man-made or natural disasters. Topics to consider include preventing criminality, containing dangerous behaviors such as alcohol-related incidents, and preparation for fires or other disasters. To learn more about campus safety, check out http://www.ope.ed.gov/security.

Tying These Factors Together: A Personal Vignette

Coach Cauthen shares his personal experience to summarize some of the above information:

I was from New York City and was used to large crowds. I attended private school from seventh through twelfth grade, however, and was comfortable with small academic environments. But I wanted to attend a college, regardless of size, in "the country." I loved wildlife and thought that one day I would settle on a farm or ranch. Therefore, I was very attracted to Alfred University (my alma mater), a small private university located in the Allegheny Mountains of western New York. It had a strong marine biology program (and world-renowned ceramic engineering and ceramic arts programs), and that accorded with my intention to major in zoology. I was less prepared—though I did adapt—for the severe winters with annual snowfalls of 200-plus inches and occasional wind chills of 80 below zero Fahrenheit. I would highly recommend that you consider your tolerance for cold, heat, rain, or snow, in addition to whether you want to live nine months in a rural or urban community.

Large universities can occur in any kind of setting. My undergraduate track and field team competed in the Nittany Lions Relays hosted at Pennsylvania State University, which is a relatively large school (over 30,000) nestled in the rural mountainous community of College Park, Pennsylvania. The University of California-Los Angeles is also quite large, but resides in one of America's largest cities—Los Angeles.

After graduation, I attended Purdue University, a school with over 30,000 students in a mid-sized city (West Lafayette–Lafayette, Indiana). I understand, therefore, the nuances of both small and large classes and campuses. Though my graduate classes were small (i.e., 5 to 10 classmates), I was a teaching assistant for classes exceeding 400 students; and regularly talked to friends who regularly attended classes with nearly 5,000 students in the same room (e.g., introduction to chemistry). Even small private colleges have large classes as well. My introduction to biology and introduction to psychology courses exceeded 100 students—certainly larger than what most, if not all, high school students are used to. The average classroom size may be important to you, as well as how many campuswide peers you want to share higher education experience.

There is nothing intrinsically or inherently good or bad about small, intimate campus communities or large, cosmopolitan scholastic communities. As with beauty, it's in the eye of the beholder. Perhaps the most dramatic difference occurs when attending basketball games and football games. Sitting in a football stadium with 30,000 to 100,000 fans significantly differs from attending a game with 6,000 fans, no matter how vociferously the fans cheer on their team—or razz the opposition.

Social distractions may be broader at larger universities and at more urban universities, in terms of the scale and diversity of activities. One can have a very active social life at a small rural college—especially if another campus is nearby or if there is a robust community of student organizations. There may be a few business establishments catering to the social interests of the students, which adequately satisfy a need to "meet-and-greet."

Summary

- Consider how your academic background, performance, and motivation fits with your college choices.
- Evaluate institutional factors such as overall university reputation, financial aid packages, and quality of specific areas of study.
- The importance of university location and proximity to family and friends should not be underestimated.

3

College Athletic Divisions

Collegiate sports are divided into several divisions, namely NCAA (National Collegiate Athletic Association) Division I, II, and III. A parallel collegiate association to the NCAA is the NAIA (the National Association of Intercollegiate Athletics). Division I football now has a subdivision called Division IA (also known as the Football Championship subdivision). Divisions IA, II, and III football teams hold playoff series to determine national champions while Division I has the bowl series. In virtually every other sport, national NCAA championships are conducted. Finally, there are two junior college divisions, the CCCAA (California Community College Athletic Association) and the NJCAA (National Junior College Athletic Association). The former only competes within California. The latter is a national system. Each division has unique characteristics. These broad delineations might also help you decide what college is best for you. Keep in mind, however, that even within each division, there is a spectrum regarding extent of competitiveness, focus on athletics, and size of budgets.

There is considerable interplay between college programs. Obviously, many junior college athletes go on to attend four-year schools. Often, based on coaching relationships, athletes from specific junior colleges tend to gravitate to specific four-year programs. This actually is not specific to junior colleges. A number of larger and smaller program coaches have their own private referral networks. Although this does not violate any regulations, understand that if a program refers you to another program in another division, it may be related to an unspoken agreement between the coaches.

NCAA, Division I

Division I is the premier competitive division of the NCAA, with over 300 schools, typically large public institutions. Division I schools are known for the following attributes:

- Catering to the most elite student-athletes. The most competitive athletes tend to seek out Division I programs, as these programs have the highest level of competition, have the most press, and provide the best ancillary services such as facilities and academic counseling.
- Offering the most scholarships and grant-in-aid per sport. You should note that college football scholarships are slightly less available at Division IA schools. The key difference between IA and I is the presence of football playoffs. Division I football programs rely on bowl games, national rankings, and conference championships to determine an overall winner. The National champion emerges out of the College Bowl Series, where a complex formula pits number "one" against number "two." Division IA has a playoff system as described above.
- Providing the most academic support and resources for student-athletes. Division I has a full staff replete with counselors, tutors, and study halls to help you stay eligible and progress toward graduation.
- Having the highest quality facilities. Millions of dollars are spent on upgrading indoor workout centers, weight rooms, and athletic training venues. Being the most time consuming and professional of all the divisions, Division I teams also tend to get the largest community, booster, and alumni support. This goes along with television contracts and media exposure.
- Having the most rules regarding recruiting, as well as the highest rates for various forms of recruiting violations. Because of the money and importance of winning, the NCAA attempts to regulate contact between coaches and athletes with hundreds of rules. Many coaches respond by breaking these rules, altering transcripts to acquire less than academically qualified players, and paying athletes, usually through alumni, under the table.

> **Comment:** As a former Division I football player says, "It took me a while to understand this, but often, they [the coaching staff] don't give a damn about you. When some of these coaches are making millions, it is all about winning." This can certainly vary from sport to sport and coach to coach. However, the reality is that Division I coaches are hired to win and are rarely part of the teaching faculty. They also have the highest pressures to perform or they will get fired.

NCAA, Division II

The second tier of the NCAA is comprised of fewer schools and is known for the following characteristics:

- Division II offers scholarships and athletic grant-in-aid; the amount of aid offered is less than that from Division I, which offers the most scholarship money per team.
- Division II has very competitive programs, but with significantly smaller budgets than Division I programs. Competition is more regional and the level of competition is not as intense as Division I, but certainly at a higher level than the other divisions.
- Division II has smaller budgets, which translates into less academic support and fewer facilities and ancillary services. There may be less access to study halls, academic counseling, and tutoring compared with Division I.
- Athletes often end up choosing a Division II school if their Division I opportunities are closed. Many athletes dream of competing at the Division I level but find that is not a realistic goal. Often, when athletes realize they will not qualify for a Division I scholarship or will not get an opportunity to compete, they turn to Division II.
- Having fewer recruiting restrictions compared to Division I; however, although less rampant, cheating does occur. Again, this is related to the financial aspects of sports. The pressures to win are not as great, but it still is highly competitive.
- Having a greater focus on in-state recruiting to maximize athletic budgets. For example, if out-of-state tuition is $15,000 and in-state tuition is $5,000, a coach in Division II can provide three in-state scholarships for the price of one out-of-state scholarship. Therefore, if you

want to attend an out-of-state Division II program and receive athletic aid, you need to be significantly better than other incoming recruits or expect to pay more.

> **Comment:** Senior associate athletic director Chuck Bailey explains that since an "in-state kid does not have to pay out-of-state tuition," Division II programs can get a lot more athletes by focusing on in-state recruiting. Therefore, "If you are out-of-state, you need to be a much better athlete and have the capability to play right away."

NCAA, Division III

This is the least athletically competitive NCAA division; this division has the highest number of schools. Division III schools are known for:

- Having no official athletic scholarships. All financial aid is based on need. This includes an evaluation of how much you and your family can afford, which academic or other scholarships you receive, and participation in work-study programs. Therefore, technically, your athletic prowess will not result in more money.
- Including some of the most academically competitive small liberal arts colleges. Many of the most competitive academic liberal arts institutions are within this division. There is an emphasis on low student-to-teacher ratios and professors—rather than grad students—teaching courses. Among academics, attending one of these colleges carries a lot of prestige. There also may be more emphasis on projects and papers emphasizing critical thinking versus the standard multiple-choice tests. The end result, as a generalization, is for most Division III programs they are closest to the ideal of being a student-athlete where the student comes first.
- Taking athletics under consideration during the admissions process. Sports can result in admissions even if your GPA and test scores are not as competitive as other non-athlete students. Many Division III programs value diverse interests, such as sporting talent, in their student population. Student athletes are also viewed as good

candidates to succeed both athletically and academically. These students also make for contributing alumni later in life. So, while athletics may help from an admissions standpoint, it legally cannot be used to determine your financial package.

- In general, having minimal ancillary services regarding academic support, strength and conditioning coaches, and facilities.
- Having the least amount of recruiting restrictions compared to other NCAA divisions. Most budgets are very limited compared to larger schools. Therefore, the result is fewer recruiting violations.
- Having coaching staffs that are much more likely to also teach on campus. Therefore, they are more likely to be a part of the school's academic mission.

NAIA

National Association of Intercollegiate Athletics (NAIA) is a division comprising more than 300 smaller, often faith-based, liberal arts colleges. NAIA colleges are known for the following:

- Offering competitive athletic programs, but typically not as competitive as Division I or Division II. NAIA programs tend to comprise smaller, private liberal arts colleges that emphasize participation and opportunities to compete rather than winning. The NAIA also touts its mission of character building through sports.

- Having fewer recruiting restrictions, which in some ways minimizes rules violations. There are fewer "blue chip" athletes who play at this level, budgets are smaller, and winning does not result in large payoffs—consequently, cheating is less prevalent.

- Offering athletic scholarships. Overall budgets are smaller, and often athletic department money is divided among a number of athletes, not just high-profile sports. Walk-ons often have better opportunities to compete at this level.

- Having smaller athletic budgets, similar to those in Division III.

- Having less extravagant facilities, ancillary staff, and academic support compared to Division I. Counselors and tutors are typically the same ones available to the general student population. Strength coaches and other sports medical personnel are a luxury, and, often, the athletic facilities are the same ones used by the general student population.

- Not having an age limit. This is a critical difference, because it draws older athletes who are part of student exchange programs compared to the NCAA divisions.

Comment: A former executive at an NAIA college sums up the division in this manner:

> The NAIA often struggles to differentiate itself. I would say that we are "champions of character." We want model student-athletes who make a difference in their community. We are second tier, but we do offer athletic scholarships and excellent athletic programs at many of our universities.

Junior College

Junior colleges are two-year colleges that can provide vocational experience as well as serving as a stepping-stone to a four-year college. The CCCAA, which comprises over 100 California community colleges and NJCAA junior colleges, falls into this category. In general, junior colleges, or jucos, are known for:

- Offering athletic scholarships. These are limited by budget and may vary by conference or school. The CCCAA does not offer athletic scholarships, but according to one CCCAA executive, the California junior college charges a minimal fee per credit. For example, some of the junior colleges are 700 dollars per year to attend, or about 10 percent of what it would cost at to attend a university within the University of California system. This executive adds that "if you don't get an education in California, you must not want to get it."
- Having smaller budgets than NCAA schools, which results in smaller ancillary services.
- Offering less time to focus on athletic development, due to the system being based on a two-year cycle. This is an important distinction, as you are guaranteed at least two moves and two coaches over a four-year period if you plan to complete an undergraduate degree.
- Being a "feeder" into an NCAA program. Many junior college programs have connections with NCAA programs, and thus can serve as "feeder" schools if the athlete wishes to transfer to a four-year school. This is a critical point to consider, according to a junior college vice chair for athletic affairs Dave Burgess. Burgess says that good programs focus as much on "recruiting away from the school" as recruiting an athlete to the school.
- Focusing on students who may not have the academic background or study skills to perform at another level. One of the advantages of a junior college, according to both students and coaches, is that its focus is on preparing students who have struggled academically or need a year or two to mature.
- Providing an opportunity for athletes interested in trades to compete at the college level. Students can learn a trade or achieve a two-year degree while competing.

- Having players whose talents vary widely. Many of the top junior college players are simply there because they could not make it academically in Division I. Therefore, some have professional-level talent.

Comment: Perry Jones, a former junior college and Division I football player and a current high school teacher and football and track coach says

> Juco has a better array of remedial classes that you can get into [compared to the other divisions]. Be honest about your study skills. If they are not up to par, then consider the juco route, as they are set up to help you prepare for another level. If athletes believe in themselves, [but] do not have the money, [yet] love the sport [they play], juco can allow them to mature as a student, and they still can end up in the program of their choice.

Canadian Intercollegiate Athletics: Want to compete outside of the United States? Consider Canada, which has two different intercollegiate systems. The Canadian Interuniversity Sport (CIS) is the larger university division with over 50 members and over 10,000 students who compete in 11 sports. The Canadian Colleges Athletic Association (CCAA) comprises smaller universities, community colleges, and technical institutes. There are over 100 members and over 9,000 students who compete in nine sports. According to CCAA executive director, Sandra Murray-MacDonell, the Canadian system's philosophy is that athletics are of the overall academic experience. International student athlete quotas do exist; consult our Web sites in the reference section for more details.

Summary

- Division I is the most competitive and has the most prestige and money.
- Division II provides the next highest level of competition.

- Division III has no athletic scholarships and is the NCAA division that often best allows an ideal balance of the student-athlete roles.
- NAIA is an alternate smaller association that provides scholarships and also emphasizes the student-athlete concept.
- Junior college associations are two-year institutions that can help prepare you both academically and athletically for a four-year program.

4

Getting Seen

After some initial consideration of colleges and their athletic programs, it is time to narrow the school selection process. If you are in a high-profile sport or if you have been a standout performer, you may have been receiving information from colleges for a long time. If not, these tips, which focus on initiating contact and marketing yourself, will get you headed in the right direction.

Initiating Contact

Except for Division I and IA football and basketball programs (which possess large budgets and ample staff), the majority of college and university athletic programs cannot adequately cover the entire country or high school talent pool. Fortunately, you don't have to wait to be spotted by enthusiastic but poorly financed coaches. Simply take the action to them. After you have researched and selected 5 to 10 colleges and universities that meet your qualifications you should begin to contact them.

First, write an introduction letter. This can be sent by mail, fax, or e-mail. All colleges now have information on their Web sites, so contact information is easily attainable. Mailing an introduction letter is our recommendation for initial contact, as it is minimally time consuming for the coach. This introduction letter is where you will make a first impression regarding your potential overall aptitude as a college athlete. Common mistakes in introduction letters include spelling errors or coming across in an arrogant manner. Let the facts and your performances speak for themselves. Coaches will be more impressed by a specific performance or award versus telling them "how good you are" or that you will "definitely start or be an all-star your freshman year" if given a full scholarship. An introduction letter is just that and no more. In essence, you are saying, "Hey, here I am, this is what I do, I am interested in your program; are you interested in me?" You might also inquire about the school's standards for

Sample Introduction Letter

Michele Smith
Milton High School Gymnastics Team
234 Willford Rd.
Greenforge, NC 27402
Ph: (555) 1234-5679
E-mail: msmith@miltonhs.com

North Carolina A & M University
Gymnastics Program
120 Bobston Hall
1601 E. Draton Street
Greensboro, NC 27411-3210

May 2, 2008

Dear Coach _____:

I am a student-athlete at _____ High School, and I am interested in your university and its athletics program. Could you please send me information on your university, your team, and scholarship/financial aid packages and opportunities (both academic and athletic)? I would also like to keep abreast of your team's activities this year.

Included below is a brief description of my most significant achievements to date. I've also included contact information for my high school head coach [*and club coach, if you have one*] and academic advisor.

The next paragraph should include a description of your interests and high-school achievements. Achievements and interests you might mention include:

- Best individual statistics
- Most significant victories or honors—i.e., varsity letter(s), highest conference, sectional, regional, state, or national finish; All-conference, state, High School Heisman, or All-American honors.
- Academic Honors are relevant too—i.e., academic scholarships, top class ranking, Dean's List, National Honors Society, Who's Who Among High School Students, number of college credits.
- Overall GPA __ Senior Yr GPA __ ACT __ SAT __ PSAT __.

My High School Coach is _____. His/her office number is _____; his/her e-mail is _____. My guidance counselor is _____. His/her office number is _____; his/her e-mail is _____.

I look forward to hearing from you at your earliest convenience.

Sincerely,
Michele Smith

scholarships, which will help determine if there is going to be sustained interest on their part.

Next, you should call or send a text message. These forms of contact are better used after an initial query letter or e-mail has been sent. Let the coach dictate the frequency of calls or follow-up contacts. Keep in mind that the amount of e-mail traffic the coach receives is considerable, and it is easy to have a message overlooked. If you have an interest in a program, don't give up or assume they are not interested. Pursue them until you get a response. Answers including "no," "not interested," "not interested in terms of scholarship," or "you may walk on," may not be the answers you wanted. However, such answers do help you with your decision making. Also, keep in mind that if you are really interested in the school, before you sign off, let them know in a follow-up letter that you would like to contact them again if you

---

Sample Follow-up Letter

Michele Smith
Milton High School Gymnastics Team
234 Willford Rd.
Greenforge, NC 27402
Ph: (336) 1234-5679
E-mail: msmith@miltonhs.com

North Carolina A & M University
Gymnastics Program
120 Bobston Hall
1601 E. Draton Street
Greensboro, NC 27411-3210

May 28, 2008

Dear Coach _____:

Thank you for responding to my inquiry about your program and university. I understand that the information requested is on the way [or I've received very informative material about your university and your team]. I look forward to communicating with you in this coming year about my scholastic and academic efforts, and about the progress of your team. I also hope that we can meet soon, via a formal home and/or campus visits.

Sincerely,
Michele Smith

---

meet their performance standards in the future. If you have a performance breakthrough, contact them again with an update. If the response is still lukewarm at best, they probably had some other reasons that they are not interested. Commonly, it may involve stereotypes regarding physical capacities, such as height or size, or other factors that are unrelated to your performance.

Another false assumption is that the better you are, the more recruiting offers will come your way. Chuck Robinson, the father of multiple college athletes at different performance levels, described how being "too good" eliminates options. "My son, Teyon Ware, a nationally ranked wrestler who was the number-one recruit in the nation, had [fewer] recruiting calls than my [other] son who went Division II." He explains that "everyone assumed, as good as he was, he would only attend the very highest-ranked wrestling programs." Surprised? This is not an uncommon phenomenon, especially with non-revenue sports.

Coach Cauthen describes an early recruiting experience to bring this point home.

> During my first major recruiting assignment, I conducted a home visit to the top female high school track and field athlete of the year. Her father told me that only a handful of programs recruited her, and that, until then, only two coaches paid her a home visit—myself included. She did not choose my program, but was a spectacularly productive collegian, winning multiple individual and relay titles, and leading her team to at least one national championship. She went on to become a multiple Olympian, winning an Olympic silver medal. I successfully recruited a number of top-10 high school seniors who were only pursued by two or more schools.

Marketing Yourself

After introducing yourself to various coaches, it's time to market yourself. Here are some different tools that may be helpful:

- Newspaper or Web articles regarding your performances. This is best for highlighting outstanding statistics and for sports such as track or swimming where coaches can compare numbers. It is hard to dispute an official performance for a shot put or a 100-meter breaststroke. These are comparable anywhere in the country.

- Footage of your performances. This is ideal for technique-based sports in which performance numbers cannot be compared. Video is better for highlighting aspects of your abilities that are not statistically relevant. For example, if you are a great defensive player, you may not generate the press or notoriety and may easily pass under the recruiting radar. Ensure that it is a quality video, echoes former junior college football player and former Division I graduate assistant football coach, Waco Blakely. He said, "Some athletes would send in subpar videos showing average performance and they would never hear back from the coaching staff. Conversely, a video demonstrating skills, speed, or outstanding play would automatically be contacted."

- Participation in all-star games. This is a great way to make yourself known to recruiters, as these games help separate you from other local athletes.

- Information letter from your coach. This should focus on your suitability as a prospective student as well as a description of your physical, mental, and performance attributes that would make you a good candidate.

- Participation in summer camps for high school athletes put on by colleges. This is a great way to get to know the coaching staff while giving them an opportunity to meet you. Keep in mind that many camps are not great for teaching. They are, however, excellent opportunities to showcase your talent and personally let the coaches know that you are interested in their program. Athletes who have not generated newspaper headlines might benefit by attending a camp.

- Paid recruiting agencies or Web sites. Be wary of these! Confirm exactly what you are getting for the price, as some can be very expensive. Be very specific regarding the extent that they are recruiting for you. Do they call coaches or programs for you? Also inquire how they will market you against other athletes who might want to play the same position and have also signed up with the agency. It may simply involve listing your name and performances along with hundreds of other athletes on a generic Web site.

- Academic information. Coaches are and should be interested in this information. Pertinent information includes ACT and SAT test scores, number of AP or college credit hours, and GPA. All divisions also have individual determinations of your GPA regarding certain core classes. Check each divisional Web site for these details. If you are not a stellar student, do not hide your current performance level. Explain why you have struggled and what you are currently doing to rectify your poorer performances. It also allows a creative coach with a smaller budget to put together a comprehensive financial package. Keep in mind that coaches work very closely with the admissions office. Coaches also know the qualifying standards for different academic financial aid packages. The more academic aid that you are given, the less the coach has to pay from his or her budget.
- Reference letters. Coaches do care about how you get along with others and that you can be a role model for their program now and many years after. Reference letters vouching for your character by a community, club, organizational, or religious leader will not substitute for poor performance. But if you are competing against athletes of equal performance levels, these factors can and do matter.

Follow Up

Between the initial contact and the final stages of negotiation, you can keep coaches abreast of your accomplishments in many ways aside from telephone calls. Continue sending updates including photographs, video (analogue or digital), blogs, and newspaper clippings that demonstrate your potential value to them. Keep in mind that it is easy to go overboard with this, and that each coach has his or her own preferences. Clarify with them what they would like to be notified about. Two suggestions include personal improvements and information about performances at conferences, regionals, or state championships, which allows the coach to assess your ability to perform under pressure.

Coaches themselves sometimes go overboard, as the perception of early and frequent contact is inappropriately construed by the athlete as "being wanted more."

Other Recruiting Opportunities to Send to the Coach

Student-athletes—especially if they are attempting to attend a nationally competitive athletic program—should consider multiple competitive arenas and venues beyond their public (or private) high school conference: This includes sectional, regional, or state championships. Coach Cauthen suggests focusing on national competitions, as well as possibly securing outstanding commendations.

In terms of competitions, junior national championships or other national or international competitions go a long way to separate you from other athletes. The most popular system is the AAU (Amateur Athletic Union). It holds state, regional, and national championships in most of the sports contested by American colleges and universities. Finalists in individual-team sports like swimming, track and field, cross-country, and gymnastics, earn All-American status. Most sports, such as soccer, tennis, and golf, also have their own junior club tours and tournaments.

Sometimes, playing a supportive role may also get attention. Many states have their own age group Olympic-style sports festivals. In many of these venues, you might catch a recruiter's eye by competing successfully in the 15-to-16 age group one year, and the 17-to-18 age group the next. For highly talented athletes, national or international invitational events such as the indoor Milrose Games in track, or the largest high school swimming invitational in the country, the Southwestern Ohio Swimming and Diving Classic, provide a great opportunity to showcase your talent, as colleges compete in these meets also. International examples include Junior Pan American Games and World Junior championships in many amateur sports. Coach Cauthen says that he has "known student-athletes to earn scholarships based primarily on their participation in some of these types of competitions."

Aim for achieving All-American or other distinctions. Each lets coaches know that you are highly regarded. Of course, there are numerous All-American programs, including the Gatorade High School All-American Program and the High School

Heisman Trophy. One finalist who was an all-state performer used this distinction to catapult herself onto a national scene. Achieving scholar-athlete awards is more important for academically oriented programs, but do not underestimate their value or the value of awards that recognize scholarship, character, or volunteerism.

> **Authors' comment:** Talk to your parents or guardians, high school coach, or local club coach about all the possibilities to develop your talent, reputation, and visibility. Don't let the limitations of the university non-revenue system limit you.

Visits

If the introductory and follow-up communications have gone well, the next critical step is the visit. This step can be budget dependent. Coaches may fly you out or come directly to your home. Even Division I schools that are non-revenue have limited funds, so this can be very revealing. Most coaches will be up front with you because if they truly don't see you as a top-caliber recruit, they will not spend money to fly you in. On the other hand, if a program provides a paid visit, it is a strong indication that the staff believes that you are highly desirable and worthy of some financial aid. For smaller schools that do not have a budget to pay for a visit, visit at your own expense. Choosing a college or an athletic program is too big a decision to make sight unseen, according to Melissa Sartin, who had a disappointing college soccer experience. Sartin, who transferred after her first year, said, "I wish I had visited first before I signed. Watching a practice or game might have helped me realize that the coaching staff was emotionally cold." Here are some essential components of a fruitful visit, whether official and paid for by the school or an unofficial visit, voluntarily paid for by you and your family:

- Meeting the coaches and any assistants that you will play for. Head and assistant coaches have varying levels of responsibility and control, which depends upon the structure of the program.

- Meeting with both the academic and athletic counselors. This is to make sure that both the opinions regarding your academic background as well as your future athletic opportunities are a good fit for you and the school.
- Spending time with teammates. Usually, coaches ensure that you spend the majority of your time with athletes who are hand-picked because they are good role models for the program and closest to your event or position. This may include rooming with and going out to planned events with specific team members. Go out of your way to meet with other athletes on the team to get a fuller picture of the program. You want to hear both the pluses and minuses. Be wary of schools that do not allow or try to prevent these opportunities.
- Meeting with a faculty member in the area of your academic interest. Faculty is often quite removed from the athletic department and will give you an honest assessment of their relationship with the program. Aside from telling you about the rigors and opportunities in the department, if asked, they might also share information regarding their perceptions of how a particular coach or program views academics as well as your major of interest. Be more wary if you are interested in a rigorous academic program such as engineering or pharmacy, which might require more laboratory or higher-level science courses.
- Observing a practice and possibly a competition. Practice is a great time to ask both coaches and athletes about training regimens and practice schedules. Most importantly, you can see for yourself how you would fit in and respond to the coaches' teaching style, temperament, and philosophy. You will spend more time with a coach at practice than anywhere else. Former softball player Jenny Branscum adds, "Coaches can be different in games than in practice. See how they interchange and treat players. For example, you can get a sense of how they respond when an athlete makes a mistake."
- At the end of the visit, ask what the coach can offer financially. If they cannot give you an answer, ask very specifically when they might let you know and what other information they need to make a decision.

- *Do not* sign or commit at this time. Campus visits can be very exhilarating and sometimes every visit seems like "this is the one." Go home, think on it a few days, and talk with family, friends, and coaches before making a decision. Good coaches may want to nudge you toward choosing their program but they will not pressure you on the spot.

> **Authors' comment:** A common question that arises is when do you let a program know where they rank on your list and ask where you fall on theirs? It is a difficult question. Coaches are very good at playing this game. Honesty is the best policy; try to establish an honest relationship about where you both are on each others' lists. Track coach AF says, "I tell my recruits up front where they are on my list." Not everyone is going to have this level of integrity but try to establish this level of communication up front.

Summary

- Be proactive: select your choices and contact them.
- Make available all the high school and non-high school opportunities to showcase your talent.
- Sell your athletic and academic strengths and follow up as indicated.
- Visit the athletic and academic programs. Watch the coaching staff and future teammates in both practice and competition.

5

Scholarship Negotiation

You are getting closer to making a final decision. The initial excitement of the recruiting process has probably worn off, and it may even have become burdensome.

Narrowing down the college options requires two things. First, do your homework regarding how you compare both academically and athletically with other prospective students applying to the programs in which you are interested. Then, get direct feedback from the coaches and programs to further evaluate what college and opportunity represents the best fit and financial opportunity. This chapter addresses that latter point: scholarships and financial assistance.

Scholarships or Financial Assistance

The term *scholarship* refers to monetary assistance provided by the school in return for your providing your skill to the university. All scholarships are scholastic or academic grants-in-aid, whether for mathematic prowess, musical talent, or athletic ability. Understanding the nuances of athletic scholarships is critical. First, there are full scholarships, partial scholarships, and financial packages that can be used as an incentive to attend a college.

Full Athletic Scholarships

Full athletic scholarships are "full rides" to attend the college. They typically include room and board, tuition and other fees, and books, and they tend to be given for revenue sports, especially football and basketball. Full scholarship allotments are often divided among athletes in non-revenue sports. Only the very best athletes get full scholarships in non-revenue sports.

Partial Athletic Scholarships

In the majority of sports, the total amount of scholarship money is divided among athletes in order to field a team. "Partials" are the only way that non-revenue programs can ensure sufficient players to field a team on budgets that are usually limited. One example might be a wrestling program that has four or five scholarships to fill a roster that enables it to compete in 10 weight categories. Without dividing the money, programs like this would find it hard to field full teams.

Financial Packages

Some programs may show more interest in you if they know that you will qualify for a combination of student loans, grants such as Pell or other government grants, academic or organizational scholarships, and work-study programs. Take advantage of scholarship opportunities based on academic merit or financial need. Grant-in-aid may not seem nearly as exciting as an athletic scholarship, but it has some pluses. Unlike athletic scholarships, grants are not tied to your athletic performance and a coach cannot threaten or pull this money if you do not fulfill his or her athletic expectations. Athletic scholarships are given on a year-to-year basis and can be withdrawn, maintained, or, renegotiated based on your performance. Typically, you have to renounce an academic scholarship or not meet the scholarship's specific minimum GPA standards, violate the law or university policy, or flunk out to lose it. With Division III colleges, which do not offer athletic scholarships, assessing the financial package is important. In many situations, a win-win circumstance is for you to receive the best combination of financial aid and the coach to get the most talent for the least cost to his or her budget.

> **Authors' comment:** Compare the total financial package to the overall cost of the school. A one-third scholarship at a public in-state school may be a better financial deal than a half scholarship at an expensive private school. Also, do not undervalue a good total financial package, which might combine athletic, academic, and grants-in-aid.

The Rivalry Factor

The rivalry factor, defined as being recruited by rival college programs, can also improve your odds with a particular college. Rivalries refer to colleges that are direct competitors and these can occur in a variety of ways. Some rivalries are within a conference, whereas others are within a state. Occasionally, you also have historic rivals or universities that have competed against each other for many years. In such cases, winning everything from games to the top recruits is a matter of intense pride and bragging rights. Be aware of the historical and strategic relationship among the various programs, as strong and bitter rivals don't like losing talent to one another, especially if the talent is from their home state. If rival programs are recruiting you, a bidding war could increase the amount of scholarship offered. There is, however, a risk of alienating one or more coaches. You should try to be as diplomatic and professional as you can. Be honest; let each program know where they stand and what your financial and academic concerns are.

Narrow Down The List

Your correspondences and academic and athletic compatibility evaluations should lead you to some conclusions and enable you to put together a short list. Research the strengths and weaknesses of each program in terms of the academic and athletic factors.

Academics

Each division has its own criteria for being academically qualified to attend a college. To find the most up-to-date requirements, do these two things:

1. Go to divisional Web sites listed in this book to see how your GPA and ACT or SAT scores compare to the requirements. This is especially important if you are a marginal student. The NCAA for Division I and Division II has a clearinghouse where you register to play. This means that you have to register with the NCAA regarding your intent and interest to compete at the NCAA Division I or II levels. A combination of your GPA and your ACT or SAT scores determines if

you qualify. Those who do not meet NCAA requirements will lose a year of eligibility if they decide to attend a Division I or Division II program, and thus are often encouraged to go the juco or NAIA route. If you are a nonqualifier, you can choose to attend without a scholarship. If you perform academically, you can qualify for a scholarship. You should also evaluate the high school classes you have taken. Ensure that you have taken the classes required to attend college on a scholarship. This is one area where your high school counselor can be helpful. Each division has its own standards, and as these can change, we suggest going to the divisional Web sites to ensure that you are getting the most up-to-date information.

2. Once you are assured of meeting divisional standards, go to the Web sites of the universities in which you are interested and compare your academic performances in terms of GPA and ACT or SAT scores and the number of AP classes you have taken with the universities' average. Other good sources of university-specific information are the athletic academic counselor and the university academic counselors. Talk with both to ensure that you receive an assessment of your potential to succeed academically. If you have an interest in a professional school such as medical, law, or business school, your grades can influence your opportunity to get into a particular program. Talk with a guidance counselor to help you assess your potential to get in. Don't forget to check out the annual college books and resources.

Athletics

The more your talent and skills fit a team's needs, the greater the chances its coach will fight to sign you. Use this four-step process of figuring out how you compare with your collegiate peers. By using the program Web sites, other resources, and talking with current athletes, you can get a good gauge of what athletic scholarship you might vie for.

First, compare performance statistics and conference championships from the last few years. Conference placing and conference championships are usually more critical to a university's funding and evaluation. Few teams achieve national rankings, but every team strives for respect in its respective conference or league. Many conferences list historical results online. Obtain annual publications of conference championship results and records as well. Ask your coach or guidance counselor for help.

Next, ask athletes on the team about their performance backgrounds as seniors in high school. Find athletes whose athletic credentials are comparable to yours and ask what sort of financial package they are receiving. Be wary regarding these answers, as some athletes may not be comfortable sharing this information or may embellish their responses. This will give you some guidance as to what a coach might offer, depending on the set of recruiting circumstances for that particular year. Also compare yourself physically and athletically with members of the team. For example, an average Division I quarterback in football or center in basketball may be 6'4" and 6'10", respectively, versus 6'0" and 6'7" in Division III.

The next thing you should do is confirm the information you learned about the athletic performance of your prospective teammates. You can use team brochures or Web sites, which often contain important biographical details about the high school and college achievements of team members. Individual event records and individual successes in important invitational or duel-meet competitions signal to interested persons the program's performance on a week-to-week basis. These can also let you know when key personnel are graduating, or perhaps transferring.

Finally, look at scholarship standards. If a team has detailed scholarship criteria, see how your performances compare. This is the most clear-cut approach, and it would be ideal if every program used such a comparison standard. Keep in mind that at very competitive programs, there may be a number of recruited athletes who may qualify. Therefore, if a coach is only looking for one recruit to fill a particular position or event, you might qualify standard-wise but still not be offered the amount of money that the standard might reflect.

Summary

- The majority of scholarship athletes are on partial rides. The exceptions are football and basketball, which boast many full-ride scholarships.
- Use academic and athletic division and individual college standards to see how well you might fit with the programs in which you are interested.
- Consider the best total financial package rather than simply comparing athletic scholarship amounts.

6

Making a Decision

Imagine that after filtering through all of your options, narrowing down your choices, and sending out applications, five colleges offered you a range of attractive opportunities. How do you choose between them? Ideally, your best choice would be the one that is the best academic institution, has the strongest team in your sport, offers you a full ride, and has teammates, coaches, facilities, and a location that you love.

If this isn't your situation, there is neither a hard and fast rule nor a formula for making the best decision. The decision making will have to come from your heart as well as your mind.

Coach Cauthen's general rule of thumb is to choose the program and institution that offers the best relative financial package in relation to everything else in the mix. However, if the program with the best financial offer falls short in terms of its emotional appeal or your personal comfort zone, pick your next best option.

Two strategies of evaluating programs can be very useful in making your final choice. The Category System, used in tandem with the Rank Order System, can make for a satisfying way of approaching the decision-making process.

The Category System

This section contains composite athlete profiles to help you narrow down your choices. They are not real people, but they do represent real situations. Any similarity to real persons or situations is purely unintended. Our experience suggests that many of you might see yourselves in one of these examples of athletes who place different emphases on their athletic and academic talents. They range from being an outstanding student and athlete to being a poorer student and a less-accomplished athlete, as well as those who shine only in athletics or academics. First, let's consider the athlete that truly has one overriding factor regarding their school choice.

Do any of the following feelings or thoughts ring true with you?

- "I just have to be close to my girlfriend/boyfriend and family."
- "My family has had five generations graduate from this college and I want to also."
- "This college has the best computer science program and I would be foolish to go anywhere else."
- "I have to be around others who share my specific religious, ethnic, or racial background."

It doesn't matter what variable you put in the above comments, as it relates to location, family, relationships, academics, or athletics. For many of you, a combination of these factors will ultimately help you decide what college you attend. If you know in your heart that there is an overriding factor, listen to your gut. Ask yourself which university settings meet the criteria that will allow you to reach your goals. Of course, situations change—relationships end, academic aspirations change—but we have seen too many athletes transfer after their first year because they did not factor these considerations into their college equation.

Stellar Academics, Great Athletics

"Jill" is an honorable mention All-American tennis player who has been making local and regional news since her freshman year. At 6'1" she has a killer serve, often hitting over 100 miles per hour. She also is a formidable doubles player and was captain of her high school team her senior year. She boasts a 3.85 GPA with an SAT score of 1,400 for the math and critical reading sections. Jill also has taken 12 hours of Advanced Placement courses. Although she occasionally thinks about a post-collegiate shot at the women's professional tour, she has already decided that one day she will attend law school, as she wants to practice business law. Both parents are professionals and she is not intimidated by the thought of competing both on the court and in the classroom.

If you are similar to Jill, you are a college coach's dream. Prestigious universities will go out of their way to recruit you. You have a shot at many of the finest universities and can also compete with the highest caliber athletic programs in your sport. A great school with a powerhouse team is within your grasp. Of course, many other less competitive programs in any division are clearly also an option.

Keep in mind that GPAs vary from school to school. Therefore, SAT or ACT scores are often a better predictor of how you will match academically with your peers at any given school. If you are average or above, even with the pressures of athletics, you should be fine.

Thinking about the pros? Give it a chance if this has been a lifelong goal, but don't squander your gift of intellect. Ask yourself which universities will allow you to make the best combination of your athletic and academic talents. Be wary of programs in which the coaches automatically prioritize athletics over academics. If you have future academic goals like Jill, consider a degree that will provide the necessary prerequisites. Otherwise, consider practical majors that may give you an edge in the sports business world. If unsure, all three authors would highly recommend a solid liberal arts degree. This is a general degree that allows you to take courses in multiple areas that will provide a good foundation for any academic pathway you decide to pursue in the future.

Stellar Academics, Average Athletics

"Jim" carries a 3.90 GPA, scored a 35 on his ACT, loves reading books on just about any topic, and wants a good liberal arts background before embarking on a graduate degree of some sort. With a lot of extra training, he has emerged as a solid varsity runner on the cross-country team. He has been a late bloomer athletically, finally placing in the conference outdoor track meet with a personal best of 4:37 in the 1,600-meter run. Jim really enjoys the camaraderie and experience of high school running and wants an opportunity to continue running in college.

Jim realizes that academics are his ticket, but he still has a desire to fulfill his athletic potential. An athletic scholarship to complement his academic ones wouldn't be so bad, either. Jim may have a dilemma, as his best bets to fulfill his academic potential may have no interest in him athletically. He must ask himself if he is willing to sacrifice his academic potential to quench his athletic thirst. In this case, walking on might be Jim's best option. See the section later in this chapter that discusses this process at length.

If Jim's situation mirrors yours, there may be another option. Use your athletic talent to leverage your chances of getting into an Ivy League or similarly competitive college. Along this line, the best fit for students in this category may be with one of the many small top-ranked liberal arts schools, which are typically Division III or NAIA. Although many of these private schools are very expensive, academics are the top priority and you will have an opportunity to participate and compete athletically.

Two other considerations are to transfer for a semester a year to give athletics your best shot. Also, many programs have less competitive junior varsity programs to complement their varsity programs. This topic is discussed in greater detail later in this chapter.

Poorer Academics, Stellar Athletics

"Steve" has dreamed of an NBA career since he was 10 years old. At 6'6" and 220 pounds, he was a consensus third-team All-American, averaging over 20 points, eight rebounds, and four assists per game. College coaches drooled over his versatility, as he could play guard or small forward. On the flip side, Steve had always struggled in school. In fact, his single parent, who is a high school teacher, had to force him to study. He had a 2.0 GPA and on a retake, he scored a 20 on his ACT.

Steve has the athletic profile that has the highest likelihood of being used by unscrupulous coaches to win championships without concerns for college graduation potential. They privately hope he will "get through" academically, so that he will remain eligible and help them win championships before turning pro. Every year, athletes like Steve who are focused on the big-time and the post-season tournament, end up ineligible due to poor academic performance. This occurs despite the personal attention provided at smaller schools or the study halls, specialized tutors, and "academic counselors" afforded by larger schools. Coaches are willing to gamble on an athlete like Steve because they figure he will only be around for a year or two, because the first two years usually involve easier prerequisites, which are much less demanding than higher-level degree courses. This is why it is important to carefully assess the attitudes of Division I coaches.

If your situation is similar to Steve's, you should be sure to compare your GPA and SAT or ACT scores to the average for the incoming freshman class and ask the program and academic counselors for an honest assessment of your chances of successfully competing academically. Senior associate athletic director Chuck Bailey says:

> Everyone thinks they are Division I material and ready to go to the pros. Even on great Division I programs, only two or three athletes may have a shot at going pro, but if you ask, all the recruits think it will be them. Unfortunately, a lot of them pass up really good Division II opportunities where they would have a chance to improve their games.

We are not discouraging you from taking an opportunity at an outstanding school, and *if* you make academics an important priority, you might well succeed. Retired high school coach Steve Sublett describes considering individual motivation when helping athletes make college choices. He said, "I had one athlete who could have done well at the Ivy League level but he did not have the fire in his belly and so I suggested a less academically rigorous path." Retired college coach Bob Timmons, who has coached multiple world record holders and Olympic champions, explained his perspective once an athlete is in the program. He said, "I really tried to look for academic maturity and convince kids that academics is what is important in life."

Two other options if you are in Steve's situation include looking at Division II or NAIA programs where you are sure to get a free ride. Both of these programs may be able to personalize their attention to help you succeed academically. Also, being a "big fish in a little pond" may give you a chance to perform well.

Finally, do not overlook two other options: junior colleges and preparatory schools. Junior colleges are a great place to improve your academic skills. As Brian Renshaw said, "Juco is good for the weaker student as it allows the athlete to develop and prepare for a four-year school." He himself benefited from this experience and is now a very successful NAIA track and cross-country coach.

Preparatory schools are essentially another year of high school following the senior year, with the focus on improving grades while allowing you to continue improving athletically. These schools, typically for sports such as basketball, are controversial. Concerns about academic integrity have been investigated by the NCAA. Some preparatory schools exist to help ineligible athletes raise their grade point averages in order to become eligible to qualify for an NCAA scholarship. These schools do not focus on college preparatory and study skills, which you need to succeed academically at a major college level.

Ask yourself the following questions:

1. Am I willing to put in the extra work to get a degree?

   Make a commitment to being the best student you can be. This involves working as hard in the classroom as you do for your sport.

2. Am I really only interested in the pros?

   This is fine, but what do you want to do later? If you have no interest in earning a degree, you might be the sort of player to go semi-pro. Remember though, very few professional athletes can live off their athletic prowess alone.

It is up to you to decide that academics will be a priority. Dr. Benjamin, an athlete tutor in college, notes that sometimes simply studying was the solution.

> I was tutoring a basketball player who was failing. When he got his first C, the teacher commended me for being a 'miracle worker' and asked what I was doing, as other tutors had failed. The truth is that I forced him to sit and read without distraction. Only after he read, would I actually challenge him or ask him questions.

The bottom line: A little effort goes a long way!

Average Academics, Poorer Athletics

"Tina" has recently taken up softball and really enjoyed playing competitively for the first time in high school. She attends a larger and very completive high school that is a perennial state champion, and thus she has mainly played on the junior varsity team. Therefore, she has had little opportunity to showcase her improving athletic talents. She believes she can get better and really has enjoyed the team camaraderie. Academically, neither of Tina's parents has a college education nor has she ever considered college as an option for herself. She struggles with standardized tests. Her ACT score is 23 and her overall GPA is 2.4. With her recent success in softball, her burgeoning academic maturity, and her improved senior GPA of 2.8, Tina now believes that college might be an option and softball may be a way of helping pay for some of the tuition.

Does your situation mirror Tina's? Use your average GPA, SAT, or ACT to ensure that you find a college that is a good match for your academic background. If you are motivated and committed, you can consider targeting a higher-profile academic college. Maturity, improved study habits, and greater concentration and focus on academics may result in better college performances compared to high school. But be realistic. If going to college is solely about getting the education to qualify for a decent job and having an opportunity to compete, you need to find a place to do both. Consider the options outlined in the previous section, such as junior college, less expensive and less competitive public Division II schools, less competitive smaller private schools—especially those in Division III and the NAIA, or preparatory schools.

The Rank Order Method

Let's assume you have narrowed your choices to five schools and want to weigh your options using the rank order method, which is more analytical than the category system. First, rank each school in terms of personal or emotional appeal. Develop a chart of the key criteria for selection. Weight the relative importance of each criterion, using a scale of 1 to 5 (or 1 to 10). Discuss the top two candidates with your parents and coaches. Sleep on it for a few days and look at your scores again. Do the scores and categories accurately reflect your feelings about the programs? If so, make the selection. If not, reevaluate the criteria. In the end, you might find that there are a number of good choices, and you might end up selecting the school that ultimately feels the best to you.

The following charts are examples of the rank order system. This first chart (Table 6.1) reflects the scores that were given for each factor based on a 1 to 5 scale with 5 being the highest rating. (The schools in these charts are fictitious.):

Table 6.1

School	Criteria					Likeability			
	Academics	Athletics	Location	Coach	Staff	Teammates	Campus	Aid	
PITU	4	3	2	5	5	5	4	5	33
TSA&I	3	5	3	5	5	4	4	5	34
UCA&T	5	5	5	4	5	5	5	4	38
OSTT	3	5	3	4	4	4	2	5	30
USA&M	2	4	3	3	4	2	1	3	22

Rate how important each factor is to you on a scale of 1 to 5.

Now factor in how important each criteria (Weight in Table 6.2) is for you and multiply this number by the above numbers from Table 6.1 which will provide an individual score for each criteria and a total or composite score which considers all the criteria.

Table 6.2

School	Criteria				Likeability				
	Academics	Athletics	Location	Coach	Staff	Teammates	Campus	Aid	
Weight	2	1.5	1	1.3	1.2	1.2	1	1.4	
PITU	8	4.5	2	6.5	6	6	4	7	44
TSA&I	6	7.5	3	5	6	4.8	4	7	43.3
UCA&T	10	7.5	5	5.2	6	6	5	5.6	50.3
OSTT	6	7.5	3	5.2	4.8	4.8	2	7	40.3
USA&M	4	6	3	3.9	4.8	2.4	1	4.2	29.3

Multiply the ratings from Table 6.1 by the "Weight" in Table 6.2.

Notice that, in this example, academics was of the highest priority and location among the lowest. So, for example, in our hypothetical situation, academics at PITU is much better than USA&M, however, USA&M's location is better. Now, going on to table 2, this athlete values academics at a 2 to 1 ratio versus location. Therefore, in terms of just these two factors, PITU comes out ahead. This method allows you to numerically classify what is important. Note that the weights assigned in the second chart reverse the order of the second- and third-ranked schools in the first chart. The weights are, of course, entirely up to you.

Notice that academics received the highest weighting. How you are prepared by your major and a university's general curriculum will most likely have the greatest impact on your adult life. The quality of your adult life, especially your earning potential, will be influenced by the quality of your scholastic preparation (and the social network developed during your college years).

Study Halls/Academic Support

You may want to ask about the kind of academic support available to students in general and student-athletes in particular. Most Division I programs have "study tables" for all student-athletes. Most, if not all, such programs require every freshman to attend study table their first semester. Those who end up on academic probation must continue to attend, and those whose grades were marginal but above probation may be asked to continue as well. You will often find that straight-A students attend study table all four years. When asked why, they replied that they wanted to maintain their high academic status. Tutors are readily available and free in such programs.

Many programs have minimum competition GPAs. Some programs require that a student continue to make progress toward a degree. This usually means that the credit hours needed to be declared a freshman, sophomore, junior, and senior, remain on track, and that once a major is declared, the student makes the recommended credit and course decisions to earn a degree within four academic years. Counselors usually keep track of a student's class attendance and individual course grade status throughout the semester. Programs that aggressively monitor and assist their students offer the best conditions for successful graduation. Learning the nature of the athletic department's advising system could be as important as any of your other criteria.

Advice to Parents or Guardians

It is sometimes difficult as a parent or guardian to know when to intervene and how best to give advice. If you have an athletic background, share your experiences about recruiting and the college athletic experience. Be careful with dictating versus advising. If you are not a sports aficionado, use your lack of athletic background to its advantage by clarifying with the coach what is offered and what the expectations are regarding the program and the balance between athletics and academics.

Timmons said, "Sometimes what a coach wants a parent to know and what a parent or guardian really wants to hear are very different. Sometimes, athletes are afraid to push regarding an issue. This is where the parent or guardian comes in. Do not leave without answers to the questions that you want to discuss."

While assisting one parent help her daughter make a choice between two schools when the recruiting pressure was on, Dr. Benjamin said, "Keep in mind there might not be a right one. Both may be good places for her." The parent commented how this was a "voice of reason" that she needed to hear at this time.

These comments are suggestive of how stressful the recruiting process can be, both for the athlete and for you, the parents. You will be more of an asset to your child by reminding yourself of the following:

1. You are not being recruited. It is your child's college opportunity.
2. More than one option may work just fine. The "right" or "perfect" school may not exist; don't force it if it truly is not there.

Walk-On Opportunities

Another consideration when weighing your athletic and academic options is determining if a walk-on program is right for you. Walking-on refers to being a non-scholarship player. Many non-Division I and many non-revenue programs rely on walk-ons to complete their rosters. The degree to which walk-ons make up a team differs based on the coach and the program.

Athletes are often identified in unusual ways. Carolyn Young, a former Division III tennis player, relates that she "was playing tennis with a friend and the tennis coach walked by and asked me if I wanted to play the following weekend in a college tournament." Young had no initial intent of playing college tennis, did not ever receive scholarship money, but genuinely enjoyed the experience. Often, classes are where athletes are spotted.

JS, a gymnast who attended a mid-level Division I school, said, "I was taking a physical education course in gymnastics. The head coach saw me and asked me to try out. I had never planned to compete in college but I did anyway and made the team." After JS realized that she was on the traveling team, she did negotiate for a partial scholarship.

Not all walk-on stories result in playing time or financial aid. Dr. Benjamin remembers seeing the optimism of walk-ons with dreams of playing on varsity followed by disillusionment of this unrealized dream. In one situation, Dr. Benjamin was given charge of developing the walk-on squad toward filling slots on the varsity. A new head coach was hired and his philosophy was essentially to only keep those who were legitimate performers at the national level. Dr. Benjamin said, "It was tough when we had to let these very hard-working guys go. But, as a walk-on, you need to realize this is a reality of college sport, especially at Division I."

Also, ensure that even as a walk-on, you are treated with respect. Talk with the team's walks-ons or other non-scholarship athletes to get their perception of treatment, scholarship opportunities, and playing time. If the team you are considering has no walk-ons, this program might not be the best for you.

The truth is that some coaches feel uncomfortable playing a walk-on over someone who is getting a full ride. If possible, try to pin the coach down to specific times or performance criteria that should net scholarship or playing opportunities.

You should also clarify with the coach what he or she would do if you were competing at an equal or better level than those who are receiving financial aid. Scholarship moneys are given on a year-to-year basis. Look for a program that allows individuality within a team concept and respects each member's contribution no matter how large or small.

> **Coach's comment:** Coach Cauthen notes that some top-rated programs have walk-ons or non-scholarship student athletes on their teams who are better than the top high school performer in a given specialty. You can earn a scholarship at one of these programs only by becoming a conference champion or becoming a collegiate All-American. Cauthen says:
>
> > I once recruited [a] top two high school half-miler. [She] passed up a visit to my institution for one to the nation's top track and field programs at the time. She discovered that her best 800 was slower than walk-ons there, and that she would have to compete with them to earn a scholarship. Feeling that she was slighted and had wasted a campus visit, she had her parents contact me, asking for a guaranteed scholarship, before she would commit to a visit. That was not how our program nor most programs operate. I don't know what ever happened to her but she did not get into either program.

Junior Varsity

Junior varsity programs are used to boost enrollment at smaller private schools and also provide practice squads for the varsity athletes. Advantages are scholarship money and more academically friendly schedules. With possibly less time committed to travel and practice, along with an abbreviated competition schedule, you can better focus on your education.

PN played Division III junior varsity soccer by choice. He said, "I was given a chance to move up to varsity but I preferred JV because we had a shorter schedule and never traveled out of state." PN, now a successful psychiatrist, felt this allowed him to focus on his academics. JV coach Mark Thompson, comments these programs often "bring students in who want the opportunity to grow and appreciate the sport." Thompson adds that some may never make the varsity but they "enjoy being a part of the team, get good grades, and come away with a great education." He adds that these students also become "great alumni (partly based on) their athletic experiences." Thompson explains that, often, very talented athletes expect to have the opportunity to compete in college and "take it for granted," whereas junior varsity athletes are very grateful for the opportunity. This "appreciation combined with their academics often leads to lifelong connections with the school."

Summary

- Compare academic and athletic suitability to arrive at your final options.
- Rank your options to select a university.
- Consider other options, such as walking on or playing junior varsity.
- There may not be one best choice. Consider yourself lucky that you have more than one very good choice.

7

Roles

Many individuals may be involved in the recruitment and scholarship process. You and your family should understand the possible influence each of these individuals may have. This chapter will help you sort out the different responsibilities of the various coaches, counselors, and others involved in the recruiting process. Knowing how each fits into the "big picture" can help you better navigate the recruiting process.

Coaches

High school and collegiate coaching staffs may be intimately involved regarding an athlete's scholarship opportunities. These are the individuals you will spend more of your college time with: they will oversee schedules, practices, travel, and competition. Unfortunately, individual factors such as personal friendships, alliances, and egos interfere with what may be best for you. Coaches are influenced by factors outside of your performance. Some of these factors include their relationships with assistant coaches or your high school or club coach.

Your high school or club coach may also have specific positive or negative feelings regarding the programs you are considering. When they recommend an athlete, they may perceive that their reputations are on the line. Coach Cauthen recalls a conversation with a high school coach who actually underreported the athlete's GPA, as the coach had other ideas about where the athlete should play. Also, junior-level coaches looking to move up to the college enhanced coaching ranks may not want to put their reputations on the line.

Head Coach

The head coach is in charge of the team and takes ultimate responsibility for the successes or failures of the program. Three important considerations are the head coach's relationship with the assistants, recruiting, and control of the practice and competitions.

The head coach assigns assistants different levels of responsibility. Assess these interactions during the recruiting process, as some assistants are more valued and some aspects of a program may have more emphasis placed on it. Head coaches tend to be highly involved with the recruiting of the very finest athletes. As one assistant coach who has coached at more than one division states quite bluntly, "You know they are interested in you when the head coach starts calling you." Dr. Benjamin says that, "there definitely is a hierarchy—the higher on the list you are, the more likely the head coach will take a recruiting interest in you." However, Coach Cauthen adds that sometimes the head coach may follow the recruiting without directly getting involved, letting assistant coaches deal with the details of the early recruiting stages. Regardless, head coaches tend to be highly involved in the final decisions, both with scholarships and playing time. Therefore, if you do not like the head coach but think you will be all right at a program because you like the assistant, you may be in for a surprise.

Assistant Coaches

Assistant coaches are critical to the success of a program. Often, the full extent of what a great assistant does for the program is not fully appreciated until the assistant leaves and a program begins to falter. Assess assistant coaches for their level of autonomy, influence over the head coach, and coaching style. Many assistants have significant control over their area of expertise. However, decisions regarding the team will most likely depend on final approved by the head coach. That said, assistants exert different levels of influence on the head coach. This varies based on the sport, the relationship, and the coaching philosophy of the head and assistant coaches. In some cases, the assistant may be such an expert in a particular facet of the sport that the head coach will leave that assistant alone to control that aspect of the team's training and performance. In other situations, the assistant coach is simply an extension of the head coach in every matter. Observe the relationship between the head coach and assistants.

Ask current teammates under the assistant that you would be working with about the coaching relationships and the level of autonomy of the assistant coach. Also observe the assistant's coaching style, just as you would with the head coach. Conflicts with the assistant will invariably result in discord with the program.

> **Coach's comment:** "Does the assistant appear happy or satisfied with his or her contribution to the team?" If the answer is no, we believe it is fair to ask the assistant coach how long he or she expects to stay with the program. Keep in mind that many assistant coaches have aspirations of being a head coach. Also, head coaches sometimes fire an assistant as a scapegoat for poor performances.

Graduate Assistant/Volunteer Assistant Coaches

Graduate assistant and volunteer assistant coaches tend to be novice coaches or graduate students attempting to gain experience to progress to an assistant coaching level. Assess them for their level of interaction in the recruiting and coaching process. Often, graduate assistants also help with the logistics of recruiting trips and with such duties as driving for the team.

The experience and expertise of this level of assistant coach can vary. Often, they might be former high school coaches looking to expand their educational as well as coaching opportunities. They might also be volunteer students or those on work-study whose sole role is to help the head coach carry out specific duties. They may have no autonomy or decision-making capacities. They also can be heavily involved in recruiting; if so, they tend to recruit athletes who are lower on the list. When a coach calls and says he or she is an assistant, clarify exactly what his or her role is to differentiate between a regular assistant and a graduate assistant. You can usually confirm a position by checking the team's Web site. If the coach is not listed or profiled, most likely he or she is a graduate assistant.

Because their level of skill and expertise varies, graduate assistants usually work under one of the assistant coaches. Their payback for this is the opportunity to be involved with the program with the goal of getting a regular assistant coaching job upon graduation. Dr. Benjamin's experiences in this role were extremely satisfying. He was given a role of identifying top younger talent across the country and also recruited extensively. He describes "coming in a few nights a week and calling athletes who were lower on the recruiting totem pole. When the head or assistant coach was out, then I would step up and call a higher-level athlete."

Graduate assistants also perform multiple non-coaching duties. Examples include driving recruits around or to the airport or back. Because of the time spent with both the athletes as well as the recruits, they often are good sources for questions and candid answers. On one occasion, an athlete on the way back to the airport asked Dr. Benjamin how well he might fit in. Dr. Benjamin told the athlete, who clearly was a poor fit with the program he was considering, that he ought to look somewhere else. In the end, "it was best for us and best for the recruit."

High School Coaches

High school coaches are typically the ones who can best speak to an athlete's abilities. In many situations, they have spent the most time athletically with the athlete and also understand what it takes to play at the next level. High school assistant coach Perry Jones says, "I try to get high school athletes to look past their career and see a realistic picture. They may really be excited about Division I, for example, but Division II may be a much better fit. I tell them about the business of college sports, and [that] you really have to love it. If you don't, you will leave—and that is a tragedy." Being a realistic appraiser of an athlete's talent, as well as a motivator, come through in Jones's comments.

Another benefit is that high school coaches knows their personnel and can sell their athletes in a realistic way to a college coach. Coach Sublett relates the story of a college coach showing interest in one athlete and ending up with another. Sublett said:

> The coach asked me about an athlete who had no interest in junior college. I said that she probably would not be interested but that he ought to look at one of the non-star sprinters who was great in relays and a team player. I remember that this athlete initially had aspirations to be a typist with no interest in attending college. After it was all said and done,

because of the scholarship money and the opportunity to further her education, she eventually became a nurse.

Sublett concluded that a particularly important role of the high school coach is to "encourage them to reach ahead" but in a realistic manner.

Watch out for personal coaching biases and possible alliances with college coaches. High school coaches may be concerned about their reputations regarding who they refer or do not refer to a particular college coach. If a coach discourages one of your choices, is reluctant to help you with a particular school, or is extra positive regarding a school that is not on your list, have the coach explain his or her rationale. Often, relationships can be related to summer camp connections or possible issues with the recruitment of a previous athlete. You don't need all the details to help you make your own assessment.

Also, consider the high school coach's passion and interest in your sport. At rural or smaller schools, coaches who are coaching multiple sports in order to fulfill a spot or a contractual obligation are more prevalent. Often, they will not be as connected to your needs in their secondary sport. John Stringer, a rural basketball player and high jumper believed he had more potential in high jumping but track was "a secondary sport to the coaches. It was frustrating as they never recognized my talent in the high jump and certainly never encouraged it." With minimal practice, he managed state qualifying marks and, had he been more aware, might have qualified for track scholarships, especially at smaller, less competitive schools. Finally, do not underestimate the role of a good assistant coach, or even other coaches—who might intervene on your behalf if the head coach won't.

Summer/Personal/Club Coaches

Summer league, club, and personal coaches can also be your advocate in the recruiting process. These coaches can have similar biases as high school coaches, however. These include having specific relationships with college coaches, concerns about their own reputations, and general interest in your welfare. Ask yourself the following two questions regarding an outside coach:

1. Do they have the background to coach and make judgments about your college future? Some club coaches have minimal coaching experience but are paid by an organization or a group of parents to coach.

2. Does an unhealthy competition with the high school coach exist? This especially occurs in situations where practice time and competitions are within the same seasons. This tends to be more common in basketball and soccer.

If the answers to these are no and yes, respectively, the club coach could actually be detrimental to your recruiting chances. High school basketball coach CC laments that club coaches "contribute to bad attitudes in athletes. They build some of these athletes up [to expect to play at the top level, although] very few can play Division I. I've seen situations where athletes end up spending their [Division I] career on the bench when they could have gone Division III or NAIA and been a star."

Principal Mark Landrith concurs. He says that when club coaches tolerate mediocrity in team play and maintaining a respectful attitude, "Kids learn [that it is acceptable] to play a selfish brand of ball [from these coaches]; they talk back to refs, and the parents are paying this coach to develop their children." He notes that club coaches, especially in basketball and soccer, focus less on the whole-person concept and simply on the club team's athletic performance. Less emphasis is placed on important values such as teamwork, respect, cooperation, and player development as a person and not just as an athlete.

On the other hand, tennis club coach Dwight Nucholls, who over 35 years watched about 100 athletes he coached go on to play intercollegiately, states that, often, he and his tennis instructors actually may spend more quality time over the years with a given player than his or her high school team coach. In these cases, your club coach may be the best person to ask for advice and help with the recruiting process. Finally, some sports in some states may not be played at the high school level and therefore your club coach has to be your advocate. Examples might be such events as lacrosse, skiing, rowing, or equestrian.

Counselors

A counselor's role is to guide athletes regarding their academic options to maximize academic potential. The three types of counselors—high school, college athletic, and college academic—can have different viewpoints as well as interest levels in helping you reach your college academic and athletic aspirations.

High School

High school counselors look out for the best interest of each student. However, some counselors may limit or indirectly prevent athletes from reaching their potential because of their own biases. The counselors may know very little about college sports and may have little interest in acquiring the knowledge necessary to help athletes navigate the college athletic recruiting process. Other biases may include racial, gender, or socioeconomic biases about your ability to succeed in college. Coach Brian Renshaw recalls that a high school counselor told him that "I'd be better off at a vo-tech because I would never make it in college." This was based on a negative perception of Renshaw and his family as they came from a blue-collar background. Renshaw proved this prediction wrong as he earned a college degree with the financial assistance of athletic scholarships.

Counselors tend to be overworked and often do not have the time for the nuances of college athletics, according to Landrith, who adds, "Tell your counselor that your goal is to play college athletics and [ask] can you help me schedule my classes with this in mind." A simple way of helping your counselor help you is to provide a copy or Web site page of the academic requirements for your divisional and collegiate choices. This will help you assess whether you have met the given academic criteria.

University Team Academic Counselors

Because of the persistent problem of keeping athletes eligible, many universities now have whole staffs funded by the athletic department with the sole goal of ensuring academic success and maintaining divisional compliance. This is also a result of the majority of non-athletic counselors having no athletic department accountability. They also interact with academic professors and departments to ensure academic eligibility. Although common at Division I colleges, these positions may be a luxury at the majority of smaller colleges.

A potential problem is that the counselor's goal is to ensure eligibility and statistically impressive graduation rates, which may be contrary to an athlete's interests or talents, according to a prominent Division III faculty advisor and former Division I university faculty representative Daniel Fulks. Fulks, who also does statistical analysis for the NCAA, states that some athletic advisors "don't want their kids talking to their academic advisors. They are encouraged to keep everything within the athletic department."

However, there can be cohesion between the athletic department and the academic side, says Glenn Quick, an assistant athletic director in Academic Affairs who works at a prominent public Midwestern Division I university. Quick states that a "cooperative partnership" with the academic side is truly the vision. He believes that, in the end, the benefits of helping athletes navigate the system while serving as a liaison between the coaching staff and faculty and administration provides an academic advisor with the "encouragement and support to help athletes graduate."

Quick also points out that athletic counselors are not there to choose majors for the athletes. "We provide a different perspective and help with an informed decision. I have never told a student that they could not pursue a major in something. At the end of the day, the student makes the decision." During a visit, get the athletic academic counselors' opinions regarding your major and how this might fit in at the specific university.

College Academic Counselors

There are also non-athletic counselors whose focus is academics. Unfortunately, many athletes never receive their input, as their advice may be contrary to the athletic department's goals. Daniel Fulks says, "Athletes are often discouraged from seeking assistance from those resources outside the athletic department. Especially at Division I, it is a real problem." Use these counselors to keep the athletic department counselors honest. This may involve requesting that the program counselor call the academic counselor to explain the demands or needs of your program. This conversation is especially important if you are interested in a major that is opposed by the athletic department academic counselor. Ideally, you want the athletic and academic counselors to form a cooperative partnership.

Keep in mind that academic counselors often have little time, interest, or dealings with athletics. However, this enables you to take their advice as an independent opinion. This is especially important if you have a specific career path in mind, such as one that involves graduate school. During your visit, corroborate what you have been told regarding your major. Clear up any discrepancies with the athletic department.

Other Personnel

It is important to consider the impact of other individuals, such as presidents, athletic directors, professors, agents, and alumni. You may never see or meet the president and the athletic director, but they set the tone for the athletic department. In the case of professors, they are extremely important to your academic mission but are often underutilized. If you are seen as having a professional future, especially in any of the high-profile sports, unscrupulous agents may contact you, even in high school. Know that these connections could quickly end a college career, especially if there are any improprieties.

College Presidents

Presidents are essentially the CEOs of the university. They oversee everything from the quality of the academic programs to the strength of the athletic programs. They also are responsible for fund-raising and for the budget of the university. Often, presidents delegate the responsibility for the quality of the academic program to the provost. It is the president's vision that is passed on to the deans and the athletic director, and that dictates the quality and integrity of programs. In the end, they oversee the mission and values of the athletic department.

James Appleberry, Ph.D., a former NAIA, Division II, and Division I college president who has served as the president of the AASCU and as a member of the NCAA President's Commission says:

> Presidents' roles with athletics change with the institution type. At divisions such as the NAIA or Division III, there is much less competitive pressure compared to Division I. At Division I, the role of the president is

to ensure the athletic program plays by the rules and maintains its integrity, while ensuring that the athletic department does not mortgage away the future of the university.

This can happen when there are a few influential alumni. Sometimes, "the president must be willing to take a stand, even at the risk of the president's job."

Athletic Directors

Athletic directors take direction from the president. They control the financial aspects of the athletic department while distributing the budget to the different sports. They are intimately tied to the financial success of the athletic department, are involved in hiring and firing coaches, and also make the final decision regarding program cuts.

JK, a former athletic director at the NAIA and Division II level, believes it is the athletic director's responsibility to stress the importance of academics during all stages of sports. He said, "It really starts with interviewing a prospective coach. We spent more time looking at retention and graduation rates as well as GPAs of former athletes if they had coached before. We also stressed going to class and community service projects, as our goal was to produce productive adults."

JK also puts the responsibility of running ethical programs on the administration. He says, "Often, it is not the kids' fault if they are not academically successful, considering they are doing what they are told. I fault college presidents who may love it when they are winning—but at what price? If coaches know up front what is expected and that academics and being a good role model is valued, usually there are no problems."

Professors

Professors are a great resource for academic information but also can provide information regarding the integrity and the reputation of the athletic department or individual coaching staff members. They can also answer questions about average GPAs and test scores for students who fare well in their programs. Anecdotal stories may also be beneficial. One professor relates an incident of flunking an athlete for academic misconduct. The professor received full support from the athletic department and the athlete did not compete in a very important game. JK echoes the importance of faculty input. He said, "Good programs will ensure you talk to a top-flight faculty member in your area of interest without any coaching staff present." David Dinneen, Ph.D., a retired dean of a French department who also served as a faculty advisor to the athletic board, adds that "along with talking with individual faculty, set aside some time to see the academic facilities, such as the library."

Agents

Even for the minority of collegiate athletes who possess the talent to play professionally, agents do not have a role in a young, college-bound athlete's life. Premature contact can negatively affect eligibility. Confer with divisional rules at the appropriate divison's Web site regarding what interactions with agents are permitted and forbidden. If an agent contacts you, refer them to the Web site or your parents or guardians. Not all agents are unscrupulous, but their aim is for you to play professionally, as this is how they make money. For most athletes, high school is not the time to "go pro."

Rob Werdann, a former NBA basketball professional of nine years who also coached in the CBA and is currently a player development specialist for the New Orleans Hornets, asserts that "Agents are not stupid. Unethical ones will scout out your background (if they see you as socioecononmically vulnerable) and sell you on the notion that you can make money fast."

TB, a Division I compliance assistant athletic director says, "First, agents should register with the state. Then so long as there are no verbal, written, or financial agreements, agents are allowed to talk with athletes." From a high school standpoint, agents are trying to get a step up so that if you perform really well, you will consider using them in the future. Do not discuss *any* commitments and be wary of unscrupulous agents, because if an agent accuses you of promising to work with them, it will be your word against theirs.

Alumni

Alumni often try to live vicariously through their alma mater's athletic programs. Thus, unbeknownst to the athlete, the seemingly supportive alumni may not act toward the better interests of the athlete. Inducements from alumni are illegal. These can range from money, cars, gifts, employment opportunities, promises of family employment opportunities, housing, or trips. According to TB, "Alumni are a challenging group, especially ticket holders and booster groups. No one wants to break a rule intentionally, but it happens inadvertently." TB adds that "knowledge is power" and she encourages high school athletes and parents or guardians to "know the rules from the front end of the recruiting process so you can recognize if a rule is being broken." In general, do not accept anything from an alumnus. If you are not sure, call the program, coach, compliance department, or the division. You can do so anonymously without naming a program if you choose.

Summary

- Ask your current coaches to help you. Get to know their relationships with the college coaching staff.
- Appreciate how the three types of counselors can help you in different ways.
- Realize that the president and athletic director determine the vision for the program.
- Get professors' opinions and be leery of alumni and agents!

8

Recruiting Factors

"I really liked that school because they contacted me first," said a current Division I athlete, when identifying one of the main reasons for her university choice. It might make intuitive sense, but should first contact dictate where you might go? Athletic budgets and the size of the coaching staffs heavily influence the recruiting process. Let's find out how this affects the recruiting methods you may encounter.

"The coach sounded really nice on the phone. But when I got there, they were totally different." SM, a Midwestern college basketball player, exposes another common pitfall. The personality of the coach who recruits you may not be the same personality you will deal with after you've joined his or her program. Look past the glitz and promises: Don't let a coach's spiels lure you to a program that is not best for you.

Budgets and Personnel

Budgets refer to how much money is available to be spent. The two types of budgets, total athletic department budgets and individual program budgets, refer to the total amount of money provided to the athletic department and the total amount of money given to the individual program, respectively. Travel, equipment and facilities, scholarships, recruiting, and personnel are key aspects of the budget. Athletic scholarships and coaching salaries can be included. From a recruiting standpoint, concepts involving the recruiting budget and the size of the coaching staff are important for you to understand.

Exact dollar figures are often hard to come by, and most coaches are reluctant to share this information. However, any university that accepts federal funds has to provide data to the Office of Postsecondary Education. This data is accessible at the Web site http://www.ope.ed.gov. This database also provides general information about the athletic programs, size and salaries of coaching staff, recruiting budgets, as well as expenses and revenues. In general, larger programs have bigger budgets. In turn, bigger budgets fund more full-time, part-time, and voluntary staff. The end result is more total recruiting time and money to mail out personalized brochures, make regular phone calls, and send text messages.

First, let's compare the total expenses and total recruiting expenses of five teams covering the different divisions. Again, these data are provided to give an example of differences in spending.

Table 8.1

School	Total Expenses	Total Recruiting Expenses
PITU (Division I)	$46 million	$623,000
TSA&I (Division II)	$4.5 million	$38,000
UCA&T (Division III)	$1.3 million	$8,000
OSTT (NAIA)	$3.6 million	$11,500
USA&M (Juco)	$1.2 million	$3,400

*This table is meant to reflect the trends in college athletics spending. Any similarity to actual college budgets are purely unintentional.

The noticeable difference is that Division I clearly outspends the others in both total expenses and recruiting expenses. Division II spends much less than Division I but significantly more than Division III, NAIA, and junior college. It is difficult to compare Division III, NAIA, and junior colleges, as there can be significant variation in athletic emphasis. There are too many subtle details that are beyond the scope of this book. Using the Office of Postsecondary Education Web site can give you accurate and up-to-date information that suits your specific needs. This Web site also allows you to directly compare the budgets of each of your final choices. Here are some key features to look at. First, compare the total revenue, total recruiting budgets, and individual budgets of your specific sport at various colleges. However, you can see that the Division I programs have considerably more money that can be spent on fliers, coaches' visits, paid recruiting trips, and phone calls and other written recruiting materials.

> **Author comment:** Some schools may have a showcase non-revenue sport. This showcase sport is given greater funding, staffing, or resources than might be typical of programs from similarly matched colleges. This is often a result of regional tradition or national prominence. Examples might include wrestling in the Midwest, lacrosse in the East, and water polo in the West.

Coaching Staffs and Total Recruiting Time

Larger NCAA Division I programs have bigger staffs than Division II programs, which have larger staffs than NAIA, Division III, and NJCAA programs. Next, Division I and some Division II coaches have the luxury of only coaching. Thus, the majority of college coaches, especially at smaller schools and in the non-revenue sports, carry out other functions. Examples include teaching (typically in the physical education department along with other administrative functions), or possibly maintaining a part-time or full time job elsewhere in the community. A coach who only coaches full time and whose only connection with the university is their coaching may have less of a connection to the academic side of the university. You can ask the coach about his or her other commitments as well as those of their assistants, or utilize the Office of Postsecondary Education Web site to assess this data independently.

Next, let's use an example to break down how a larger and more athletically related coaching staff translates into a greater capacity to recruit. A good method is to use the concept of "coaching recruiting hours," defined as the total amount of hours that the program can spend on recruiting.

For example, let's assume that a Division I basketball program has one full-time head coach, two full-time assistant coaches, and three part-time assistant, graduate assistant, or volunteer coaches. For this program, total coaching time per week is 40 hours for the head coach, 120 hours for the three full-time assistant coaches, and 60 hours for the three part-time coaches, which equals 220 hours of coaching time per week. Now compare this Division I staff to a Division III basketball program with a part-time head coach, two part-time assistant coaches, and two graduate assistant or volunteer coaches. For our Division III program, total coaching time per week is 30 hours for the head coach, 40 hours for the two part-time assistant coaches, and 40 hours for the two part-time graduate or volunteer coaches, which equals 110 hours of coaching per week. Again, coaching staff motivation toward recruiting and time spent beyond the standard 40-hour workweek commitment can vary.

The next step is to compare total hours of recruiting per week. One of the biggest complaints of Division I coaches is the amount of time they must spend on the recruiting process. In fact, the bulk of their time may be spent recruiting— some Division I coaches estimate 50 percent or more—compared to coaches in smaller divisions, who might spend between 20 to 30 percent of their time on recruiting.

Using the data above, 50 percent of 220 hours is about 110 hours per week spent on recruiting versus 30 percent of 110 hours per week or 33.3 hours per week for smaller programs. Next, let's see how this correlates to the practical aspects of recruiting that shape your perception of the recruiting process.

Recruiting Numbers: Seniors versus Underclassmen

The pattern continues: Larger schools and revenue sports with bigger budgets and larger staffs are able to make earlier contact with recruits, have more frequent contact with recruits, and make more paid recruiting visits; they also have a higher number of athletes being actively recruited their senior years, and make more actual contacts per week. Let's compare the number of high school seniors and underclassmen contacted in men's basketball and track and field, based on some coaches' observations of this aspect of the recruiting process. One coach who has coached at more than one level said, "Most Division I schools pay for recruiting services and then send letters to 200 to 300 kids. In terms of early contact, there are some Division I colleges now even sending letters to coaches of eighth graders." In comparison to these numbers, at junior colleges "possibly 50 athletes are contacted and rarely before their senior year," according to this coach.

Now consider a non-revenue sport such as track and field. Current high school athletic director and former Division I track coach RB remembers sending out recruiting letters to anywhere between 500 to 1,000 athletes, many of them being highly touted freshmen. Dr. Benjamin recalls sifting through data from every state high school meet to identify qualified athletes who met specific minimum standards. On the other hand, an NAIA coach, WS, believes these numbers are closer to 200 total athletes contacted, and rarely are these athletes underclassmen.

Now, remember that very first letter of interest that you received. It was probably generated by someone like Dr. Benjamin, who as a graduate assistant coach was given the task or identifying *every* potential underclassman in the country who one day could *potentially* be a scholarship athlete at the Division I level. "The whole key was to get to the athlete first," said Dr. Benjamin.

A Coach's Dilemma

Coaches are very aware of the impact that volume of contact and early contact can have on the perception of desirability. For programs with large staffs, coaches may "pour it on" with incessant phone calls, e-mails, and text messages. If inundated, let coaches know what your limits are and make clear that your final decisions will not be based on volume of contact. With this clarification, you might be surprised as to the sigh of relief on the other end of the phone and the increased time you have toward your homework and other activities.

Coaches who know that they cannot compete in the volume game are proactive by directly discussing staff issues as well as how they spend their time. Athletic director and former coach David Burgess said, "I tell kids right at the start that as a recruiting staff of one, I cannot call you every night or show up at your games on a regular basis." Coach AF echoes this sentiment, adding:

> I tell kids and their parents that I will answer every question they have, and with the advent of e-mail, I can do this quickly. I also remind them that I have a philosophy of putting the majority of my attention into each of my current athletes. If they expect to be called every week, I tell them that this might not be the best fit for them.

The bottom line: Acknowledge the excitement regarding programs which contacted you first. Temper these feelings with the knowledge that first contact does not necessarily translate into automatic desirability or the best fit. Also, do not compare apples to oranges as a larger Division I program in most cases will clearly have more resources and funds to "out-recruit" programs that are from smaller Division II, Division III, or NAIA. The key questions, which are difficult to gauge, are twofold:

1. How much are they contacting you compared to other athletes who play your position? Comparisons of universities within the same division will be more accurate, as schools will have the same financial or personnel resources.

2. What level coach is contacting you? If it is the head coach or the top assistant coach in charge of your specific event, you are highly regarded. If it is a volunteer graduate assistant, there are most likely others who are being recruited ahead of you.

Summary: Big and Small

- Larger schools, especially Division I revenue programs, have larger budgets.
- Smaller schools have smaller budgets. The trend of revenue or high profile sports having significantly larger budgets compared to non-revenue programs persists.
- Some schools may have showcase programs that might get a larger proportion of the budget than would typically be expected.

- Larger budgets translate into more personnel, who can contact you earlier and more frequently.

Spiels

Good recruiters are salespeople, and selling the program is what the recruiting process is all about. You expect the coach to stress the program's strengths while minimizing the negatives. There is no perfect program, college, or situation! What we view as being less-than-honorable are the blatant attempts to conceal issues or problems that would result in a bad fit for you. Most coaches are quite ethical in that they follow the rules and are generally well meaning. Remember, coaches are under great pressure to win. They are competing against hundreds of other qualified coaches for your attention. Spiels allow them to stand out and be unique. A few prominent types of spiels include purposely focusing on mutual non-athletic interests, appeals to unique concerns, promises of a professional career, deliberately overstating their emphasis on academics, and playing up a winning tradition.

Anything but Sports

"Their head coach was so cool. He was the only one who never talked about running during the recruiting process. We spent hours on the phone talking about the outdoors." This comment was divulged to Dr. Benjamin by a former All-American high school runner during a recruiting trip.

This connection "with the outdoors" was enough to convince this runner to attend a high-powered distance program. Problems arose very quickly as the program's philosophy of running 100 miles per week was a radical departure from his high school training of 30 to 40 miles per week. He finished out the year and transferred to a program that he had previously overlooked, even though his new coach was not quite the fishing expert.

Other examples might include the coach who is a stand-up comedian, places special attention on your parents or guardians, or attempts to sell his or her unique educational backgrounds. Also overemphasized are aspects of the "coach's aura," aimed at convincing you that the coach is a "confident winner" on and off the playing field. These include great eye contact and firm handshakes or expensive clothing and fancy cars.

You certainly want a coach to show an interest in other aspects of you. It makes you feel good when you believe your coach is like a "buddy," but make sure you really know enough about the program to make a choice, especially if you feel so enamored with the coach that nothing else seems to matter. Talking to athletes on the team as well as getting a sense of the day-to-day expectations will help you sort out what this experience will be like after the honeymoon period.

The bottom line: Do not make a decision based on an aspect you value in the coach that has nothing to do with the sport or the program. If you are drawn to a coach for a love of the outdoors, as in our above example, proceed with caution.

Appealing to Gender, Religious, Racial, or International Concerns

Another avenue a coach may take to convince you to join his or her program may be to appeal to gender, religious, cultural, or international concerns. Is this necessarily problematic? Absolutely not, so long as it is *authentic*. Authenticity refers to a legitimate, sustainable interest, desire, or concern regarding your background or situation. In the paragraphs that follow we provide some examples to think about.

One former coach confidentially described recruiting African-American athletes by overfocusing on their mothers. Upon arrival to the program, after a few months, some of the African-American athletes came to the conclusion that the coach really did not care for their racial background. In fact, they believed that perceived prejudices did interfere with the coach-athlete relationship, and indirectly affected their athletic performance.

Female athletes may be enticed by more of a "nurturing figure," according to a former women's college assistant coach, Dona Zanotti. This is based on her own collegiate playing experiences, coaching career, and the mentoring of two daughters who participate in athletics. Again, ensure that this caring coach during the recruiting process will still be caring a few years and thousands of hours into your career.

International athletes should be wary of coaches that claim to be more culturally sensitive than all of the other coaches you have met. Some coaches learn a few catch phrases in your native language. We applaud this effort, but cultural sensitivity can be better reflected in acceptance of different styles of play or different attitudes or beliefs about the world around you. Zambian soccer player GA relates that, although he was respected, he had to adjust to a more "American" style of playing, as "the African game emphasizes more creativity. Our style of play is different. It was initially hard to adjust."

The Promise of Reaching the Pro Level

"Of 25 kids that might come to many Division I or II football programs," laments Chuck Bailey, "25 will think they are going to the pros, and they don't want to hear differently." Bailey points out that even at prominent Division I programs, very few athletes actually have a legitimate shot at a professional career.

No matter how good you are, be wary of programs that guarantee this. Yes, state-of-the-art workout facilities, large travel budgets, and continuous television and media exposure sound nice. However, reflect on how many of the great players you idolized are currently playing professionally.

Ask about the percentage of former athletes who play professionally and the percentage who played more than five years. The majority of professional careers last less than five years. As Coach Werdann reminds, "Playing professionally was a great ride, however it needs to be coupled with the understanding that *it could all end tomorrow!* Today's athletes are sold on the fame and making money fast. I chose a college with a great communications department because I knew one day that my professional career would be over."

Percentages are more important, as many coaches single out one very successful athlete that they have coached to an extremely high level. In these cases, an extraordinary athlete can make any coach look good. Also, clarify regarding professional leagues as these could refer to semipro, or professional opportunities in other countries. Some programs also have outstanding assistants who are very successful at coaching a specific event or position. Before you are sold on this reason, ensure that you fit the mold of player that is professional-bound from the program.

Promising Plenty of Time for Academics

Academics should be your number one priority at college. However, when you add up the hours of practice, travel time, other ancillary time such as weight-training, voluntary player-only practices (which really aren't so voluntary), and the importance of winning or competing at a high level, the emphasis is on athletics.

Verify claims that a coach or program cares more about your education than others do. Be wary of programs that try to dictate your major, plan your courses, or prohibit you from taking classes that may cut into practice time. One athlete playing at the Division I level said, "One coach told me that it was great that I was thinking about pre-med, but she indicated that this might not work out well for the team. She then told me that I could not take any classes after 1 P.M., which would eliminate a lot of mandatory lab classes."

Paul Duren describes spending 30-plus hours per week devoted to football during the season. He said, "I managed over a 3.0 but if I was interested in pre-med or pre-law, I just don't know how I would have done it. I believe my GPA would have been a lot higher without football."

If you think this happens only at the Division I level, think again. GA made a decision to quit playing NAIA-level soccer his senior year as "I was intent on getting my degree in mechanical engineering. When I came to the United States, I was really excited to know that sports could pay for my education. But in the end, I dropped out, lost my scholarship but ended up with my degree." GA's story is ironic in that he had to attend three different colleges to find a combination of collegiate soccer and an engineering program, but to maintain his grades in such a challenging major, he had to give up his athletics because he "wanted something meaningful after I stopped playing one day." GA shares the concern that often an athlete's major tends to be less challenging. If you have specific academic goals in mind, be concerned if all the current athletes are attempting the same major or if very few seem to match your academic fervor. If the actions and attitudes don't fit academically, cross the school off your list.

To assess this topic, find out about the graduation rates of the program. Also, ask to talk to other athletes who are majoring in your area of interest. Ask them about the support they have received from the coaching staff. This information is critical because many of the revenue college programs, especially football and basketball, also have poor graduation records. There are too many athletes who opt not to get a degree because they did not think they would ever need one. Don't sell yourself short.

Tradition: Look What I Have Done in the Past

You might hear some of the following claims as you explore different athletic programs:

- "We are among the most competitive athletic colleges in the nation."
- "We have won the most championships since the 1950s."
- "We have over 100 All-Conference or All-American athletes."

These facts reflect a commitment to athletic success and can make a difference if you want to play at a certain program because of their history or reputation. Maybe you have always dreamed of playing in those colors at their specific arena since you were eight years old. This institutional idealization is very powerful.

Coaches and programs also are aware of how much easier it is to recruit for a program with a winning history or a great reputation. AF says, "I have actually sought out about 10 athletes over the last four years. The school reputation recruits for itself." Tradition can be blinding. You cannot go wrong by assessing the coach's connection to the tradition and evaluating for individual and/or team improvement.

Coaches can be the main reason for a tradition, be part of a continued tradition, or simply inherit a tradition-rich program. In the first two situations, you at least know that the coach can take some credit for the program's success. In the latter situation, be wary of the coach's use of tradition to give him- or herself a leg up in recruiting or to possibly ward off scrutiny of his or her previous record.

Check the statistics or records, which can indicate that the current program is living up to its storied history. This can be very difficult to do if the coach is in his or her first or second year. In this case, research the coach's prior records if possible. Many times, assistants or coaches with no prior college head-coaching experience may step into the head coaching role.

Again, evaluate programs based on the overall individual improvements of their athletes from their freshman to senior years. For example, if the majority of swimmers have swum faster and improved their personal bests over the coach's tenure, this should give you some confidence. Break this down further if you can look at your specific event or events. One of the best ways to do this prior to a visit or to talking with coaches is to review the programs and online statistics, which typically are readily available. Your chances are better of maximizing your talent if indeed others also have improved.

Consistent success is more indicative of your chances to continue to improve. Keep in mind that great programs can bring in a lot of great athletes, but not all will reach their potential. A former high school All-American told Dr. Benjamin that he thought he would really improve by going to one of the best programs with a Hall of Fame-level coach. Instead, he says, "I got injured every year trying to keep up with the top athletes."

Author comment: A great question to ask coaches is, "What do you think prevented the athletes who transferred, got injured, quit, or did not improve from being more successful?" This is a tough question to ask, but what you are really looking for is a coach who can take some responsibility for not all his or her athletes improving. If a coach brands all of these athletes as "losers," be cautious—that "loser" might be you one day.

Summary

- Ensure that each coach's style is "really them" and is applicable to the sport itself.
- Four of the most common spiels can encompass other-than-sports topics; appealing to a racial, cultural, or

gender stereotype; misrepresenting how much time there will be for academics; promising professional playing opportunities; or relying on tradition

- See through the spiels. Judge the overall academic and athletic opportunity rather than simply the messenger.

SECTION II

Individual Issues
and Values

1

Association Stated Values

You now have a better appreciation for the technical aspects of recruiting. You know how to spot a sales pitch by a coach. You understand how recruiting truly is a game unto itself.

This section focuses on matching your values with that of the coach and the program. However, these factors are program and coach dependent. When distortions of these values occur, the stated values commonly associated with athletics are negated.

We will discuss gender, racial, ethnic, international, and other related issues that arise as sports attempt to embrace greater diversity. The last chapter in this section emphasizes the need to assess a school and its athletic program for medical safety. No amount of scholarship money or glory is worth chronic medical problems or putting your life at risk.

Before we address the finer points, let's take a look at how the different organizations view athletics as a part of the university experience.

NCAA

According to its Web site, the NCAA's ideology is reflected in a core purpose of governing athletics in an ethical manner and integrating athletics so that "the educational experience...is paramount." Core values listed include integrity, sportsmanship, excellence in academics and athletics, inclusion that "fosters equitable participation for student-athletes" and the role of athletics as being a supportive role in "the higher education mission." According to an NCAA representative, GD, "Student-athletes have exceptional values...which include great time management, perseverance, determination, and the will to succeed in academics and athletics." GD also points to the "camaraderie" with teammates and engagement in "community projects" that produce future "productive role models."

NAIA

On its Web site, the NAIA focuses on its Champions of Character program aimed at teaching character development through athletics. Core values include respect, responsibility, integrity, student leadership, and sportsmanship. An NAIA executive says that the NAIA teaches its coaches to "intentionally teach about the importance of character and learning the right lessons." The Champions of Character program is campus based with plans to create a Web-based curriculum. Former NAIA coach WS gives an example of how two related track events are designed at the national championship event to encourage participation. WS explained, "By placing the 800-meter run very closely to the 4 × 800-meter relay, coaches use more athletes, as one cannot compete in both."

NJCAA and CCCAA

On its Web site, the NJCAA sees its purpose as providing regional and national level competition "...consistent with the total educational program." It also emphasizes drug-free sports as well as gender equality. In its position statement, the NJCAA points out that it takes drug-free sports very seriously. Also, there is an emphasis on giving women opportunities to both compete and coach. This is also true for the CCCAA, according to a CCCAA executive who says that "there are no athletic scholarships given so financial aid is not based on athletic skill." This, along with an emphasis on competition in California that culminates with a California championship, ensures an emphasis on academics.

In summary, all divisions envision athletics as an important part of the educational process. They view athletics as an additional way to teach some of the values that are listed above.

Does Reality Belie The Stated Values?

Reflect for a second: Do you believe that college athletics follows the stated intent or core values as described above? During the recruiting process, assess the programs regarding the divisional as well as the stated institutional credos. If they indeed match up, this is a good sign that your athletic experience is truly a part of a complete educational experience.

Summary

- Each Division has stated values, which should dictate how the athletic departments should conduct their business.
- Values statements arose to try to ensure that athletics follow the academic setting.
- Reflect on whether athletics really follow the stated values of the given institution.

2

Unethical or Distorted Values

When you combine big business with the pressure to win, unethical behavior can be rampant. This is a fact that, unfortunately, can come into play during the recruiting process. The desire to win also drives many coaches to behave in less than ethical ways: for them the low incidence of being exposed and the potential upside of recruiting a "blue chipper" outweigh the risks and penalties. Non-revenue and non-Division I or -Division II programs are not immune. We divide this chapter into three often-interrelated sections: cheating, excessive focus on athletics, and troubling athlete-coach relationships.

Cheating

Cheating is the most obvious form of unethical behavior, usually the result of a "winning is everything" mentality. What follows are a few examples of cheating in terms of the categories of academic, contact, financial, and unethical promises. Also mentioned and discussed in more detail are performance-enhancing behaviors that break the rules.

Academic

Any alteration of the typical academic process constitutes cheating. This involves tampering with high school transcripts or test scores or being aided on tests or papers. Creation of false courses such as those in some post–high-school preparatory schools also is illegal. In the end, falsifying these sorts of documents only leaves you without the skills to pass on your own and increases your risk of failing, even if you get into college.

Contact

Inappropriate levels of contact is one of the most common ways of cheating and is often incidental in nature. This is also how many coaches hope to get an edge. Each division and sport has certain limitations on phone calls, texting, e-mails, face-to-face meetings, and official visits. Again, because these rules change on a routine basis, it is necessary to check divisional Web sites for the latest information. Ask each coach what his or her understanding of the rules is—then clarify with the divisional headquarters if necessary.

Financial

Financial payments or other material inducements, typically in high profile revenue sports, are used to convince you to sign with or remain at a given school. Know the allowances of recruiting per division as, for example, an NAIA coach can buy you a lunch or a snack, which might not be acceptable at the Division I level. Any monetary benefits that exceed what is allowed by the existing NCAA division rules are problematic. This includes under-the-table payments or payments for work that is not performed. Also, accepting exorbitant pay at a wealthy alumni's business is also against the rules and can result in ineligibility. Sometimes, these clearly occur with the coach's approval or with the coach turning a blind eye; in other cases, unethical and wealthy alumni may be involved without any knowledge of the program.

Unkept Promises

Coaches can promise anything. Some promises are illegal whereas others are simply unethical. Illegal promises include telling you that they can guarantee a scholarship for five years. "Scholarships are year-to-year renewable financial assistance," according to TB. Promises of jobs or jobs to family also fall under an illegal inducement. In addition, beware of the unethical but not illegal recruiting practice of lying. Verbal commitments relating to position, playing time, opportunities for a friend or buddy to also play, or guarantees to start are all examples of verbal promises that may or may not be honored.

Verbal commitments regarding scholarships in the future are also tenuous: just like you cannot guarantee your freshman year performance, it is impossible for a coach to promise you any changes in financial aid. If it is performance based, get it in writing! This actually is a good way to ensure that coaches are willing to put their money where their mouth is—most coaches, if they are making a promise they don't intend to keep, will never put it in writing.

Here are some tough questions for the program and coaching staff. If uncomfortable, have your parent or mentor ask them.

1. Have you or any of your staff ever been involved in a rules infraction?

   Wording the question in this manner will result in a better response than using the words "cheating" or "illegal recruiting," which are confrontational. This open-ended style also gives the coach an opportunity to elaborate if indeed a recruiting scandal has occurred.

2. Has any program that you have been associated with ever been on probation? If so, what happened and how was this problem corrected?

3. Has any program that you have been associated with ever been investigated?

The point here is that investigations also can reflect potential unethical behaviors. A possible red flag is if the coach has a penchant for moving or leaving programs. Stability of the coaching staff is often difficult to assess.

Ask the coaches or the athletic director about potential ethics issues until you are satisfied. These questions may help you differentiate between a remorseful coach who takes responsibility and demonstrates the value of following the rules versus one who views rules and regulations as getting in the way of winning. Remember that coaches do make mistakes. Current and former athletes may also add some insight regarding these topics. Research the Internet and news media for information about current or prior infractions or investigations. Also, some divisions such as the NAIA or NJCAA actually list member institutions that have committed recent infractions.

> **Author's comment:** The ramifications of cheating are grossly unfair to innocent athletes. You may be directly and indirectly punished for a coach's ethical breaches. The program may have to forfeit past victories and titles, be forced to give up some scholarships, and may be ineligible for postseason competition. The coach, who might have blatantly broken the rules, may transfer to another university without any real consequence.

Excessive Athletic Focus

"College sport is a full-time job" says Paul Duren. "High school athletes need to realize that it is not just about fun." We have already described the level of commitment and the difficulty of maintaining a balance of athletics and academics. Three areas of excessive athletic focus, all related to doing everything to win, include extra "voluntary" training, excessive training used as punishment, and treatment of the athlete based on performance.

Excessive Practice

"Optional" or "voluntary" sessions are used to bypass divisional regulations regarding the number of hours per week during the season or off-season that can be athletics related. However, training beyond the rules is used to get a winning edge. Realize that optional or volunteer sessions may not be so "optional." Duren suggests that you consider playing, traveling, competing, taping, film time, and athletic training time in the total time commitment. Ask current team members if these sessions exist, how often they occur, and if they are purposely kept hidden from the public. Also inquire if anyone has lost his or her scholarship for not attending.

Exercise as Punishment

The use of excessive training or exercise can be used as an unethical means to "help" an athlete who has not lived up to his or her promise decide to quit. This is called "running someone off the team," but it could include any sort off physical or mental punishment. Obviously, on occasion, coaches do use a few extra laps or pushups as a consequence for a poor practice or game performance. However, when the exercise is used to single out a particular athlete with the intent of getting him or her to quit, get injured, or rescind his or her scholarship, this clearly crosses the line.

Troubling Athlete-Coach Or Athlete-Athlete Relationships

This section discusses some types of demeaning behaviors toward athletes. These include performance-based treatment, which deflates self-esteem and contributes to problems later on in life, and negative behaviors including hazing. Hazing, aside from being degrading, can also be dangerous and life threatening. The sections below summarize the data compiled by one of the top hazing research sites at Alfred University, to help ensure that this does not happen to you.

Performance-Based Treatment

Coaches have a right to express pleasure when an athlete performs well or displeasure with a poor or sub-par performance. But this reaction should be aimed at the performance and not aimed to demoralize the athlete. Contrary to some coaching philosophies, telling you how bad you are will not help you perform better! Look out for coaches who give athletes the "cold shoulder" after a poor performance or who make humiliating, debasing, or abusive comments.

One coach confided anonymously how he has witnessed this sort of behavior. "The head coach would allow the high-performing athletes to ride in the head coach's car. If you did not perform well, the punishment was to ride with the assistant. It really made the athletes feel bad about themselves and not just their performance." The problem with this technique is it really was meant to degrade the athletes who did not perform as well. The other aspect is that this is suggestive of poor coaching relationships as the above situation devalues the assistant coach.

Coaches are often held to a lower standard of behavior than other faculty and many are allowed to behave or speak unprofessionally, especially in losing situations. Can you imagine a professor swearing at you because you made a mistake during a test? Excessive or persistent anger and negative or abusive treatment should not be tolerated. Certainly, everyone has their own personal tolerance levels for these sorts of behaviors. Make sure the coach does not exceed yours.

Star Athlete Treatment

Many of you have received special treatment because of your athlete status. This can be amplified in many programs. Unfortunately, programs that allow their star athletes to act any way they want instills in athletes a belief that they can do no wrong and often results in demoralizing fellow teammates. Investigate if this is a potential issue in a program by asking non-starting athletes how the "stars" of the team are treated compared to the other players. Also, inquire how athletes who break team rules are dealt with. Does the coach mete out consequences in a fair and consistent manner? Be concerned about programs in which athletes are not held accountable for their actions. Ask yourself if these are the values that you want to be surrounded by.

Other Negative Behaviors

Compared to non-athlete college students, student-athletes are more likely to be involved in negative behaviors, including drinking more alcohol, smoking tobacco, carrying weapons, and being the perpetrator of sexual abuse. These surprising facts come from studies such as those found in the *Journal of the American Medical Association*; such studies reflect that prestige plus the perception of "untouchability" puts athletes at higher risk for hazardous behavior. It should also be noted that it is a stereotype that the only students getting into trouble are kids from revenue sports who come from disadvantaged backgrounds. As Katherine Redmond, founder of the National Coalition Against Violent Athletes (NCAVA) says, "there is correlation with athletes who act out and revenue, (as revenue) brings entitlement."

Hazing

A landmark 1999 study conducted by researchers at Alfred University determined that hazing entails "any activity expected of someone joining a group that humiliates, degrades, abuses, or endangers regardless of the person's willingness to participate." These activities typically involve the freshmen class as an "initiation rite" that is supposed to "foster a feeling of belonging." This study, which included 244 colleges, suggests that up to 80 percent of college athletes have experienced some level of hazing. Interesting findings include that women's hazing had a higher involvement with alcohol. The most dangerous or illegal forms of hazing was linked with football, especially at Southern and Midwestern campuses. Behaviors that qualify under this term include the following:

- Behaviors meant to humiliate, such as verbal abuse or being forced to act in an embarrassing manner.
- Excessive consumption of alcohol or other substances.
- Lewd sexual behaviors or physical assault.

These last two categories have resulted in multiple deaths. These behaviors should be banned by the president, athletic director, and the coaching staff. In fact, some states have anti-hazing laws, as hazing has resulted in alcohol-induced death from excessive forced or coerced drinking to sodomy with different objects.

Unfortunately, many times, it is the players that organize this behavior unbeknownst to the coach. A former female athlete who competed in a non-revenue sport at a prestigious NESAC college described hazing that occurred in many sports. Even though there was constant scrutiny by the administration, the coaches would look the other way. She described a lot of the behaviors relating to "alcohol and making fools out of yourselves." However, she added, "you could opt out and you were not looked down upon. You didn't have to partake."

When visiting colleges, be sure to ask about possible hazing rituals. Here are a couple of suggested questions:

Ask the coach, "What is your policy on hazing? Are you aware of any hazing behaviors and if so, what did you do and what have you done to prevent this from occurring?

Ask freshmen and sophomores on the team if they experienced any "rites of passage." If so, can they describe these behaviors? What happens if I don't participate?

The truth is that despite the pressures, you *do not* have to participate in hazing rituals. In fact, you might earn the respect of those around you if you decide that your health is more important than fitting in. Peer pressure and the desire to be a part of the team are strong motivators to comply even if you know better!

It is important to differentiate between specific team rules where underclassmen may have certain responsibilities that upperclassmen do not have. Draw the line based on whether these additional duties are functional versus demeaning. For example, acceptable demands might include tasking freshmen to get the water buffalos ready for practice. Not acceptable, in our judgment, would be the freshmen having to clean the seniors' uniforms on a weekly basis.

> **Coach's comment:** Hazing is sadistic and can be life threatening. Do not tolerate practices that aim to demean or that involve alcohol, sexual acts, or physical assault.
>
> For details, including examples of hazing as well as the geographic regions and sports that are most likely to participate in these behaviors, check out Alfred University's study of hazing at: http://www.alfred.edu/sports_hazing/introduction.html.

> **Author's comment:** For those of you who expect a clean athletics environment, do your research. One parent describes how his son, who initially received a full ride at a Division II football program, began his pre-college summer experience. He found himself surrounded by alcohol and rooming with two other athletes who had pregnant girlfriends. "It was not an atmosphere that he was used to and might have contributed to why he left." His son transferred and walked on at another Division II school as a wrestler.

It's important to try to determine if your values fit with a program's culture before you commit to that school. Ask the coach: "What are your teams' rules regarding illicit substances, alcohol, partying, and tobacco? What happens if an athlete is caught and has this happened recently? Ask athletes a slight variation of the same question: "What are the rules and how many of our teammates drink alcohol or use drugs?" These questions can also reflect any other behaviors that you desire to vet. One former junior college basketball player who went on to compete at the NCAA Division I and II levels, told Dr. Benjamin he felt out of place in his program as "just about every player on the team used weed. I didn't and so I would stay to myself."

You need to assess how your values and behaviors fit with the program. Other athletes already in the program will give you the real scoop. Coaches often have a standard to maintain and may turn a blind eye to some behaviors (such as underage drinking) so as not to alienate athletes who will help the program win.

Summary

- Academic fraud, under-the-table payments, illegal contact, and unkept promises are common ways of cheating during the recruiting process.
- Excessive athletic focus on non-sanctioned practices, exercise as punishment, and distorted coach-athlete relationships reflect programs where athletics and academics are out of balance.
- Programs where athletes are given special treatment, are above the law, or engage in higher than typical rates of negative behaviors may reflect an athlete worship culture.
- Hazing is common in college athletics and aside from being degrading can be dangerous.

3

Desired Values

One of the main functions of college athletics is to promote positive values. This is accomplished through teaching and role modeling. "What we are really looking for in a coach is a good mentor. The coach is really taking on the role of a parent away from home," says Steve Scruggs, a father to two high school wrestlers. Academics, safety, and maximizing athletic potential are three other facets to consider as part of your evaluation of a program. As you are reading through this chapter, think about how you perceive an ideal coach and then evaluate how prospective college coaches match this ideal. Ask parents, family, and high school coaches what they would seek out in a college coach. During conversations with current and former athletes, you can judge if these values hold true.

Teacher/Mentor

Good college coaches are great teachers and mentors. Coaching is unique. While professors typically interact with students during lectures and academic hours, coaches spend hundreds of hours with you during practice, travel, and competition. College coaches have a unique opportunity to be a role model and a teacher.

> When looking at a program, ask current athletes the following question:
>
> 1. What have you learned from the coach unrelated to the sport or winning?
>
> If current athletes have difficulties coming up with any answers, there is a good chance that this coach is solely about the sport.

Role Model

Role modeling refers to the feeling that your coach is someone who you would look up to and be like some day. Many winning coaches are horrible role models. Athletes from these programs leave with nothing beyond their actual competitive experiences. However, a good role model can influence the rest of your life. The definition of a great role model depends on the individual. Consider a coach at a small religious college versus a coach at a very liberal, public university. Which one is better? The answer depends on your vision of the admirable qualities in a coach. There are many aspects of role modeling that might be debated, and there are many that are very clearly not in this category.

Two examples relate to safety and substance abuse. For example, driving exceedingly fast or recklessly puts you at risk. In most programs, coaches do the driving. Some are risk takers and show little regard for such rules.

Abuse of alcohol or illicit substances is another area where poor role modeling can occur. Reports of coaches getting drunk at athlete parties are not uncommon, nor are reports of coaches accumulating DUIs. These coaches tend to be younger in age and experience and try to be friends or buddies to the athletes instead of parental figures. Ask athletes about these issues and, in general, get a sense if athletes ever feel unsafe physically or emotionally around their coaching staffs.

Important Qualities in a Coach

There are many adjectives used to describe superlative coaches. For simplicity's sake, if a coach cares about you as a person and is honest and fair, you can't ask for much more.

Caring

Does the coach want what is best for you first as a person and then as an athlete? Often, athletes find this out when faced with relationship, family, or academic problems. Ask yourself and current teammates if you would be comfortable talking with the coach about an emergent personal situation. Caring does not mean that your individual interests and needs will always come before the team's. It does imply that your physical and emotional health is paramount, and these should come before the team.

Honesty

You want honesty both during and after the recruiting process. In fact, dishonesty during the recruiting process suggests a bad future prognosis with the coach over the next four years. Honest coaches deliver what they promise and do not promise what they cannot deliver. This may include financial or scholarship issues, playing time, or other guarantees of a personal nature.

Fairness

Coaches have to make many tough decisions. Seek out a situation where teammates believe the coach strives for fairness regarding the individuals and the team. One way that this can be assessed is regarding team or competition rules. Ask athletes if these are acted on consistently and across the board for all athletes.

What Do Coaches Teach?

Coaches are always teaching by their actions and how they interact with the team. If a coach emphasizes teamwork, sportsmanship, discipline, and independent thinking, you will be ahead of the game.

Teamwork

Working well with other members toward a common goal is something that sport can teach better than most other activities. The capacity to work smoothly on the playing fields regardless of your off-court or off-field relationships teaches emotional maturity. Emphasizing a team focus rather than individual statistics represents healthy self-sacrifice. Coach and coauthor Patrick Donnelly said, "With so many different personalities and a 25 percent turnover rate every year, being a team player is extremely important."

Sportsmanship

No one likes to lose. But this is no excuse to behave like an idiot. You will not get away with this in a business meeting, and such behaviors should not be tolerated in athletics. Does the program have a reputation for winning with humility and losing with dignity? Rebounding from loss and persevering are also life-defining values.

Discipline

Successfully combining a rigorous academic and athletic schedule cannot be achieved without discipline. Proper execution of your sport at a high level also requires this attribute. Learning discipline will help you long after you stop competing.

Independent Thinking

A cornerstone value of higher education, independent thinking is often underemphasized and even punished if implemented by an athlete. Many coaches over-control athletes to maximize the opportunity to win. They do this by herding athletes together under the auspices of team building through eating and study halls that are only with other athletes. Part of the college experience is to make mistakes, take chances, and explore new ideas. This does not mean that you do your own thing in a play-off game, but coaches should allow you to grow as part of the athletic process. An example might be to give the athletes a voice in the creation of the team rules, as well as the consequences for violating them. This, along with leadership, can also be taught through the creation of positions such as a team captain or position representatives. The capacity to have training input as a senior is also a sign that this trait is valued.

Academic Emphasis

Graduation rates are much publicized, as are team GPAs and student-athlete awards. Studies from the NCAA reflect a pattern of lower graduation rates in the revenue sports compared to the non-revenue sports. These statistics are confounded by players leaving early either to transfer to go to the pros, or players who actually come back to finish their degrees. GPA numbers can also be inflated, as some athletes may be guided toward easier majors, pre-selected classes, and athletics-friendly professors.

Look for programs that have a sustained emphasis on academics throughout your college athletic career. Two key things to look for are that class schedules are valued over practice, and that athletes are clearly free to choose their major.

Acceptance of occasional classes or labs that interfere with practices should be a given. In general, big-time programs are less tolerant of classes and labs that interfere with the practice and game schedules. However, at smaller, less-competitive colleges, especially where coaches also teach and are part of the academic process, this is better accepted. Assistant coach Mark Thompson described an athlete whose major required a class one afternoon per week. "It makes it difficult to work around but we do alter individual practices to make this work." Acceptable responses might be finding alternatives if available, taking the class in the off-season, or seeing if there is an online option. But, if pressed further, the opportunity to take a class should be allowed without negative consequences.

The ability to decide your own major is also important. Although uncommon, there are situations where everyone on the team has "chosen" the same major and takes the exact same classes with pre-selected athletic department friendly professors. This is where conversations with the academic counselors can be very instructive. Also, if your academic vision is completely different than everyone else's on the team, this may also be a warning sign, especially if your choice is a much more challenging major.

Suggestions regarding a potential major are reasonable, especially if you do not have one in mind, but it needs to be your decision. With any suggestion, clarify what you can do with the degree and ensure that it meets your personal needs. If for example, you cannot stand the sight of blood, nursing as a major might be out of the question.

Author's comment: Do not hide your academic aspirations—especially if you are interested in an esoteric field such as astrophysics. If you get a negative gut response, confirm how the coach will feel if you embark on such a major. Talk with professors in this specialized department regarding your athletic aspirations. Most will give you truthful answers if they have had problems with the program or athletic department.

Maximizing Athletic Potential

This is one of the main reasons you compete. Let's help you assess your prospects for maximizing your potential. This concept can and should be unique from one individual to another. To form an overall impression, you need to consider the skill of the coaching staff and assess your own capacity for individual improvement and that of your team.

General Considerations

It is essential that you identify the aspects of your athletic opportunities that are most meaningful to you. The first aspect is to judge your personal opportunity to compete and experience college athletics. The second is to evaluate how prepared the coaching staff is to help you be a better player and athlete. However, consider your starting athletic level when projecting your future potential as a component of this decision making process. Remember that the closer you are to your full potential, the less improvement you will see, no matter where you go. Consider how much time and effort has been spent training in high school. If you play multiple sports, began playing late, or maintained lower levels of training, you most likely possess a greater potential for improvement. For example, if you shoot 89 percent from the free throw line as a result of shooting 500 free throws a day, no school is going to take that percentage much higher compared to someone who shoots only 55 percent and only plays basketball in season.

> **Author's comment:** Be honest with yourself regarding your potential and current performance level. Request trusted family and coaches' opinions regarding the above questions. At the end of your college athletic career, you want to look back with a sense of personal satisfaction regarding fulfilling your potential. This is as much individual perception as fact.

Playing Time versus Team Potential

In the best of all worlds, your talent will match exactly the level of play within the division of interest. In addition, you will play as a freshman, be a superstar, and play on a championship team. Unfortunately, it typically does not work out this way, so ask yourself—and get input from your coaches and family—where it is your greatest talents and interests lay.

So, how important is the opportunity to participate and possibly be a "big fish in a small pond?" Individually, would you prefer playing time as part of an average team or riding the bench on a championship team? If you have always been a role player, this may not be as big a deal, but if you have always been center stage, being on the sidelines might be more difficult. A follow-up aspect is your need to be a superstar. Would you prefer to be pushed by the competition but only finish fifth in a large school conference championship or possibly perform below your full potential but win most meets at a smaller school? In addition, consider how your talents compare to current teammates to judge if you will get an opportunity to compete as a freshman or sophomore, versus waiting your turn and competing as a junior or senior. In team sports, your individual performance may take a back seat to what is best for your team. A common example is the high school basketball player, who is accustomed to being a star player and scoring 20-plus points per game but is asked to be a role-player or a player that will not be in the spotlight at the college level. This is a tough transition as "you are now playing with a bunch of great players in college," says basketball coach CC. Again, defining what it means to maximize your potential in team sports is more difficult.

Another aspect to consider is your preference for a particular playing style or training philosophy. Each sport has different styles of play. Make sure yours matches up well with the programs you are considering. Many sports also have different training philosophies regarding volume of training, number of sessions, use of ancillary training techniques, and intensity levels. How does the coach make decisions regarding individual success versus that of the team? Ask about relays or participating in a number of events in track and field or swimming. Ask coaches and confirm with athletes regarding how the coach envisions opportunities to maximize individual performance versus scoring points for the team.

Authors' comment: We advise caution with playing where you are either so good or so clearly outmatched. Frustration can occur especially in team sports when your teammates are well below your playing capability. However, learning how to make those around you a better player is also a worthy learning experience. On the other hand, if you are overmatched, be able to resign yourself to a practice team with limited playing time. In addition, trying to keep up physically with those way ahead of you often carries a higher risk of injuries.

Judging the Coaching Staff

Considerations include the knowledge of the coach as well as the personal athletic background of the coach. Finally, assess for improvements in performance for current athletes. The first is often underrated and often assumed, while personal athletic exploits and careers of the coach can be overrated. However, consider the factor of attrition rates in the equation. Remember that even the most successful programs will have athletes who are dissatisfied, unmotivated, or who will transfer or quit. Most important are rates of these occurrences along with the reasons why they occurred.

Knowledge

How knowledgeable is the coach regarding your sport? Some coaches simply imitate what they have been taught or what worked for them without much regard for the latest in sports science. No one expects coaches to hold a degree in exercise science or kinesiology, but an interest in understanding how science relates to performance is not only helpful but safe. As tennis instructor Dwight Nuckolls says, "Tennis is governed by two things: proper biomechanics and the laws of physics." According to Nuckolls, a lack of understanding of these two issues will result in poor performance and injury. Nuckolls described a former tennis player who was "trying to do what the college coach was telling him. Unfortunately, the advice on how to serve was wrong. A good service motion is essentially a good throwing motion. The improper technique resulted in a shoulder injury and cost this young man his season."

This is true of every sport to some regard, as physiology, kinesiology, and sports mechanics are interconnected. A willingness to explain the "nuts and bolts" reflects a general attitude of openness about the philosophy of training and competing. Any coach whose answer is "Do it because I tell you" is behind the times. Everyone also has different learning styles and sometimes visual, demonstration, or kinesthetic learning techniques might be more beneficial for you.

The Coach's Past Athletic Experience

The issue of the playing background of the coach can be a double-edged sword. Often natural athletes are great in spite of themselves. They often possess a gift for competing under pressure or picking up specific athletic skills very quickly without a real understanding of the "hows and whys"—they simply are able to perform at a very high level. On the other hand, their competitive experiences and appreciation for the subtle nuances of the game can be invaluable. However, some coaches who were not as athletically gifted choose to study the game to maximize their potential. These types can teach what they have learned. Again, judge each coach individually and not simply by his or her own abundance or lack of athletic talent.

Gauging Improvement

The most underrated way to assess a program is to evaluate the improvement of individual athletes. If athletes improve, this is a good prognosis for your own athletic experiences in the program. If, however, you notice a trend of athletes not getting better or—even more concerning—getting worse, this might not be the ideal athletic opportunity. Ways to assess this potential for improvement include actual individual performances, general physical conditioning tests, and improvement in measurable sport specific skills.

1. Gauge improvements in the performance of the athletes. This is an easy tool to judge or compare programs, especially in primary sports such as running, skiing, or swimming. Very specifically, you want to be in a program where over the course of their college careers, athletes' personal bests improve. Although statistics can be manipulated, our adage is that if the

majority of athletes that are in your event are improving under a certain coach, you have a good chance of doing the same. We focus on improvement rather than performance because the best teams get the best athletes. Thus, it is important not to get caught up in one great performer, as that athlete may be a former high school All-American. Seek out competitors whose performances out of high school mirror yours.

2. Technique-oriented sports require deeper digging. Inquire about stroke velocity or accuracy in baseball, golf, or tennis. Specific examples might be pitching, teeing off, or first serve velocity in the above three sports respectively. Technique or skill improvements may be more difficult to assess, but players often know the difference. Examples might be improved shooting range or dribbling better with the opposite hand in basketball, utilizing a jump serve in volleyball, running better routes as a wide receiver in football, or more accurate corner kicks in soccer.

3. Assess for improved general fitness performance. No matter what the sport, most programs have some sort of fitness and conditioning program. No matter how technical your sport, maximum speed, strength, endurance, and flexibility are necessary to reach your full potential. Therefore, consider changes in performances in the 40-yard dash, number of pushups in a minute, vertical jump, or throwing velocity. You can ask what the athletes' initial performances in these areas were and what they are now. Often, strength and conditioning coaches will have this data.

> **Author's comment:** Compare individual athletes' best performances in high school to their current college performances. Thumb through previous programs' Web sites to get a sense regarding athletes who have quit, left, or transferred. High rates of athletes leaving the program may reflect a "one method fits all approach."

Summary

- Values are individual. You cannot go wrong with coaches who rightfully pride themselves as being good teachers and role models.
- Balance academics and athletics. Optimal performance in both areas is a worthy goal.
- Define your version of athletic success. Evaluate athletes' improvements compared to high school in terms of these parameters.

4

Gender Issues

Imagine attempting to attend a university on an athletic scholarship prior to 1972, when only about 30,000 women athletes competed. Since the passage of Title IX, a law that ensures equal spending for women's athletics as men's athletics, this number as of the 2004–2005 academic year was greater than 205,000 women athletes. This stands in contrast to the over 291,000 men competing during the same time frame. These numbers are difficult to compare, as football has the greatest number of athletes per team and there is no women's sport that has comparable roster sizes. The bottom line is that although the number of participants and the amount of spending has increased for women's athletics, Title IX proponents would argue these figures still lag compared to those for men. One study from 2001-2002 reflected that at the Division I level, the average women's budget was about half of the men's budgets.

The benefits of healthy sport participation among women include improved physical health, self-image, and self-confidence, along with an increased chance of graduating from college. However, the emphasis should be on the word *healthy,* as there are a host of issues that can negatively affect you as a female athlete from both a physical and emotional standpoint. These issues include weight management and related medical concerns, increased risk of knee damage, and sexual misconduct.

Before you (or your daughter) are put in such negative situations, find out whether that pleasant voice on the phone during the recruiting process will translate into a knowledgeable and caring coach over the next four years. You want someone who has an eye out for such issues and will handle them with sensitivity and expertise. In this chapter, we describe some of the major concerns and how to assess and hopefully avoid them. First, let's look at some issues that may be specific to females.

Concerns for Women Athletes

Research and discussions with women athletes and male and female coaches confirm that there are concerns that are unique to women athletes.

Confidence

Women athletes may not be as confident in their athletic skills as their male counterparts. Athletics has typically been the domain of males and some attributes necessary in sports—including aggressiveness and an emphasis of winning or beating others—can be discouraged in girls and young women. An encouraging coach may be the solution. Interestingly, participation in competitive sports may provide for some life-long benefits, according to former collegiate soccer player Megan Duncan. Duncan said, "Sports is a big part of who I am. It has really boosted my confidence and made me more 'thick skinned.' In sports, when you make a mistake and get criticized, you learn from it and apply it instead of focusing on the mistake."

Dual Roles

The perceived dichotomy between being an athlete and being a woman is especially evident in sports that involve direct physical contact such as basketball, soccer, field hockey, or lacrosse. This may result in a role conflict regarding qualities such as aggression and competitiveness, which may go against society's view of what is feminine. Though there has been progress toward gender equality and on women having the same opportunities as men, girls and young women are still sometimes raised in circumstances and environments that do not always support these notions. Good coaches reinforce the notion that being competitive in athletics and being a woman are not mutually exclusive.

Reflections on Coaching

Dona Zanotti sums up these differences accurately. She says, "Women are raised not to be dependent but to be interdependent while men are encouraged to be independent." This quality might be borne out in relationships with coaches and other teammates. JS concurs and adds that as an athlete, women stress the "whole person concept and are more interested in the sport being a part of the complete educational package." This is reflected in higher graduation rates for female athletes than for male athletes and a more realistic appreciation that a professional career is not very likely. Mark Croghan, a former steeplechase Olympic finalist and current Division I college coach who works with both men and women agrees. Croghan said, "I notice a gender difference in that female athletes are more realistic about professional athletic opportunities and consider academics first."

Weight Issues

The weight gain of a typical non-athletic female college student between freshman and senior years is about 15 to 20 pounds. This can be attributed to college stressors, a lack of exercise, and poor nutrition, but it may also be related to healthy maturation. Maintenance of an ideal athletic weight is understandable, but beware of coaches who perceive any weight gain as an impediment to performance. Your coach does have a right to ensure that you are fit, and weight is one criterion used as a training indicator. The goal should be peak performance, which is the result of optimal training. However, when weight becomes the overriding focus, this can lead to tragic physical and emotional consequences. Athletes in sports such as gymnastics, rowing, and track and field are at a greater risk for the "female triad" which includes eating disorders, menstrual problems, and osteoporosis. Men in these sports, along with wrestling, are also more prone to eating disorders.

Eating Disorders

The combination of perfectionism, excessive focus on weight, and excessive exercise are associated with two eating disorders, anorexia nervosa (AN) and bulimia nervosa (BN). Both are not uncommon in women athletes, with some studies suggesting that 5 percent of women athletes have one of these diagnoses compared to 1 to 2 percent of the general female population.

In AN, a person develops a distorted view of his or her body and focuses on weight loss to such an extent that it becomes physically dangerous and emotionally unhealthy. Restriction of food, use of laxatives, diuretics, or other weight loss products, and excessive exercise are used to maintain an unhealthy low body weight. In BN, there is an increased focus on binging and purging to maintain a normal weight. The bottom line is that performance and fitness levels become unimportant, as low body weight and eating patterns become the only focus. These problems can contribute to depression, breakdown of muscle, electrolyte abnormalities, seizures, heart problems, and death. In addition, according to Randy Sansone, M.D. professor of psychiatry at Wright State University's School of Medicine and an international expert on eating disorders, the combination of unhealthy eating, athletics, and a new college experience is concerning. He says, "Coaches who are not familiar with eating disorders are a risk factor, as college tends to be a time of symptom exacerbation. An athlete's ability to tolerate a new environment away from home is critical to a healthy adjustment. Participation should be based on weight stability and menstruation." In addition, symptoms including low body weight, as reflected in a body mass index (BMI) of less than 18, excessive preoccupation with food, or excessive exercise beyond what is required in training are cause for concern.

Amenorrhea

Amenorrhea is defined as an abnormal cessation of menstruation. Amenorrhea occurs in about 10 to 20 percent of women who exercise vigorously and can be the result of either too low a body weight as a result of caloric restriction or excessive exercise. Prolonged, this can lead to osteoporosis, or significantly decreased bone mass, and an increased risk of bone fractures.

When visiting colleges, you should ask how the athletic department and program monitor the health of their athletes: How do they address the issue of athletes dropping their regular menstrual cycle, as well as other factors in the female triad? Does the program have access to a physician and dietician who is knowledgeable regarding these topics? If you have an eating disorder or have a history of unhealthy diet and exercise patterns, this topic should be high on your priority list when selecting a college. College sports can trigger some of these symptoms. Access to knowledgeable experts is crucial.

Warning Signs

A red flag should go up if you hear that prospective coaches use any of the following tactics, rituals, or practices related to weight:

- Establishing eating tables, which provide indirect or subtle ways of controlling an athlete's food intake. This is important, as the "control" issue is critical in eating disorders.
- Utilizing excessive exercise as a way of weight loss or punishment for an athlete not within the coach's weight expectations.
- Coaches tying scholarships to strict weight standards. Scholarships should only be tied to performance.
- Instituting daily weight checks as a form of punishment or reward. Also, be wary of coaches that encourage methods such as food diaries, which can over focus the eating aspects of training.
- Coaches or fellow athletes who accept making inappropriate comments, derogatory remarks, or special treatment based on falling short of a specific weight goal.
- Connecting self-esteem or self-worth to an athlete's weight.
- Teammates seeming more concerned with their weight than with their performance. This often reflects an undercurrent of the importance of weight placed by the coaching staff.

ACL Tears

Injuries are a risk of sport participation; however, excessive injuries as a result of poor coaching practices may be an issue that you as an athlete or parent should consider. The anterior cruciate ligament, or ACL, provides the majority of stability to the knee joint. An ACL tear occurs when the ligament is overstretched, usually as a result of quick stops or torque, or twisting motions, on the knee. Women are excessively prone to this type of ligament damage; some theories for this phenomena relate to women's higher levels of estrogen, which result in ligament elasticity, as well as the angle of the hip and femur toward the knee. High rates of this problem require some scrutiny and may reflect a poor prevention or preseason conditioning program or excessive exercise that leads to a chronically overstressed ligament.

Sexual Harassment

Although sexual harassment happens to both men and women (and is perpetrated by both men and women), this issue tends to be more pertinent for women. This problem can come across in numerous ways. One of the most prevalent is harassment from authority figures, such as a coach harassing athletes on his or her team. It is important to acknowledge that strong emotional bonds can form between the coach and an athlete, as it is typical to spend a great deal of time with each other while practicing, traveling, and competing. However, it is a mature coaches' responsibility to ensure that he or she always maintains "proper boundaries" and does not utilize the coaching position in a sexually inappropriate manner. Despite the secrecy attempted by the offender, teammates often are aware of any unethical behaviors. Ask current and past team members about the occurrence of any of the following:

- Sexually inappropriate comments.
- Inappropriate sexual contact, including inappropriate touching, massages, or other behavior.
- Pressure on athletes to be alone with a coach in non-competition settings. This excludes team parties but refers to situations where an athlete is singled out or treated in a special manner.
- Sexually inappropriate material which is viewable as part of a public forum/practice environment or exposure to such materials.
- Coaches dating athletes or having reputations of being sexually promiscuous.
- Scholarship upgrades or promises based on sexual favors.

Also, it is fair to directly ask the coach and athletic director about their specific policies and personal stances on sexual harassment. Ask them if this has been a problem in the program and how it was addressed. These questions send a strong message to the potential coach about your resolve and knowledge as an athlete or as a parent.

Harassment from Fellow Athletes

It is important to be aware of the possibility of sexual harassment among fellow athletes. Over the course of your college playing career, you will get acquainted with a lot of other athletes. This connection may be because of similar athletic living facilities, traveling together for competition, or seeing each other in the specialized training facilities such as weight rooms. Therefore, you may be at higher risk of sexual harassment or assault from other athletes.

Many athletic departments and coaching staffs have cavalier attitudes toward women and assault, most likely as a result of a glorification of aggressive male behaviors. In fact, according to Katherine Redmond, founder of the NCAVA, college athletes commit one in three alleged college assaults. To make matters worse, since many athletes are placed on a pedestal, the victim may be concerned about the risks relating to a case involving a high-profile athlete. Therefore, the victim may decide not to testify, which allows the perpetrator to go unpunished. The knowledge that others will "look the other way" then fosters the attitude that athletes can get away with anything, possibly including rape. Statistics also bear this out, as a study cited by NCAVA notes that the conviction rate for non-athletes committing assaults is 80 percent while for college athletes it is 38 percent.

This attitude of invincibility is more common with more aggressive sports, such as football. However, the most common denominators are teams that have high prestige or notoriety on the given campus. This may vary, as lacrosse at an Eastern school or volleyball at a school on the West Coast may have a greater risk of having players who are perpetrators than similar programs at other schools.

We are not implying that you are responsible for the criminal actions of another athlete. It is important, however, to consider taking preventive steps to avoid a very dangerous and possibly life-altering situation. First, be aware that other athletes in high-profile sports may have a higher risk of being perpetrators. Be especially cautious about athletes who have a reputation of disrespecting women or who act as if they can date anyone they choose. Second, be aware that alcohol is a common factor in many of these situations. If you are legally allowed to drink alcohol and this is your choice, be aware of your surroundings and always drink responsibly, especially in a dating situation.

Pregnancy

The risk of an unplanned pregnancy in female college students is another rarely discussed topic; in many cases, an unplanned pregnancy often results in the woman athlete being pressured to make a decision influenced mainly by her worries of the pregnancy's effect on her scholarship status.

One college athlete described a situation where her teammate got pregnant. Out of fear of losing her scholarship, she felt pressured into having an abortion. After this occurred, it was never discussed again and the coaching staff was never told. It is important to know that pregnancy is classified as a medical condition and, technically, your scholarship cannot be rescinded because of it. However, this is a taboo subject and you do run the risk that a coach may attempt to rescind your scholarship or financial aid.

Women-Only Colleges: Another option for women athletes? Some seek education at a women's college. According to Susan Lennon, executive director for the Women's College Coalition, there are over 50 women-only colleges in the United States. Interestingly, Lennon states there are "no data profiles" regarding women that choose this setting versus a coed college but points to studies on their Web site that reflect increased opportunities for leadership and academic success. From an athletics standpoint, one of the challenges is that some universities and conferences are leery about competing against women's colleges. One former women's college graduate said that "there are many women who thrive in this environment, but for some, it can affect their relationships when it comes to dealing with men."

Concerns for Males

The topic of the long-term consequences of being treated as a special person on campus has previously been discussed, although many programs in the women's department such as women's basketball have now joined the high-profile status previously only conferred to men's programs.

With a continued push toward gender equality, athletic departments are notorious for discontinuing men's non-revenue sports. Sports such as track and cross-country, wrestling, golf, tennis, and swimming and diving are the most common sports cited, especially at the Division I level. This happened to Brad Johnson, who was ready to move from the Midwest to the West Coast to play college baseball. "They canceled the program two weeks before the start of the season. I had passed up other scholarship offers so I was pretty upset." You cannot completely prevent this from happening but at the same time, when you ask the coach if he or she plans to be there for the next few years, ask the same question regarding the program.

The Government Accountability Office (GAO) has looked into this issue and highlights of two GAO studies reflect the complexity of this situation. First, GAO-07-535 noted the trend between 1991–1992 through 2004–2005 has been for participation increases in both men's and women's collegiate sports, although there have been greater increases with women versus men. In addition, for men's sports, there have been greater increases in participation opportunities at the Division II and III level versus Division I during this same time period. Discontinuation of programs also seems to have some gender differences according to GAO-01-297, which surveyed college athletic directors. Insufficient student interest and inability to field competitive teams were the rationale for the discontinuation of women's programs, whereas gender equity requirements and the need for resources for other sports were cited as more common reasons for men's programs to be discontinued. See more details at the GAO Web site.

A final issue that affects males more is the transition or loss of a sport at the end of a career. According to Zanotti, "Athletics often plays a larger role in the identity of males as this is how they are socialized. The thought of having to give up their sports aspirations of playing professionally can be difficult." Part of making a healthy transition is using the academic environment to help transition the athletes' energies and focus toward a non-athletic career. This remains difficult if the whole academic experience is centered around athletics.

Summary

- Be aware of gender-specific concerns such as eating dis-orders, ACL tears, and sexual harassment.
- Males may face more transitional issues and their non-revenue sports are more likely to be discontinued.

5

Racial Issues

Sports may be color-blind but sadly your coaches, administrators, and teammates may not be. Racism can extend into the recruiting process and college athletics. Dr. Benjamin recalls situations where athletes' poor performances were blamed on their bad attitudes. After hearing the coach make some racially insensitive jokes, he understood that there was a coach-athlete disconnect that was affecting the athletes' performances. Coaches' attitudes regarding your racial background can affect their perception of you. Understanding the ways that racism can play a role in academics, athletics, and the recruiting process, can help you avoid programs that might make you feel uncomfortable. This chapter mainly focuses on African-American issues, although racism can be directed toward any racial background. Even though there are laws against discrimination, racial tensions can sap the enjoyment of your collegiate experience. Rather, screen out programs based on concerns addressed in this chapter.

Academics

If you are a male African-American college football or basketball player, your odds of graduating are less than 50 percent, especially at major colleges. This rate is lower than your white counterparts for multiple reasons, which include coaches' negative perceptions of your capacity to succeed academically. You are ultimately responsible for meeting your academic requirements, but it is crucial that the university and coaching staff be supportive and provide the opportunity to carry out your scholastic pursuits. Beware of coaches and programs that minimize your chances for an education by either attempting to choose your major or divert you away from a major of interest that is perceived by the athletic staff as difficult or time-consuming. This may even start during the recruiting process. It is not unusual for programs to seemingly have degree tracks where the coursework and faculty are athletic department friendly. Often, these may be in the physical education department or it may be a generic major that may not have any direct applicability to your interests or goals. There is nothing wrong with any degree, but beware of racially motivated academic counseling that is geared to keeping you eligible, maintaining an acceptable NCAA graduation rate, and winning games for the coach rather than challenging you academically. This may be a result of perceptions regarding your family academic background or the stereotype that you as an African-American athlete do not value an education and are simply there to play sports.

Two African-American athletes who did not let anyone sideline their education are Jabari Wamble and Corey Finch, M.D. They both stayed the academic course while competing in athletics at a Division I and a Division III program, respectively. Both came from families that valued academics, and they let their coaches know from the onset of the recruiting process that graduation and graduate school was a definite part of their future. Wamble is now an assistant attorney general and Finch is a physician. Wamble developed an interest in pre-law and used "my undergraduate courses to prepare me for law school." Like Wamble, Finch believes that you should be loud and clear regarding academic aspirations. Finch said, "I made it very clear that my ambition was to go to medical school. I chose my school partly because my coach was very supportive of my academic aspirations." As you look at different programs, talk to current team members about how they chose their respective majors. Also, find out how these decisions were made. Further, ask other African-American athletes if there are any negative stereotypes regarding intelligence and academic aptitude or if they felt pressure to choose certain courses of study over others. Ask the coaches for a breakdown of the majors on the team; if the majors seem to break along racial lines, inquire about that. You should also ask the coaches about the graduation rate of team members and inquire about any discrepancies between the graduation rates among different races. Again, there are many reasons for poor graduation rates and choices of major and the coaching staff may not necessarily be the problem. However, you need to be assured that your graduation opportunities are maximized. This question also sends an important message to the coaching staff that academics are important to you.

Athletics

Although African Americans only make up about 7 percent of all undergraduates at NCAA Division I colleges, they make up about 55 percent of the NCAA Division I football and 63 percent of the basketball players. About 2.5 percent of head football coaches are African American; in basketball, the percentage is significantly higher—over 25 percent. Racism exists in sport although much of this is subtle. Watch out for negative stereotypes, the practice of channeling, and race-targeted recruiting styles.

Stereotypes

Everyone has biases or beliefs that are unfounded. The capacity for a coaching staff or team to have open discussions about racial issues should be commended. However, stereotypes may reflect a coaching attitude that does not have your best interests at heart. Beware of racial epithets and stereotyping, racial slurs, or derogatory jokes that are often expressed behind closed doors or only in the presence of staff. Comments from players that are tolerated, accepted, and possibly even encouraged, may reflect an undesirable precedent. Athletes may have their own prejudices, but you want to ensure that the coaches have a zero-tolerance policy regarding such comments.

Stereotyping of African-American athletes regarding personal or social attributes also can negatively influence the coach-athlete relationship. Personal attribute stereotypes are directed at the individual level and might include being assumed to be unintelligent, lazy, or irresponsible. Social attribute stereotypes are directed at a group as a whole and might include assuming a whole group is sexually promiscuous, or involved with gangs, crime, or illicit drug use. These attitudes may extend to academics or to the concept of channeling.

Channeling

Channeling is the placement of an athlete in a specific position or event based on a racial or ethnic profile rather than on the unique characteristics of the athlete. This practice is often based on the stereotype that African Americans are better athletes than whites, or that Asians are more intelligent and team-oriented.

An example of channeling would be an African-American quarterback who has the leadership, arm strength, and intelligence to play quarterback but is automatically switched to another position, such as cornerback, which can reflect the stereotype of speed and aggressiveness.

Channeling can also run the other way, with the white sprinter who has run similar times as non-white sprinters being asked to compete at longer distances because of the perception that a white athlete cannot compete in terms of raw speed. This problem is not infrequent, argue two white former collegiate athletes, both of whom requested anonymity. The first athlete felt that "even if your statistics and play are superior, it's sometimes not given the same level of recognition as your African-American counterparts."

The second athlete also notes a geographic factor along with perception and expectations. He said, "It seems that there are low expectations of white athletes along with a higher perceived potential for the black athlete. This is also true in that in some places, for example in the Midwest, kids might grow up believing they are going to play for a specific regional team. Also, it might be the norm to have major college coaches on campus asking about athletes." They both believe that this bias does affect the recruiting and scholarship process, especially in sports or events where there is a predominance of African-American athletes. The other bias may be more geographic in that you might be given an edge, for example if you are a West Coast water polo or volleyball player, a Midwest wrestler, or an East Coast lacrosse player.

Another athlete who is African American believes it is about "winning," and not race per se. "If a white kid is clearly better, I don't think this comes into play. However, if you are recruiting

---

This question may be helpful during the recruiting process. You can also talk with other athletes to see if channeling is prevalent in the program.

What position or event do you envision me playing?

If the answer is not what you expect, you might ask why he or she thinks you are better suited to the position or event they suggested. Gauge if there are some logical reasons for a change. Look for subtle cues regarding any stereotypes he or she might hold involving speed or athletic quickness, temperament, and intelligence.

two kids of similar abilities, then this is where these perceptions can make a difference." Sometimes as you transition to the collegiate level, position changes may be warranted, but your racial background should not eliminate you from a position or event if you possess the skills to succeed at them.

Recruiting Factors

Beware of recruiting strategies based on race or ethnicity. For example, with the case of African-American athletes coming from single-parent backgrounds, a common ploy is to woo the mother; in the case of Asian-American athletes, the ploy might be to overemphasize academics based on the stereotype that Asians are bright and academically motivated. Your parents or guardians should be involved in the recruitment discussion. However, excessive pleasantries toward a parent or guardian will not make up for four years of incompatibility with a program. Recruiting practices based on racial or ethnic backgrounds often reflect insincerity and manipulation rather than honesty and integrity.

Another recruiting strategy involves using athletes of the same background to talk up the program. It is not uncommon to spend time with athletes of a similar background, and therefore these opportunities allow for honest discussions regarding the team and race issues. Take this opportunity to assess any racial bias. If, for example, you are an African-American distance swimmer and the rest of the distance team is white, then you should seek out experiences and opportunities to talk with swimmers who you will train alongside, regardless of their background.

Recruiting visits also allow you to assess general comfort levels. One African-American athlete noted that a particular coach was uncomfortable around black people. "The assistant coach—who was black—came to see me for a family visit. I later found out that the head coach had never interacted with anyone of color until he was over 18 years old. I now understand why he may not have been comfortable around black athletes." This perspective is interesting, as interpretation of such a comment can have a lot to do with your perceptions of a coach. This coach seemingly was attempting to be honest and reach out by discussing race in an open manner. Consider your own biases as part of the recruiting equation.

Team Factors

It is important to evaluate the race relations and interactions among your teammates and coaches. Good coaches should treat everyone according to his or her unique attributes as an athlete, which is unrelated to background. Therefore, assessing these factors while being recruited can help you know what might be experienced the next few years. Ask athletes on the team if they feel the coaching staff treats them fairly and judges them based on their talents rather than their race. Ask for specific examples, which can help differentiate between bias and an athlete's dissatisfaction with the program. For instance, it is not unusual for a 6'5" high school basketball center to be switched to a forward position in college, or for an athlete to get less playing time in college than in high school. These are often the realities of playing at a higher level. You should also ask if athletes and coaches from different backgrounds get along. Remember that every team has its cliques and different levels of bonding, but if all the athletes of one race feel excluded from the rest of the team, it may be cause for concern. A parent of a former African-American tennis player shared her concern regarding her son's experience at a public Division I Southern college. Everything seemed to be fine on the courts but "on the weekends, the whole team would go out but my son was never invited." The implication was that her son was fine as a teammate but not as friend. This social isolation reflected a level of subtle bias and this athlete transferred to another school where player-imposed racial segregation was not an issue.

College Factors

Your background, expectations, and personal experiences influence what sort of community and surroundings you desire in a college environment. If you have grown up in a mixed racial setting, the atmosphere of the college may not be as critical. However, if college atmosphere is a factor, ask what percentage of the student body versus the athletic population is of your particular group of interest? These numbers will help you appreciate whether your racial group is represented as a part of the student body or if they are simply there to help the athletic programs. Meet with a minority faculty member unrelated to the athletic department who might be able to tell you about attitudes toward students of your particular background.

You might also want to ask what social and educational opportunities are available for different minority students. Are there academic studies, social clubs, counselors, and community programs that fit what you are looking for in a college atmosphere? Depending on your background and experiences, being a sole or "token" minority on campus may be a lonely experience.

African-American Colleges

There are over 100 self-identified historically African-American colleges along with a number of colleges where the student population is 75 percent African American or higher. These colleges vary in terms of academic and athletic reputations. These colleges are an option if being a part of this particular racial minority is important to you. Despite the setting, do not assume that you are automatically safe from all of the racial issues discussed above. African-American coaches may harbor similar biases. Just because someone appears similar to you, do not assume they will automatically be the best coach for you.

Author's comment: Coach Cauthen notes that often African-American students who grew up in the South have an ambivalence regarding whether they should go to a historically African-American college to show support to their culture and history or go to a school at which they would be a minority and get what some may perceive is a better education. Coach Cauthen uses the word *perceive,* as he cites one study reflecting that, compared to other state colleges, the college with the highest economic impact in a particular state was a historically black college. According to Cauthen, this reflects that for every dollar given to the university, there was a significant return back to the local, regional, and state level in terms of economic benefits. This would include spending, job creation, innovation and research, and employment benefits. Cauthen believes this is suggestive that your opportunities for future occupational success will be there regardless of this choice. No one is suggesting making decisions based on one study, but do not eliminate these colleges as a possibility simply because they cater to African-American students.

Asian-American Athletes

The truth is that the percentage of Asian-American athletes is quite low and little research has been done regarding this group and the racism they face as athletes. Also, the term *Asian* encompasses a broad group. The prevailing stereotype of an Asian-American athlete is of a person who might not have the finest physical skills but who is very smart. If your performances are equal to those your white or African-American counterparts, but you are not getting the same offers, consider that you might be fighting a stereotype. This may not be the case in traditionally more expensive sports such as tennis, golf, or fencing, for example. In these sports, where athletes are often self-selected based on social class and the costs of participation, it can be more difficult sometimes for Asian-American athletes to be given a fair look. However, Megan Duncan, a Korean-American former Division I soccer player, believes that positive stereotypes such as persistence and intelligence can be beneficial. Duncan said, "If you can play, then an Asian background might be seen as an advantage. Also, as a minority, I would stick out on the playing field and this can be helpful if coaches are recruiting at a particular game." This may be a reflection of the physicality of the sport as you may be given an edge in "finesse" sports. In these situations, Asian-American athletes may indeed be recruited less vigorously.

Summary

- Racism exists for both minorities and white athletes. Know how some of the factors are different.
- Channeling and stereotyping are two forms or racism.
- Consider minority factors if you are concerned about the team and the college.

6

Religious and Cultural Issues

As the United States becomes more diverse and a growing number of international athletes participate in college sports, a greater number of college athletes will have religious and cultural values that are different from those of the coaching staff and the majority of other athletes on the team. Research and our personal experience suggest that coaches tend to be individuals who have benefited from the status quo. This in itself is not problematic, but if you are from a minority religion or culture, here are some guidelines to help use the recruiting process to ensure that you will compete for a program that will respect your culture and values.

Religious Issues

Oxford's Atlas of the World's Religions estimates that there are up to 40,000 new religious movements throughout the world. New religious movements include mainstream religions along with the many variations and ways that they may be practiced. We cannot cover all of them, but we can provide themes to look for and some examples so you can reflect on your own personal beliefs and project how these beliefs and practices may fit with the programs that you are considering.

There are two main topics that you should consider. The first relates to the religious convictions of the program and the second involves ensuring that any personal religious beliefs or practices are accepted prior to attending and playing at a particular college.

The Program's Religiosity

Despite laws that dictate a separation between religion and public university settings, many coaches, staffs, and athletes believe athletics is a way of spreading their personal religious beliefs. Many private colleges have a religious mission, and if this fits with your beliefs and you know what to expect, that's fine. However, even at large secular institutions, you may encounter fundamentally religious coaches who indirectly recruit based on "how good a Christian" they perceive you to be. These situations can be uncomfortable for more secular athletes. In fact, there are some coaches who may make church attendance or routine prayers a requirement, which although against the law in a public institution, may still happen. You may love the school, the environment, and the opportunity to compete but feel alone if religion plays a larger role than you expect with the coaching staff and teammates. This may not seem important, but this can play out regarding rules on common issues.

Clarify the policies on the following topics if these are of concern to you. The bottom line is to identify your specific values and ensure that you seek out a college environment where you will be comfortable.

- Substance policies. Some colleges and programs may prohibit any alcohol, caffeine, or tobacco use. Most prohibit illicit substances but may have radically different approaches to the extent that they perform random drug screens, enforce rules on use, or have an attitude— especially with marijuana —that so long as it is done privately and with discretion, they don't want to know about it. We are not advocating any of the above, but if you drink alcohol or caffeine, or use tobacco (including smokeless, cigarettes, or cigars), check with the coaches and athletes about the specific policies.
- Dating policies. Some colleges may prohibit or strongly discourage premarital sex, cohabitation, and even cross-cultural or interracial relationships. It is important to know how the college's rules and values compare with your values.
- Attendance at chapel or other religious functions. Some colleges require mandatory classes in a specific set of religious beliefs. If you are considering a college that has a religious affiliation and you are not of that particular denomination, do not practice your religion in the same

manner as the college desires, or are more secular, this attendance and participation may become problematic. The opposite is also true. If your faith, and that your faith is practiced in a similar fashion by those around you, is of central importance, a smaller faith-based college might be best for you.

Religious Practices

Before choosing a college it is important to identify specific religious practices that are important to you and to determine how well they fit with the colleges you are looking at. General considerations include holy days or periods, dietary restrictions, dress requirements, or bathing regimens. If any of these are observed in a strict manner, they might impinge on your participation in numerous practices or competitions. Therefore, you may have to ask to be accommodated, which colleges are legally required to do. Ask yourself how comfortable you are speaking up, standing out from others, and dealing with any prejudice you might encounter. It is better to bring such issues up before you attend than after you get there. It is outside the scope of this book to cover every religion and variant that might affect your college sports opportunities. Rather, our goal is to provide examples that will allow you the chance to assess your own beliefs and how these may come into play.

Holy Days or Periods

Holy days or periods vary based on the religion and its practice. These periods, which can range from a day to a couple of years, reflect the expectation of performing specific rituals or not participating in any events that are not religiously related. It is these specific practices that you need to consider in terms of how they might affect your ability to practice and compete.

For example, many religions have holy days or weekly Sabbaths, which might not afford you the option of practicing or competing with the rest of your team. In both the Jewish and Seventh Day Adventist traditions, Sabbath is from Friday at sunset to Saturday at sunset. Many competitions are on Saturday afternoons, and as Amber Chambers, a devout

Seventh Day Adventist and former college softball player discussed, there is an inherent divide in maintaining some religious beliefs in a secular competitive environment. Chambers selected a Seventh Day Adventist college. "My faith was important to me and my family and I thought it would be easier to compete at a college which would honor my beliefs. Unfortunately, they were starting up these sports programs and it was not organized nor what I expected. We practiced year around but the program was unable to schedule any games. After this experience where I was not given an opportunity to compete, I transferred closer to home and attended a Seventh Day Adventist college that did not have a softball program." Despite the religious similarities, the poor fit between Chambers and the athletic program resulted in her transferring after her first year. She never competed again, with regret. Chambers said, "Honestly, if you play on a team, there's not a lot of flexibility. If you don't play, they will just go to the next person. I made a tough choice based on my religion but I regret it. I feel I had a God-given talent to play college softball and never got an opportunity."

Some religions involve periods of fasting. Examples include the Muslim and Bahá'í faiths. Both involve no eating or drinking from sunrise to sunset for 30 and 19 days, respectively. This practice alters your capacity to be at your physical or mental best. Shawn Khavari, a former high school tennis player of the Bahá'í faith, explained his struggle and final compromise. He said, "I had a very supportive coach and initially tried to fast and still play tournaments—but I found this was impossible, as I had no energy and would get dehydrated. I finally made a tough decision and would forgo my religious practices on tournament days."

Finally, some religions may involve extended periods of time away from competition such as with the Latter-Day Saints (LDS) faith. Mission work away from the college setting is typically performed for a two-year stint. Many LDS athletes attend an LDS university for the reason that they know that this sort of work, typically achieved in the early 20s, will be accepted and understood. Thomas Wood, a freshman at an LDS university explained, "Many of us as we enter college really see the mission as a very important part of our religious experience." Coaches who are accepting of their athletes fulfilling their mission also recognize that they will have a more emotionally and physically mature athlete. However, this may be a harder sell to a non-LDS program.

Other Considerations

Examples include prayer rituals, dietary restrictions, possible clothing or bathing restrictions, and possibly some medical constraints. Prayer rituals may vary based on daily or specific holy practices. Muslims may pray five times a day and Jewish athletes may not compete during the high holidays around Rosh Hashanah and Yom Kippur.

In terms of dietary restrictions, if you adhere to these practices, discuss alternative options with the coaching staff as well as the team nutritionist if available. For example, Muslims, Jews, and Seventh Day Adventists do not eat pork products, and Hindus do not eat beef. In addition, vegetarian or vegan athletes, regardless of whether or not their dietary preference is related to religious or spiritual beliefs, might want to share his or her concerns with the coaches. Honoring dietary practices may not be an issue during practice but may be harder to adhere to while traveling.

Some Muslim and conservative sects of Judaism and Christianity may require women to wear specific more conservative clothing. Also, many cultural and religious groups are not as comfortable with open bathing stalls and may require their own private bathing facilities. Medically, members of the Jehovah's Witness religion may not accept blood transfusions and Christian Scientists often choose to eschew most medical interventions. Rare is the need for emergency surgery that requires a transfusion, but coaches and the medical staff ought to know about any specific wishes.

Questions of Tolerance

Each of you express your religious beliefs in very different ways. The intent is not to stereotype but to help you reflect on what is important to you. The following questions might help you gauge how your faith may interact with the athletic program.

1. Will your religious practices supersede the demands of the sport? To what extent?

2.   How tolerant will the coach and staff be toward your religious beliefs in terms of how they affect your availability to practice and compete?

For example, if you have issues with competing during your Saturday Sabbath, this may be a difficult issue to resolve. However, some coaches may work with you regarding dietary restrictions, other practices, and occasional days off.

EB is a Jewish athlete and Maccabi games medalist who attended a public university. She said, "It [prejudice against my faith] was never overt but I always felt pressure to go to church or participate in team prayers. I had even discussed how important my faith was to me but it was given lip service."

3.   How comfortable are you regarding your faith with your teammates and staff?
4.   How comfortable are they regarding your faith?

Usually, these two are interconnected but not necessarily. You may be faced with a tolerant team but an intolerant assistant coach, or vice versa. Examples may include team prayer and church rituals. Dr. Benjamin recalls one particular recruit, a non-denominational Christian athlete, who fell asleep while at a "voluntary" prayer ritual during a recruiting visit at a public secular university. He realized very quickly that his belief system did not match that of the team's and crossed the school off his list. Less overt but equally insidious is the feeling of subtle pressure of conforming, constant preaching, or even suggestions of conversion to another religion.

Agnostic or Atheist Athletes

For the religious yet secular athlete, opportunities abound, but what about the atheist or agnostic athlete? First, seek out a secular program at a secular college, an inclusive college, or at least a college that doesn't require a religious commitment or is overtly affiliated with a church. Second, be aware that prejudices against atheists can run high. A former collegiate athlete who attended a secular college stated, "I never told the coach or my teammates. I just lowered my head and closed my eyes when the team prayed out of respect for their belief." This athlete also cautions against what to divulge. He said, "I strongly advise not telling teammates about a lack of belief. I believe that people are more biased against atheists, more so than any other group."

Cultural Issues

Cultural diversity is as broad as religious diversity and we cannot possibly assess every cultural aspect that may intersect with athletics. Two prominent cultures in the United States that we will highlight are Native American and Latino cultures. Many athletes from these backgrounds who are scholarship eligible are often passed over by recruiters and coaches because of concerns that the athletes might not stay in school, as the cultural barriers may be too much of a hurdle to overcome. Addressing possible stereotypes or cultural misperceptions as part of the recruiting process will enhance your college chances.

Native American Students

Many talented Native American athletes go unrecruited and the ones who attend are at high risk to not successfully complete their college careers. One study cites a 36 percent graduation rate for Native Americans, compared to 56 percent for the total population. Jerry Tuckwin, retired athletic director and former basketball and track coach at Haskell Indian Nations University (formerly named Haskell Indian Junior College), believes the reasons for this lack of recruitment revolve around the issues of "scholarship" offers, stereotypes, and goodness of fit.

The Perceived Scholarship Offer

When you are looking at programs and weighing financial aid offers, you should clarify that the scholarship offer is truly a scholarship offer or an expectation that you will receive a Native American grant and not need the scholarship. Tuckwin said, "It would irritate me when coaches would exploit the situation and offer 'scholarships' when they really were counting on the athlete getting a minority Native American grant. The truth was they did not want to risk spending any of their scholarship money." According to Tuckwin, this relates to stereotypes of Native Americans.

Stereotypes of Native Americans

Stereotypes of Native American athletes are related to effort and motivation, capacity to adapt to a non-Native college environment, and high dropout rates. Awareness of these perceptions will allow you to understand what you have to overcome during the recruiting process to achieve your athletic and academic goals.

A perceived lack of consistent effort may reflect what the above study noted as a "lack of persistence." The study concluded that social isolation and lack of academic preparation may leave many Native American students at risk academically. This perceived lack of commitment may be interpreted as not being as motivated or competitive. Emphasize to coaches about your competitive drive and willingness to work hard. Coaches' letters, tryouts, and camps are ways to demonstrate your work ethic.

The capacity to "fit in" is another area of trepidation for many coaches. Indeed, this may be very pertinent and possibly accurate, even though only about one-third of the approximately 2 million Native Americans live on reservations. Tuckwin states that "the transition of the Native American athlete, especially for those who come from a very strong cultural background, can be very difficult." Ask yourself how prepared you are to attend a non-Native American college or even a Native American college. As Tuckwin points out, "Native Americans are as different as any other group but sometimes we get lumped in all together." If you are integrated into the larger society, emphasize this fact during your recruiting conversations. If you have lived most of your life on a reservation and spent time with only Native American people, consider what it might be like to play on a team with non-Native Americans. Geographic considerations may also be a stronger reason to maintain a connection with your particular tribe, if pertinent. Even though this is a consideration for every recruit—finding the balance of familiar surroundings and new experiences that suits you—keep in mind that there are over 500 tribes and over 250 recognized tribal languages. Tuckwin also adds that the differences and variation among the hundreds of tribes are significant.

Traditionally high dropout rates in Native American students also scare off many coaches. These dropout rates, as discussed above, may reflect the difficulty with transitioning to a non-Native American setting as well as any issues occurring back home, according to Tuckwin. Consider this when thinking about proximity to home as discussed in Section I. Consider interactions with teammates also, as these can have a great impact regarding decisions to quit competing. One athlete that Tuckwin recalls improved dramatically in junior college, which allowed him to be successful at a four-year college where he felt very accepted by the coaching staff and teammates, none of whom were Native American. Finally, consider if your level of college preparation is adequate for the college setting that you are considering.

Goodness of Fit

As you look at programs, assess the coaches and team members for stereotyping and general respectfulness during the recruiting process. This will help you determine if you will be treated as a person first rather than as a Native American.

One of the first clues is the use of negative stereotypes by coaching staff. "I have had former athletes describe being asked to do 'rain dances,' 'hoop dances,' or 'powwows.' The coaches and other athletes found these sorts of comments to be funny, but the lack of sensitivity was part of the reason that these particular athletes transferred," according to Tuckwin. He adds, "There are certain programs where Native American athletes are just not accepted and they should watch out for these."

Look for programs that display general respect. Tuckwin strongly believes that simply reflecting on how the coaches treat their athletes as people is critical. "Forget about whether you are Native American, or an athlete, or a student: Do they show respect for you as a person?" This subtlety can come out in a Native American context. Tuckwin describes an athlete who shared a goal of wanting to be a "medicine man" after graduation. This goal evoked ridicule by team members, much to the athlete's chagrin. "This position is still highly revered [in] Native American tribes and on reservations but it was denigrated by the coaches and athletes." In this situation, the athlete transferred.

College Decisions

When making decisions on college, a consideration on background and family connections may help. If you have little bond to your tribal heritage, your Native American background may have no bearing on your college choice. If the bond with your Native American heritage is a major part of your everyday life, attempt to clarify for yourself what is important to you in terms of tribal opportunities, language, and proximity to family and tribal cultural events. Therefore, if being close to a particular tribe is important, ensure that your college opportunities reflect this. Do not minimize the chance to compete at a Native American college as HR did. "I actually walked on the football team and played fullback for two years. It was a great experience and being around an Indian environment made me feel more at home." There are 24 recognized tribal colleges, at least half of which have athletic programs; the majority of these are junior colleges, according to Carrie Billy, CEO of the American Indian Higher Education Consortium (AIHEC). According to Billy, you should research the different sports programs, scholarship opportunities, or tuition waivers that might be available, despite limited funding. Find their Web site in the online resources section.

Hispanic and Latino Students

Hispanics and Latinos now comprise the largest minority in the United States. They clearly are a heterogeneous population. Nevertheless, you may encounter stereotypes involving family, economics, and legal status as you navigate the recruiting process.

What are seen as traditionally strong Latino family connections can be either beneficial or obstructive when it comes to college athletic opportunities. According to JG, a Hispanic soccer coach, what the family wants often "will dictate what the player does. So if the family is not supportive of college or college athletics, the athlete may choose not to go." National Hispanic University college mentor Arnold Melgar agrees. He notes that, "Since we were children, we [were] taught to respect our elders and often we [would] not take opportunities such as a college scholarship if they are not supported by our families." Discuss college options early on with your family to make sure they know what you want and also so you can be aware of what they expect. Early in the recruitment process, have coaches espouse to your parents the benefits of a college degree. Another aspect relating to family might be language. If English is a second language, effective communication is crucial. Language should not be a barrier that prevents you from getting a scholarship.

Sometimes an emphasis on the immediate economic benefits of entering the work force straight after high school may also impede the odds of you realizing your college athletics dreams. The need to work may win over scholarship opportunities. As Melgar says, "In Hispanic culture, we are taught to value hard work and helping the family above all things, including academic opportunities." Focusing on the increased long-term economic opportunities as a result of a meaningful degree may be the best approach if you want to play and you experience familial resistance. Engage your coaching staff to point out the long-term benefits of an education.

Questions regarding your legal status may result in concerns from the coaching staff. Many athletes who play high school sports may never have their status questioned. However, financial aid forms and the college application process request much more identification information and this, according to JG, is when the recruiting process "can go south when applications for college ask for Social Security numbers or other forms of [proof of] legal status." These questions might prevent the athlete from continuing the recruiting process, as, according to JG, "The athlete may be legal but if other close family members are not, they may not want to risk bringing attention to themselves." Coaches may also have concerns regarding legal status but may not know how to broach this delicate topic. Don't wait for the coach, bring this up with a simple comment such as, *"Coach, just in case you were wondering, I am a legal resident or an American citizen, and do not foresee immigration status being an issue."* If you are not a legal resident, clarify what needs to be disclosed with your high school counselors. Also, most coaches are interested in winning and not addressing legal issues regarding immigration. There may never be a need to discuss a family member who has a questionable immigrant status. So don't!

Other Cultural Experiences

It is well beyond the scope of this book to describe the thousands of cultures and sets of experiences that make up our diverse nation. Decide what is important to you and judge if the environment, program, and coach have the tolerance and combine to create an atmosphere in which you can to thrive. Identify what, if any, cultural events and observances are important to you. Does the college you are considering have a community in which you can participate in your cultural celebrations? Do your cultural traditions or customs require you to make a trip home, or do they otherwise affect your attendance in class or at practice? What will your professors' and coaches' attitudes be if you miss class or practice?

The observances, traditions, and celebrations of some cultures are of a significance comparable to what Christmas or Easter represent for many Christian faiths. Examples include the Chinese, Vietnamese, or Persian New Year. The latter, which occurs during the spring equinox in March, is for Persians the most important family celebration of the year. This may conflict with spring practice or a spring break competition trip.

> **Author's comment:** Be up front and honest about cultural practices that might have an impact on your participation in a sport; this should open a dialogue with the coach. If a coach is uncomfortable discussing these issues, it may be a sign to look somewhere else.

Summary

- Consider the specific religious practices that are meaningful to you. How might they possibly affect practice and competition?
- Native American and Latino athletes should be ready to counter stereotypes that might negatively affect the extent of recruitment by some coaching staffs.
- Do not underestimate the importance of ensuring tolerant coaches and teammates.

7

International Athletes

Every year, thousands of exchange students from around the world come to the United States to participate in intercollegiate sports. (For brevity's sake, these students are often referred to as "international students" while they are in the United States and that is the term used throughout this book.) In fact, a number of programs in sports such as ice hockey, tennis, track and field, golf, basketball, swimming, soccer, and cross-country can rely quite heavily on international athletes. International recruitment is a controversial issue. Bob Timmons, former Kansas University track and field and cross-country coach, feels that this "takes scholarships away from American athletes. I felt that any way you cut it, not enough money was there to go to American athletes." Vince Westbrook, a Division I director of tennis, holds the opposite view, "The world is shrinking. No one ever says not to do international business. Our job as coaches is to secure the most talented kids, and I want an international mix." Regardless of your viewpoint, it is a reality that has implications for you whether you are an international or American prospect.

In this chapter, we consider what the prospective international student-athlete needs to know. Unlike American athletes, you may not have a chance to visit and you may know little about certain aspects of American college life—a challenging task, especially if you have not done your homework. As an American athlete, at just about every division and in most sports, you will be competing with international athletes. We want to ensure that you know how to maximize this experience and how to get the attention you need to be successful.

International Athletes' Perspective

As an international athlete, you are in a college athletic program to provide a competitive boost to programs that may not be able to attract the finest American talent. From a global perspective, these opportunities provide far-reaching growth and learning experiences for athletes and coaches alike. Even though the majority of international athletes do not feel exploited, John Bale, a professor at Keele University in England and the author of *Brawn Drain*, recommends that you consider several factors before leaving your homeland.

Coaching Factors

Many good coaches recruit international students. Unfortunately, others who are good "business" managers and recruiters see international talent as an excuse not to teach and coach. This is because some international athletes have superior skill levels and are therefore competing at a high level even before extensive collegiate coaching. Whether you are an international or an American student, you need to assess whether the coaching staff is really committed to coaching.

From a recruiting standpoint, coaches experienced in international recruiting know that only 1 in 15 students actually come to the United States, according to Bale. Therefore, a coach may send out lots of feelers. There is a perception that recruiting internationally is difficult, but there are some coaching benefits. First, for international students, the recruitment process might cost less and provide instant competitive success. Recruiting may involve merely a phone call or e-mails but no recruiting visit costs. From the coach's standpoint, the cost of a full scholarship, while expensive, will result in instant team success.

The downside to being an internationally recruited athlete is that you may lack awareness of the implications of any promises made to you. First, you need to realize that you are possibly trading your skill level to help a program for the opportunity to garner a college education. According to Allen Thompson, an Ethiopian American who came to the United States at age 14, "Understanding this is critical because coaches *are* counting on your skill level; no matter how good your personality and how stellar your grades, if you do not perform athletically, you will end up on a plane back to your country of origin." A college coach agreed, confiding that he is up front with international recruits. The coach makes it very clear that if they do not perform at a full scholarship level, the scholarship will not be renewed. The end result can be transferring to another college or being sent back to his or her country of origin.

Also, clarify what exactly you are getting in return. Some examples of pure charlatanism, according to Bale, include being "offered free meals at a casino, guaranteed entrance into a specific university," and lack of clarity "regarding scholarship amounts and benefits." Also, remember that the coach who is recruiting you may not be the one who will work with you. Ensure some contact by phone, e-mail, or mail to gain a sense of comfort with the coach with whom you will be working most closely. Ask the coach for e-mails of other athletes on the team, especially other international ones or possibly those from your country. Often, coaches have recruiting contacts or "pipelines" set up in certain countries and it is not unusual to see a number of athletes from the same country on the same team. This is often done intentionally, as the coach has the philosophy that having a few athletes who share a common culture and language may prevent loneliness and ensure that they will stay.

Team Factors

As an international recruit, you might be perceived as "taking away" scholarship opportunities from American teammates, so asking questions regarding how well teammates get along and how the coach attempts to create a cohesive unit are well worth asking. Jealousy factors arise when international players are promised things such as playing time before competing for the position. A former collegiate soccer player from a Western African nation said, "American athletes realize that you are on a full scholarship, and not all athletes are welcoming of foreigners." Before signing, it is crucial that you talk with both international and American athletes regarding the coaching staff's ability to fairly integrate the team. Westbrook concurs. He said, "A challenge, but also a big part of my job, is to mold a team including international and American athletes." Westbrook does this by ensuring that there is quality interaction among athletes away from tennis.

Another factor may be age related. Unlike the NCAA, the NAIA and junior colleges allow athletes of any age to compete. You should consider what it would be like to be an older, more mature athlete, spending time with much younger teammates.

Finally, the concepts of practice and competition may be very different. For example, the concept of running a number of events to score points for the team as is expected in American track and field often is different from the individual notion of track and field as seen in international or non-American track and field settings. Also, many countries' training programs, standards, and coaching philosophies may vary greatly. For example, South American soccer player Anderson Cristian Fernandes stated that he was "used to a more fast and agile game, while in America, it is more about power." GA agreed, feeling that the African soccer game is "more creative and skills-based; initially, it was hard to adjust." If you are sold on a particular philosophy or style, you may run into problems if your coach then alters your training and technique. This issue goes back to whether the coach is a coach or a manager. Know what you are getting as well as what you are wanting.

Preparation Factors

You need to be aware of the technical aspects of immigration as well as the recruiting factors. In terms of immigration, you should fully understand your visa status, requirements, and limitations. Immigration standards have gotten considerably tighter since September 11, 2001, so give yourself plenty of time—it may take up to 18 months or more to finalize your student visa.

Further, do not underestimate the importance of comfort with the English language. First, you will be required to pass the Test of English as a Foreign Language (TOEFL), an English-language proficiency test required to get admission to most colleges. Even if you are from a country where English is a common second language, do not underestimate this exam. Another tip is ensuring that you are computer literate or savvy. So much academic activity, from online classes to comprehensive papers, requires competent computer use.

Initial Recruiting Factors

On the recruitment side, consider how you were contacted. Often, your initial contact may be with a university representative, a former athlete, or a school alumnus, and these people often have the school's interest in mind. The motivation regarding school pride in sports stands apart from any other academic or athletic system in the world and does not make sense to many outsiders. In Canadian John Gill's case, it was his high school coach who realized that an American scholarship opportunity might be just what Gill needed. Gill, currently a high school athletic director and coach said, "I did not know what an athletic scholarship was. My club coach knew that without a scholarship, I would not be able to attend college." Gill, who was the first college graduate in his family, "wouldn't trade the experience for anything."

There has been a rise in recruiting agencies that you pay to secure a connection between you and a prospective college. These agencies can easily promise a lot—but once you are in the United States, if things are not what you were told, none of these agencies are going to pay for your ticket back. Confirm and clarify everything that you have been told, first with the coaching staff and then with current players, especially international ones.

Individual Factors

There are two aspects to consider when deciding to study and compete in the United States. The first is identifying why you want to study in the United States and the second is determining what individual characteristics will ensure a good fit for your college experience. In terms of what drives you to come to the United States, Bale points out that some of the factors include a lack of facilities, coaching and training opportunities, and competition in your home country. Another factor is that, unlike many countries where only a privileged few have the opportunity to attend college, there are many levels of academics and opportunities in the United States. If you have athletic talent but were an average student, your athletics may open some academic doors that you would not have had access to before. Often, the perception about the United States as being a land of opportunity can also spur a move.

In terms of what will allow a good fit, an honest look or discussions with those who know you well might be helpful. Bale points out that the traits for a good fit are similar to those of anyone open to new experiences. The capacity to accept change and differences, the view that there is an opportunity to learn, and an ability to be culturally open and adaptable are critical to making the transition. Fernandes agrees, stating, "First, you have to love your sport. You will be away from everything you know: family, relationships, language, and culture. I like new experiences, am open minded, and willing to try everything.

This attitude is what has helped me survive." Laura Lochner, Ph.D, a clinical psychologist who has reflected on both her own study-abroad experiences as an undergraduate and her experience working for a Division III study-abroad program, noted three common stages that study-abroad students would typically undergo. Lochner described that "initially, students are enamored by the opportunities and experiences of a new country. Next, once the newness has worn off, students often begin to dislike their host country and focus on the differences between their homeland and where they are studying. Finally, a new level of emotional maturity sets in where students can appreciate the differences, strengths, and drawbacks of each setting." Lochner adds that the time frame for this triphasic response is individual and if "problems occur, it usually is in the first six months."

Appropriate expectations are also important because no matter how things go, you should expect an adjustment period, especially in the first month. Full adjustments may take six months to a year. It is also important to figure out if there are resources on campus that are geared to international students. Ask for help during this critical transition period.

Social Factors

Adjusting to a new country, academic system, and athletic system is daunting. Factors to be considered include social issues, discrimination, and campus rules. You will be more likely to spend your free time with athletes than with people from your cultural background. Bale points out that the more similar your background is to your teammates', the better your chances are of staying the course. Gill agrees. He said, "Being Canadian, there was not a lot of difference coming to the States." On the other hand, one international athlete with a non-European background commented about the negative responses he got when he began dating an American Caucasian female. He believed that ethnicity and being "non-American" were both factors in this attitude, even though he did not experience or feel any prejudice while attending class, competing on the team, or spending time with American friends.

How you fit in with your teammates will be critical. Other factors include loneliness, homesickness, and boredom. For possibly the first time in your life, you will be away from your family and friends, typical routines, and familiar haunts. This in itself is a tough enough transition without the added pressures of academics and having to perform well to maintain your scholarship money. Holiday times and vacation breaks can add another layer of isolation, especially in the first six months, before you really have met people that you are comfortable around.

How well you manage these issues will dictate how successful your transition will be, according to Bruce Lochner, Ph.D., a psychologist who is assistant vice president for student affairs and director of student counseling at a Division II university. Lochner says that "in order to optimize athletic performance, you need to be comfortable in your new culture, and this does not happen immediately." Other concerns include dealing with administrative issues, motivation to study, mood changes such as depression, climate adjustment, financial difficulties, and the feelings of being obliged to perform for your education. Allen Thompson adds that "the coach can really help with the transition by being upfront with some cultural factors. In many countries, people don't wear deodorant or might eat with their hands and not utensils. It can be very embarrassing once an athlete finds out that others have been making jokes about them behind their back. Ask your coach what they think you should know about the cultural differences and practices." Many schools have specific religious dogma that dictate their policies and often dictate who will come to the school. Review the information in the previous chapter. Discrimination as described in other sections can also be problematic and is typically worse the more different you are from the typical student. In addition, the coach can always "send you back home" if things are not going well. Discussing these issues up front and getting into some e-mail dialogue before getting on the airplane is critical.

School or Academic Factors

Many of you are looking for educational opportunities. Unlike many countries where only the top students or ones with a lot of money or status are given a chance to go to college, just about anyone can go to college in the United States. The United States also offers many levels of college options ranging from junior college through Ivy League, as well as public and private options. However, simply having a degree from the United States may not be enough, so find out if your particular degree will mean anything in your country. An example is that associate degrees are almost worthless in many countries, though working toward an associate degree will keep you eligible from the coach's perspective. Also, you may be tempted to make a hasty decision based on having a friend at a particular school, being offered a scholarship, or having a perception of a specific location or climate.

You need to ask yourself why the school is recruiting you in the first place. Often, it may be that the school is perceived to be undesirable by many American students. Also, if you have not been in school for a while, unless you are very motivated academically, enduring the studying process again may be difficult. Bale points out that international students' majors tend to be in the social sciences and not in physical education, so make sure your coach is clear on and supportive of your academic goals. On the other hand, Westbrook believes that the intensity of academics in many countries sets international students up to perform well. Westbrook said, "International student-athletes really appreciate the educational opportunities that they get. I have seen some barely pass the TOEFL but because they are well educated and motivated, maintain over 3.0 GPAs."

Cultural Factors

It is important that both you and your prospective coach are able to clearly assess how cultural factors might affect your time in an athletic program. It is helpful to know if you are part of a recruiting pipeline through which other international athletes have joined the program you are considering. If so, talk with other international athletes, keeping in mind that the more similar your culture is the easier the transition will be. Cultural biases can also be problematic in that a coach may assume that, for instance, all Kenyans are alike—not taking into account both regional and individual differences. Along this line, national stereotypes also can affect the recruiting process. For example, Kenya and other East African countries are known to produce distance runners, whereas Nigeria and Western Africa are known to produce sprinters. If you are a Kenyan sprinter or a Nigerian distance runner, you might experience some bias. Cultural differences can also be problematic in the recruiting process of colleges that have a religious mission. Ensure that you know what you are getting yourself into and that your values and expectations fit with those of the college. An assistant Division II tennis coach asked Dr. Benjamin how to help one of his South American players whose family member had recently died. He was not sure why it was taking this player so long to recover. Whereas in the United States, athletes keep competing, this athlete felt just the opposite. The athlete's open expression of grief, as well as the belief that competing would be disrespectful to the recently departed, was underappreciated by the coaching staff. Dr. Benjamin's suggestion to allow the athlete to grieve in his own way and even sit out a tournament or two, helped this athlete recover without feeling anger toward the coaching staff. The expression of grief and how it is managed with regard to athletics is just one example of the many issues that an international athlete might face over a four-year collegiate experience.

> **Author's comment:** According to Bale, the majority of foreign athletes do not feel exploited. Henry So, a Chinese Australian who played tennis at a Division II university, agrees. So, who is a tennis instructor in Hong Kong and enjoyed a brief stint on the professional tennis tour, stated, "to receive a scholarship of any sort is an honor and should be cherished. [Scholarship recipients] should understand [that] it is an agreement [and] that they should always give their 100 percent in both their academic studies and their field of discipline. I have seen too many people after receiving a scholarship abuse that privilege." So concluded that he experienced no prejudices and "felt welcomed with open arms."

American Athletes' Perspective

As an American athlete, you may have an international teammate and may well compete against international athletes. First, there is a perception that international athletes are recruited because they are superior, but this is false. The majority are not as good as any of the blue-chip athletes in any given sport. But, in certain international sports such as hockey, soccer, or running, many of the recruits are above average and may compete well because of age, talent, and experience or maturity. You need to consider such things as the coaching philosophy, a global perspective, competition factors, and possibly the experience of being a minority. All these factors should be considered when considering a program that extensively recruits international athletes.

Coaching Philosophy

As noted, it is important to ask the coaches why they recruit overseas. One female soccer player told Dr. Benjamin that "Our men's team recruited international athletes and they were better for it. We wish we had a couple of international players on our team!" However, ensure that the coach does focus on player development, because if their recruits can win with simple management and minimal coaching, their feeling might be, "why teach?"

Westbrook added that the coach should be helping all of his or her athletes. "In order to be successful, you have to constantly be developing your talent." If the coaching staff is only interested in winning with proven international talent, there will be no incentive to develop your athletic skill set.

Global Perspective

Part of the college experience is to meet people from places that you have never been. It might be cool to have teammates who have experienced different cultures, music, or ways of life. From a practical side, an increasing percentage of our interactions in business and economics is global, as Westbrook alluded to earlier. Training, engaging, and competing with international athletes provide these real-life experiences, which truly is the college experience at its best. On the other hand, if you view these experiences as being irrelevant and irritating, or believe that this philosophy takes opportunities away from American athletes, then being part of an international team may not be for you.

Competition Factors

Older athletes may have maturity and experience that make them frustrating to compete against or with. In some sports, age is a partial determinant in performance, as strength, endurance, and skills improve into the late 20s and early 30s. Therefore, it is quite an awing experience to know that this new 25-year-old freshman was on his or her Olympic team and has experienced international competition. When the international player is a star, it may take away from your opportunities to compete against what you would perceive to be your typical American player. On the other hand, assistant Mark Thompson sees a distinct advantage from a competitive standpoint. Thompson, who ran with and against international athletes and also has coached them, said, "A few international athletes really can improve the level of competition. This brings everyone's game up a notch. It is good for the American athletes as well as the international athletes."

Minority Perspective

For many of you, it might be a very different experience competing on a team where you are the lone American athlete or a part of a minority contingent. For some, it is a very lonely experience as, all of a sudden, English is not the primary language on the team or there might be multiple cliques based on similar backgrounds or cultures. This may be an eye-opening experience, but you need to be aware of how you might adapt. If you are being recruited to an athletic setting where this is the case, spend some time with both your international and American teammates. Do not allow yourself to be only entertained by one group or the other, as you want to assess the way that the different groups get along. Ideally, you want to see a mix of players spending time both on and off the playing field. During a visit or when talking with current athletes, inquire how the coaches treat them and confirm that rules are consistently enforced for all players. Also, as the United States has been and continues to be a land of opportunity, there is a good chance that some of your coaching staff may also be international. Ensure that communication styles and coaching philosophies are compatible.

Summary

- International athletes have the opportunity to attend college as well as have access to possibly great facilities.

- International athletes often know very little about their college choice and, unless they are adaptable, may have a difficult transition.
- American athletes benefit from the additional competition as well as global experience.
- American athletes should ensure opportunities to compete while looking for programs where the coaches coach.

8

Other Issues

This chapter focuses on categories of athletes who have legitimate concerns about how their uniqueness will fit with a college program. These groups include athletes who have disabilities, are gay or lesbian, or were homeschooled. At most schools, differences such as these, even if not accepted by the college majority, do not prevent you from getting an education. In addition, at most large campuses, you typically have a large number of individuals who share these qualities that you can connect with.

Athletics, however, is more limiting, as compatibility with coaches and teammates may be another issue. Athletes who are disabled have different challenges that are based on the type of disability. Athletes who are gay or lesbian often suffer in silence as they struggle for acceptance. Finally, it is a challenge for students who were homeschooled to display their athletic talents. The sporting world tends to be a conservative one in that the focus is on performance and winning. Therefore, often, situations or individuals who require more work in terms of fitting in with a team are often overlooked, as the opportunity to teach about differences is undervalued. You have seen this theme throughout the book. In addition, athletes and coaches, when compared to the student or faculty population, tend to garner a lot of attention and campus fame. Therefore, there is less of a tendency for the athletic world to "want to rock the boat," as acceptance and tolerance have little to do with winning. We discuss the unique challenges that face this group of prospective athletes.

Disabilities

The Americans with Disabilities Act, which was passed in 1990 to prevent discrimination against people with disabilities, also ensures educational access at the college level. A disability is defined as "a physical or mental impairment that interferes with one or more major areas of one's life." It should not prevent you from being academically successful. This may be true on the academic side, but you should not assume this is so on the athletic side. If you are talented enough to compete at the college level in spite of your disability, which many athletes have done at all divisions, seek out a coach and teammates who are accepting of your disability. Without attempting to be all-encompassing, let's look at sensory, physical, and learning disabilities.

Sensory Disabilities

Sensory disabilities include people who experience some level of hearing, sight, or speech impediment. It may be unreasonable to expect that the coach knows sign language, but access to a sign language interpreter might be a reasonable request, especially at larger programs. A coach's willingness to "see you as a player and not a disabled athlete" is critical, according to Chad Robinson, a former NAIA baseball player. Robinson, who has had a hearing disability since he was 18 months old, defied the odds and played football, wrestling, and baseball in high school. Discrimination was noticeable, however, and Robinson believes his hearing disability prevented him from getting other offers. Robinson added that "My college coach was aware of my disability. I turned down a Division I offer as I could tell that not every coach was going to treat me as a regular player. That was the key—a coach who treated me like everyone else but did inquire how to meet my needs. The staff asked me what I needed and as I could follow hand signals and lip read, I was in pretty good shape." Chad's father, Chuck Robinson added, "This type of coach is very unique and special." In terms of special services, Robinson did utilize "special note takers for classes" and recommends ensuring these services are available. Talk with athletic and academic counselors as well as the faculty and staff in your intended major. Every university also has an office for disability services. If you have concerns regarding how the program or school might or might not accommodate your needs, stop by this office as part of a recruiting visit.

From a coach's perspective, "patience" is the one standout quality, touts Jason Gordon, a former volunteer club coach who worked with a deaf high school high jumper. Gordon added,

"The coaching process took extra time to get across what I wanted her to try to do. Being able to demonstrate is also an asset," as a picture or the use of visual cues may truly be worth a thousand words.

Physical Disabilities

Athletes with physical disabilities have competed successfully at every college division. Just ask current Paralympics world-class sprinter Roderick Green. Green, who had a birth defect that resulted in the amputation of his right foot when he was two years old, plays sports with a prosthetic foot. With the improvement of technology, along with the same hard work as any other athlete, Green first earned a junior varsity basketball scholarship to a Midwestern NAIA school. Green moved up to varsity, and after graduation, he became exposed to Paralympics track and field and has not looked back since. Green believes that actions speak louder than words in terms of naysayers. He advises athletes to expect coaches to not recruit you because of a physical disability but not to be deterred in your efforts. Green said, "I was initially told that I should play at lower levels, but this just lit the fire within me to prove them [coaches] wrong." In terms of recruiting, Green believes that you should look for a program where you are allowed to "take care of yourself and take care of your technology." He points out that although you should not expect to be treated differently than other athletes; you may know when your joint or prosthetic has "had enough." This is a big part of injury prevention, and working with a coach who cares enough to be interested in being educated about any special needs is important. Green's comment about the care of your prosthesis is important. Wear and tear or damage can occur. You want to be able to have a quick turnaround if necessary so factor in the closest location to a competent sports prosthetics expert.

In terms of teammates, Green believes that if you are accepting of your disability, others will be too. "I can pick up any discomfort by a stare, a look, or a verbal comment like, 'How did you do that?' I joke that if I wasn't an amputee, I would have made it to the NBA. Be confident but know that you are different. Let your teammates come to you by letting your game play out loud. Don't get mad, as getting angry will put pressure on you and you won't play as well."

Learning Disabilities

Learning disabilities include such conditions as adult attention deficit disorder, and people with this condition might require more time to finish an exam, for example. Other learning disorders involving dyslexia, math, or reading, often require special classes, which need to be assessed in terms of how they are accommodated at the college level. Tutoring and a counseling center equipped to help students with learning disabilities are critical to the success of the athlete.

Another issue, according to *ESPN Magazine,* is that a number of high-profile programs are using the learning disabled (LD) tag in an attempt to lower the academic criteria to keep their athletes eligible. If you truly have a learning disability going into a college, ensure there are services to help you succeed academically. If not, do not let yourself be labeled for the benefit of the athletic department. Request testing and confirm this diagnosis with experts outside of the athletic department.

NS, a parent to a prospective college player, believes that the coaches' involvement regarding her son's diagnosis of attention deficit hyperactivity disorder (ADHD) was necessary to ensure his college academic and athletic success. She said, "It is hard to be forthcoming to the coaching staff as you don't want your child to be labeled. However, sometimes, you have no choice when your child is tagged as not following directions, working hard, committed, or motivated—all possibly because of his ADHD." NS recommends that finding a coach who can "build confidence, provide the ample structure, challenge in a positive manner, and prides themselves on finding a diamond in the rough" is necessary when it comes to a good fit for a child with learning disabilities.

Sexual Orientation

According to estimates, anywhere from 1 to 10 percent of the U.S. population is gay or lesbian. But according to Helen Carroll, a former athletic director and national champion women's basketball coach and current director of athletics issues at the National Center for Lesbian Rights, "the percentage of gay or lesbian athletes is unknown because this is considered such a taboo subject." Often, college is the first time that individuals explore their identity and realize that they are gay or lesbian.

The loneliness and internal suffering can be great, not only related to the locker room, where coaches and teams privately and publicly bash gay or lesbian athletes, but also regarding the considerations of disclosure to the coaching staff and teammates. For the high school player who is already out, it is much easier to bring this up to the coach during the recruiting process versus the athlete who has not acknowledged his or her orientation yet.

Gay stereotypes also can be used to bash opposing coaches during recruiting, as one coach may make subtle or not-so-subtle allegations regarding the sexual orientation of an opposing coach or team. These stereotypes are especially used in women's sports, particularly softball and basketball. Other common stereotypes are that all women athletes are lesbians, that there are no gay male athletes, and that gay and lesbian athletes will be looking at other athletes in the showers. Carroll laments that even though there is no mechanism to ensure that you will choose the right school, she does recommend that you ensure that the athletic department respects your rights, that there is diversity education and training, and that you find support on campus.

Regarding the athletic department, Carroll suggests two criteria be in place. The first has to do with the athletic department policy and the second involves continuing education for coaches and players regarding diversity training. Carroll said, "Look for the specific words of *discrimination based on sexual orientation is prohibited*" within the athletic department bylaws" of any potential university. Second, "Ensure that diversity training is included as an educational component for staff, coaches, and athletes." Confirm that the diversity training includes topics regarding gay and lesbian issues. Finally, ongoing support and advice from those who are connected to this subject is important. This can be sought through organizations such as the Women's Sports Foundation. In addition, campuses often have a Lesbian/Gay/Bisexual/Transgender (LGBT) center, which can provide some campus support. Unfortunately, because of the high-profile nature of collegiate athletes, a lack of anonymity prevents many athletes from using this resource. An alternate suggestion is to seek out faculty, counselors, or other staff who may have designated stickers by their phones or windows that are lesbian or gay friendly. These individuals can provide a safe space.

On an optimistic note, more coaches and programs are interested in ensuring that their locker rooms are safe places. It may be unrealistic to find a team where everyone is comfortable with your orientation; however, it is especially important that you seek a place both academically and athletically that is accepting of your orientation.

How do heterosexual athletes feel about this issue? There is the full spectrum ranging from bigotry, complete neutrality, and acceptance. In the end, however, performance talks. As a non-lesbian player anonymously states, "I don't know any softball players who have not been asked if they are lesbian [because of the stereotype that softball players are lesbian]. As a straight athlete, if the known lesbian player was good, her sexual orientation did not matter."

The Homeschooled Athlete

As one of over two million homeschooled students, you need to be proactive in seeking out opportunities to showcase your athletic and academic talents. As we note in Section I, Chapter 4, "Getting Seen," in addition to initiating contact with schools and sending video of your recent performances, you need be focused on creating chances to compete against known public school talent. This may involve open meets and regional and national homeschool tournaments. Tim Flatt, the National Christian Homeschool Basketball Tournament coordinator and club coach of a homeschooled team, says that, especially in a major sport like basketball, you need "to get exposure, and this means playing against college-bound competition" or having some "unique physical characteristic [that] makes you stand out." If you are a 6'7" female volleyball player, you may be given the benefit of the doubt simply because your height is in demand.

Some other topics to consider include revenue versus non-revenue sports, opportunities to compete with a high school team, and convincing the coach that you are academically and socially prepared for the collegiate challenges ahead.

Flatt argues that many non-revenue sports have the "advantage of open meets or tournaments. You can compare times anywhere," which allows for direct comparison to public or private school athletes. Homeschooled athletes who compete in revenue sports and especially team sports require more work to get seen. Some options include possibly competing for your local high school team, as some state and district rules allow homeschooled athletes this opportunity. Other options include specific homeschool and club-level tournaments that give you the opportunity to showcase your talent against the best players in the state, region, and country. As Flatt emphasizes, use any venue that gives recruiters a chance to see how you fare against those who are known blue chippers.

Also, you should be aware that while you may not question your academic and social abilities to get along in a college atmosphere, a college coach might. If you have been homeschooled for religious reasons, attempting to attend a college of a similar denomination may not be problematic for either you or the smaller private college that desires your entrance. However, if you are considering a larger public institution where you will be exposed to all types of people, there may be a perception that you might not be able to cut it academically and socially. Take the PSAT, SAT, and/or ACT to leave no doubt that you are on par academically with your competitors. Also, ensure that your academic program is accredited. LC, who has been instrumental in helping a homeschooled student gain acceptance to a very prestigious Northwestern university, said, "It is helpful to use an accredited school program as well as document the curriculum and classes used. Having the student attend a college class or two helps solidify the notion that the homeschooled student can compete academically."

Coaches may question how you will fit socially in a non-controlled environment. This is a fair question and one that you should be comfortable addressing directly during the recruiting process.

Secular Homeschooled Athletes

The stereotype of homeschooled students is that they are religiously conservative. This is a false assumption, as Flatt explains that over the years, the common ground of wanting a home-devised educational experience has overshadowed the differences in the reasons why. This evolution, according to Flatt, has essentially allowed all homeschooled students the opportunity to compete side by side regardless of their religious, political, or philosophical beliefs.

Summary

- Athletes with physical, sensory, or learning disabilities need to ensure that both the athletic and academic aspects of the university are motivated and equipped to help you succeed.
- Gay or lesbian athletes need to look for specific non-discrimination clauses in the athletic bylaws.
- Homeschooled athletes should be willing to go the extra step to prove that they can compete academically and athletically, and cope socially.
- Ensure that any unique individual expressions are respected and tolerated by the program.

9

Medical Concerns

Because unsafe practices can result in chronic injury or, in rare cases, death, an assessment of a program's medical services needs to be part of your overall evaluation of a college's program. First, we will examine the typical common injury patterns for each major sport. Next, we will cover life-threatening medical conditions, other sport-related medical conditions, and performance-enhancing drugs. Finally, with this information in hand, consider your own athletic medical history. For example, have you ever suffered from heatstroke, had a concussion, or a specific joint-related injury? For most athletes who train and compete at an intense level, certain injuries are not uncommon. While reflecting on your own injury history, along with your knowledge of injury patterns within your sport, and other considerations, we will summarize some simple rules when assessing a program in terms of medical safety.

Common Injury Patterns for Different Sports

Injuries are a part of sports. However, each sport has some common injury patterns usually related to where the sport puts stress on the body. In conjunction with your own personal medical history, you can ensure that your university of choice takes your injury history seriously and focuses on prevention. In no way are we attempting to be a comprehensive medical text and also, like you, we are aware that any injury can occur in any sport.

Life-threatening Medical Concerns

The top four conditions that result in the majority of medically related sports deaths are asthma, cardiovascular or heart problems, heat stroke, and sickle cell disease. If you have a history of any of these conditions, it is important to discuss them with the coaching staff and the associated medical personnel before you begin playing. Parents, do not minimize these risks. To

Table 9.1 Common Sports Injuries

The following is a cursory list of typical sites of injury for each sport.
Ankle—basketball, fencing, skiing, soccer, volleyball
Athletic triad—cheerleading, gymnastics, racquet sports, track and field, wrestling
Back—golf, gymnastics, racquet sports, rowing, swimming and diving
concussions—football, soccer
Head and neck—equestrian, field hockey, swimming and diving
Knee (including ACL)—basketball, racquet sports, skiing, soccer, volleyball
Multiple joint (individual or multiple)—football, hockey (field and ice), track and field, wrestling
Shoulder—baseball, tennis, softball, swimming and diving, water polo
Wrist—golf, gymnastics, racquet sports, rowing, volleyball
Upper extremity—equestrian, cheerleading, golf, gymnastics, racquet sports, rowing

keep this simple and relevant, we will define each condition, explain its sports connection, and briefly discuss screening and or prevention that should occur.

Asthma

Asthma is the inflammation or narrowing of your lung vessels, which can lead to a number of symptoms, including chest tightness, wheezing, or shortness of breath. This condition afflicts about 20 percent of the population. In addition, exercise-induced asthma affects between 12 to 15 percent of athletes. An acute attack leads to sudden death more commonly than heart disease and is the leading killer of young athletes. Exercising at over 80 percent of your maximal effort, cold air, or environmental allergens can precipitate attacks. One way to monitor when you are exercising moderately hard is to recognize when you cannot carry on a conversation because your breathing is labored—this is another estimate of 80 percent of your maximal effort. Outdoor sports and those requiring continuous exertion place you at higher risk.

One of the most commonly misunderstood phenomena is that you do not have to have asthma in order to have exercise-induced asthma. Screening for this condition involves some minimal non-invasive testing. The easiest way, rather than getting elaborate pulmonary function testing done, is simply note if you have wheezing, shortness of breath, or increased sputum production that only occurs at moderate to maximal exercise efforts. This is suggestive of exercise-induced asthma. If you have these symptoms, consult your physician.

Athletic trainers should be made aware of a diagnosis of asthma in either form; access to medication and treatment from a physician is key to managing these conditions. Although preventing exposure to asthma triggers can be difficult, coaches should never force an athlete to "push through an attack."

Cardiovascular or Heart-related Conditions

The four most common heart conditions involve abnormal coronary arteries, abnormal heart wall thickening, arrhythmias, and infections of the heart. Each of these conditions has a unique set of participation limitations and requirements that are beyond the scope of this book. If you have a known history of any of the above, ensure that the program has the capacity to medically monitor and assess you. In addition, coaches should be willing to respect your medical requirements, as the consequences of ignoring them can be dire. Medical supervision, preferably with a cardiologist, is paramount. According to Phil Adamson, a cardiologist who is an internationally known expert on sudden death and is a cardiology consultant for a large public Division I Midwestern university, says, "Programs should follow the American Heart Association recommendations, which focus on yearly screening all athletes. Most programs are not going to have a cardiologist as part of the medical team, but there should be a low threshold for further evaluation with a cardiologist for any athlete who registers a positive (for example, an abnormal EKG or chest pain while exercising) or has new-onset heart problems." Adamson also believes that athletes are best served "if there is buy-in from the coaching staff and trainers that medical problems are taken seriously. The old-time thinking that kids who complain about physical symptoms are babies puts the athlete at risk." Also, like other sports medicine experts, Adamson strongly urges that "physicians should have the last authority regarding medical clearance."

Exertional Heat Illness

Heat exhaustion and heat stroke refer to a set of symptoms that are the result of excessive heat combined with the body's inability to cool itself. Many athletes, typically in strenuous outdoor sports, are affected each year. One study concluded that there were one to two college football deaths per year. Important risk factors include increased ambient temperature and humidity along with reduced fitness levels and poor weather acclimatization. Research also notes that body weight over 250 pounds—a weight not uncommon for a football lineman—puts you at additional risk. In fact, according to Scott Anderson, the head athletic trainer at a Division I program, 90 percent of these cases are football related, as "the larger the mass, the greater the surface area, which leads to the inability to dissipate heat." Anderson adds that 50 percent of the cases in football occur within the first day and 75 percent within the first two days," especially when teams practice twice a day. If you live and train in moderate to cooler environments and plan to attend a warm weather school, allow yourself a few weeks of transition with your workouts to prepare for exercising in a warmer climate. In addition, collegiate training regimens are much more rigorous than high school training. Ask for a summer training plan to prepare you.

A quality program should also provide and insist on proper hydration and special care with training in excessive heat, especially in the critical period of the first three to five days as well as within the first 10 to 14 days. These gradual changes in exercise include both intensity and duration of training. There should be an icebath close at hand to relieve players in danger of heat exhaustion or heat stroke. Also, realize that if you have had a problem with excessive exhaustion to the point of losing consciousness, or if you know you are sensitive to the heat, discuss this during your recruiting visit. Other preventive factors include wearing light-colored clothing and minimal equipment, and abstaining from energy drinks or other caffeinated drinks. Beware of any coach who has a "tough it out or you are wimps" mentality.

Sickle Cell Trait

"Sickle cell trait" refers to a gene inheritance pattern in which the shape of the oxygen-carrying red blood cells become abnormally bent, or sickle-shaped, in situations of sustained intense exercise. This trait is present in about 8 percent of African Americans and is more common in those of Mediterranean ancestry, although this blood disorder can afflict individuals from any background, according to sports hematology/oncology expert, Dr. Randy Eichner. Eichner explains that individuals with sickle cell trait commonly have no symptoms in the resting state, during short bursts of exercise such as wind sprints, or during prolonged slow exercises. However, when intense sustained bouts of over two to three minutes occur, a lack of oxygen results in the deformity, or sickling, of the hemoglobin molecules in the red blood cells. The result of this sickling is often blood clotting, which leads to about 5 percent of all athletically related sudden deaths.

National sports medicine and trainer consensus is that athletes with this condition can participate in all sports, but there needs to be awareness within the program so that coaches and trainers can act on this problem if symptoms arise. Eichner says, "As cheap as the test is, all athletes should get this test." As a precaution, check your medical records, as this test is often performed as part of a childhood medical record. If not done, get this simple test independently and provide the results to the program, especially if you have the trait. Do not play at a program that does not take this condition seriously.

Non-Lethal Conditions

Several conditions that are not life threatening can nonetheless have a negative impact on your athletic career. If you are aware of these during the recruiting process, you can assess how seriously the coaching staff and program takes these conditions, how they follow known prevention guidelines, and if they are equipped to deal with these situations in a medically appropriate fashion.

Chronic Overuse Injuries

Chronic overuse injuries include muscular, joint, tendon, and ligament injuries and can range from mild bruises and strains to fractures and tears. Data from a 16-year study of all NCAA athletic programs suggest that pre-season is the period of highest injury risk compared to in-season and post-season. Division I had a higher rate of injury compared to Division III. In general, the three most common reasons are a lack of preparation for pre-season workouts, poor injury prevention training prior to an increase in duration, frequency, and intensity of training, and poor progression from easier to harder conditioning exercises.

The majority of injuries are contact-related and affect the lower extremities, mainly the ankle and knee. Women in basketball, soccer, and volleyball had the highest rates of anterior cruciate ligament (ACL) tears. Injuries can also be part of a repetitive overuse pattern, common in running as well as throwing sports. Daniel Kulund, M.D., a former professor and sports orthopedist says, "A good sports medicine program focuses on education, including trainers, coaches, and athletes. With education comes prevention."

Concussions

Concussions, or mild traumatic brain injuries, are on the rise in athletes. There is no specific data just for college sports, but estimates suggest over 300,000 concussions per year related to all sports, with over 60 percent linked to football. These increased numbers are reflective of a much lower threshold for the definition of a concussion or a mild traumatic brain injury. The research on concussions now indicates that having your "bell rung" for a few seconds can do harm, as the intensity of your experience may not fully reflect the level of damage within your brain. The only way to determine this is through a neurological exam and using enhanced imaging processes such as computer tomography (CT), magnetic resonance imaging (MRI), or functional MRI (fMRI), which in most situations will not be available at a practice or game site. Therefore, regaining consciousness does not mean that you are medically ready to go back into a game. Keep in mind that with head injuries can also come cervical or neck injuries that need to be evaluated.

> **Author's comment:** The greater number of concussions that you have experienced, the greater your risk in the future for chronic neurological changes, possibly in your memory, concentration, mood, and even personality.

You should expect the program to have a specific policy regarding concussions and medical management. A complete assessment should be performed, often by a neurologist, and the medical staff should be the *only* ones to clear you to go back to practice or competition. Recommendations lean toward being more conservative. For example, 92 percent of repeat concussions occur within 10 days and 75 percent occur within the first week. Therefore, the American Academy of Neurology recommends a seven-day waiting period to prevent recurrent trauma and complete assessment. This conservative position may not be fully appreciated by the coaching staff. Symptoms of concern, aside from loss of consciousness, include being dazed (even momentarily), or taking a hard hit to your head. Changes in personality, memory, attention, or focus may also reflect a need for further testing. Once you start practicing again, you should progress slowly from general non-contact exercises back to your normal level of participation. The coaching staff should not make or pressure decisions regarding the safety of the athlete. Prevention focuses on proper use of quality equipment and proper technique. Some data also support headgear for soccer players who head the ball, but research in this area is inconclusive.

Methycillin-Resistant *Staphylococcus aureus* (MRSA) Infections

Methycillin-resistant *Staphylococcus aureus* (MRSA) infections are bacterial infections that become difficult to treat because they are resistant to antibiotics. In most situations, they do not pose a danger unless the bacteria get into the bloodstream (bacteremia). You are at a higher risk when you have lacerations or cuts and when using unclean, shared equipment and locker rooms and training rooms. A recent study in a prominent medical journal named football players (especially linemen and linebackers), wrestlers (because of the skin-to-skin contact), and fencers (because of the shared equipment), as carrying higher-than-average risk for contacting this possibly life-threatening disease. MRSA occurs when the normally benign bacteria present on your skin gets access to your bloodstream and causes an infection. According to Dr. James Kirk, an infectious disease specialist, what appears to be a simple cut or boil enlarges quickly and becomes painful. Other symptoms suggestive of a systemic illness include increased heart rate, fever, and shortness of breath. At this point, it is life threatening, often requiring hospitalization and intravenous antibiotics. Athletes at all levels have died from what starts out as a minor cut. Do not underestimate the importance of prevention.

In terms of prevention, remember this three-step process. First, be aware of the possibility of infection with seemingly minor wounds. Then, use the simple first-aid technique of cleaning any wound quickly and well. Finally, cover the wounds to prevent reinfection.

From a recruiting perspective, Kirk suggests that "you seek out a program that maintains clean facilities and equipment and takes even small cuts and bruises seriously." There appears to be a correlation with increased risk of MRSA linked to getting the typical flu—therefore, immunizing athletes every year in the late fall may be helpful.

Mental Health Conditions

It is important to be aware that at any given time about 10 percent of any college population has a mental health condition This encompasses mood, anxiety, eating, or attention deficit disorders, as well as substance abuse disorders. There is a perception that athletes are invulnerable to mental health disorders and that, if they have one, they are weak. This is a dangerous notion, as suicide is among the leading causes of death among college students. Here is a three-step process to help you with this topic while on the recruiting trail.

1. Do you have a diagnosed mental health condition, including substance abuse? Does this require ongoing treatment or was this a one-time issue that has since been resolved? For example, bipolar disorder may require lifelong treatment, whereas difficulty coping with a family situation such as a divorce may only require limited treatment. If unsure, ask your current mental health treatment professional what ongoing treatment you may need at college. Help him or her understand the demands of college athletics, as many may not understand the realities of college competition.

2. If you have an ongoing problem, how do you perceive that the coach and program will respond regarding this situation? Eric Morse, M.D., a sports psychiatrist who works with professional, college, and younger athletes and is current president of the International Society for Sport Psychiatry (ISSP), says that recruits "don't share this information out of fear that it will negatively impact their ability to get a scholarship." However, these issues need to be a part of the "goodness of fit" equation and, according to Morse, "Asking what the program has done in the past with athletes with a mental health history" will allow you to judge the coach's response. If the coach demonstrates a lack of interest, has no answer, or states that "they haven't had any" athletes with mental health conditions, you don't want to be there. College is stressful enough and the addition of athletics may result in the recurrence of symptoms at some time during your career.

3. What sorts of services are available to help me if I need it? Many programs are associated with sports or team psychologists, whose focus is performance-related or, according to Morse, "Punt care to the university general counseling center," which is often ill equipped to handle the requirements of a student-athlete. However, according to Bruce Lochner, Ph.D., most college student counseling centers are "well equipped to help you with normal problems that do not reflect serious mental illness." Ensure that they will have the background to deal with your particular set of issues. Otherwise, access to a specialist in the local community is important. In addition, if medications are warranted, it is important to have access to physicians who are experts at prescribing medications who also understand athletic performance.

Substance Abuse

Athletes who are committed to maximizing the strength and size of their bodies may be tempted to use a number of substances that are illicit or harmful. These include alcohol, marijuana, cocaine, and a number of other drugs. Dependence on narcotics or painkillers, which may initially have been legitimately prescribed for an acute injury, can occur. Addiction or the compulsive need to use a substance even despite damage to health or performance is very powerful.

Alcohol

About 60 percent of NCAA athletes drink alcohol. There is no data reflecting the exact percentages of those who experience problematic drinking or regular drinking. You will more than likely spend more time with your teammates in and out of practice, and your beliefs regarding alcohol will affect your socialization practices. Therefore, screening the program to assess if there is a relatively good match between your beliefs and the program's is important. If you do choose to drink and you personally see nothing wrong with it, it is equally important to find a program and college that does not restrict consumption. Some states also have laws regarding drinking ages. A lot of drinking occurs regardless of state laws on a lot of college campuses, but realize that as an athlete, whether you want it or not, you will be held to a higher standard. For example, a typical college student who has a DUI will attract little attention. An athlete with a DUI, however, especially if he or she plays a higher-profile sport, will quickly become fodder for the news.

Illicit Substances

Although rates of illicit substance use for both college students and college athletes is much lower than that of alcohol, it may be higher than you might imagine. For example, about 20 percent of college athletes use marijuana and 2 to 3 percent use cocaine. All programs ban these substances, and some schools and coaches have a zero-tolerance policy, which means you may get kicked off the program and possibly out of school if you are caught.

That said, many coaches overlook use of some substances, especially marijuana. One former junior college basketball player confided in Dr. Benjamin that he did not know this before joining the team but that the "majority of players on the team smoked marijuana." The coaching staff either did not know or turned a blind eye to this problem. Coaches have very different policies and those within college sports know that drug and alcohol use goes on at higher rates than they are willing to admit. Ask both the coaching staff and the athletes on the team about policies regarding alcohol and illicit substance abuse.

Morse's experience suggests that administrators and trainers often know the programs at any given college where alcohol or illicit substance use is problematic. He adds, "Often, it is a team culture issue. Players recruit other players and if they sense that you as a recruit are not going to use with them, they will often let you know that you shouldn't come here."

Regarding treatment, asking for help regarding alcohol issues is often seen as acceptable. However, this is not always true regarding illicit substances. This is because they are indeed illegal. Also, there is a stigma regarding addiction to illicit substances, especially drugs like cocaine or heroin. Treatment options range from the local counseling center to intensive inpatient treatment programs followed by therapy or support groups focused on coping skills and prevention. Depending on the situation, medications might be necessary as part of a comprehensive treatment program. Most coaches will not be pleased that you might need to miss a significant portion of your season, and this unspoken understanding that "*nothing interferes with the season*" is also what prevents athletes from bringing up these issues as they arise.

Conversation with the Coaches About Substance Abuse

There is no doubt that there is a stigma associated with mental illness and addiction. Therefore, the decision as to whether to divulge these conditions may be a difficult one. There is no right or wrong answer to this question, as being honest may result in coaches viewing or treating you in a different way, or possibly not recruiting you.

If you have dealt with this issue and there are no pertinent or current treatment issues, leave it out of the picture. If, however, this is an ongoing issue and you need continued follow up, an honest discussion about the problem, what you have done to address it, and how you see your future may be beneficial. Some coaches may even respect your honesty, integrity, and maturity. A way to approach this might be along these lines:

> "Coach, I want to bring up a difficult topic for me to discuss. About a year ago [time frame for problem], I had some problems and used alcohol [or other substance] to cope with it. I got into some trouble and since [give approximate date], I have been receiving treatment consisting of [current treatment plan]. I have not used any [explain, or if alcohol, define use] and I have every intention of being the best student-athlete that I can. I also have these plans in place if I feel that I am slipping [discuss your prevention plan, consisting of support system, ongoing mental health or substance abuse treatment, etc.]."

As with mental health treatment, you can choose to hide struggles with addiction, but it can be difficult to get the treatment you need without a supportive coaching staff. Also, Morse believes that despite NCAA requirements that programs have specific substance abuse policies, most don't. Therefore, if you relapse, programs can either "kick you off the team or get you in treatment. You want to attend a school which offers treatment." Morse adds one other line of subtle questioning. He said, "Ask the coach if they have ever given a redshirt year to an athlete because of a mental health issue. If the answer is 'yes,' you know that you are dealing with a coach who is sensitive to mental health problems."

> **Author's comment:** Confidentiality is also very important. Address this directly with the coaching staff if you do not want teammates to know.

A Note to Parents

Substance abuse rates are higher among athletes than non-athletes. In addition, often, first alcohol and drug experiences occur in a pressure-filled campus setting. Discuss this potential with the coaches to ensure the level of supervision if your athlete is staying in a special athletic dorm or on road trips. Coaches' attitudes and opinions regarding alcohol and drug use vary, though they may all issue the stock line against it. It is not unknown for junior level coaches to be drunk at college parties with athletes in attendance. Not the type of role model you want! Remember Morse's comment about "team culture," as it often starts at the top.

Weight Loss

Within 33 days in 1997, three college wrestlers died due to improper rapid weight-loss techniques. This led to the NCAA Wrestling Weight Management Policy, which all member schools are required to follow. Although wrestling is used as an example, any sport—although especially gymnastics and distance running—can have an excessive emphasis on weight maintenance.

Peak fitness requires you to be at your best competitive weight *that is healthy for you*! We cannot stress this last part of the equation enough, as coaches often have a mindset about what an ideal weight is for their athletes, even though one size does not fit all. As discussed in the "Gender Issues" chapter, excessive focus on weight simply results in poorer performances and lower self-esteem in the athlete. Already discussed are patterns to watch out for. Here, the focus will be ensuring that your program of interest follows approved guidelines within the sport as well as within the sport medical profession guidelines.

First, is or has weight been a concern for you? If so, realize that you are at higher risk for this issue to recur with the coaching staff during your career. You should address it during the recruiting process so you are personally comfortable with what to expect.

Now, let's consider healthy weight-loss guidelines, which include a focus on a healthy body mass index (BMI), which factors your height and weight relative to healthy norms. Being above or below these norms can be medically hazardous. Furthermore, weight changes should occur over a period of time and should rely on healthy exercise and nutrition. Guidelines also suggest avoiding gimmick or short-term programs, as well as unapproved and often unsubstantiated herbal substances. Healthy weight maintenance that focuses on appropriate weight for your height and body type is the key to all treatment and prevention interventions. Aside from your coach, consult with your physician and a sports nutrition expert, as these professionals can sometimes help educate the coach, who may have a simplistic view on what each of his or her athletes should weigh.

Performance Enhancing Substances

Herbal products to enhance athletic performance have been used throughout history and were documented earliest in ancient Greece, Rome, and indigenous South African tribal societies. Recently, there has been an influx of products claiming to improve energy, speed, or strength. Many of these products may lead to improved short-term performance, but the medical, physical, and emotional consequences—including death—are not worth the risks to you. Keep in mind that supplements may be encouraged or used by the program's weight training or conditioning programs.

Often, head coaches are purposely "protected" regarding these practices but are aware that these performance enhancers are used. The "I wasn't aware of this" response isn't good enough. An enforced "no steroids" policy is what you should expect!

Many new and modified supplements are coming out on a regular basis. These usually fall into one of two areas. The first is muscle building or strength promoting. The second is better endurance or improved energy. No matter what is written on the label, all medications, synthetic products, or herbal or natural products (which are not approved by the FDA), work through neurotransmitters and body chemistry. Don't be fooled by labels touting no risk. In fact, studies suggest that often products are tainted by other contaminants, including steroids, as well as other ingredients that have resulted in death. Both Dr. Morse and Dr. Eichner agree with world-renowned strength coach Istvan Javorek (interviewed in Section III), who recommends staying away from performance-enhancing products, although the pressure to use them might be great.

Muscle-Promoting and Strength-Building Drugs

Multiple products can be taken to increase muscle mass and recovery. Three discussed include steroids and steroid-like products, creatine, and growth hormone. These are marketed under many different names. Clarify what exactly is being given to you, either by staff or teammates. We strongly suggest looking up supplement information rather than taking anything blindly or on faith.

Steroids or synthetic products with steroid-like effects have multiple systemic effects, including increased muscle mass. Side effects and risks include numerous physical changes, including breast development in males or deepening of the voice in females, as well as emotional instability, including an increased risk of suicidal thoughts. Athletes often get them from a prescribing physician, but a number of steroid-like products and mass-building products are readily available on the market. One former junior college football player who never took steroids himself describes teammates who would go across the border to Mexico to get steroids over the counter. He said, "It was readily available, teammates knew about it, and it was never discussed with the coaching staff."

Creatine is a natural product that creates short bursts of energy. Taken at high doses, there is some evidence that it might help with events that are of a short duration. Risks, however, include weight gain, dehydration, cramping, overload to your kidneys, and, rarely, kidney failure.

Growth hormone is another natural product that has been synthetically produced with the intent of improving strength and muscle mass by increasing protein synthesis. Side effects and risks include facial changes, diabetes, arthritis, and muscle abnormalities.

Energy-Enhancing Products

Two commonly used energy-boosting products are ephedra and caffeine. Ephedra is also used to help with weight loss but has multiple negative side effects, including increased risk for stroke and heart-related incidents, including heart attacks and abnormal heart arrhythmias. One study suggests that male athletes use ephedra more for improved athletic performance, whereas female athletes use ephedra for its weight-loss properties. In 2004, the Food and Drug Administration (FDA) banned the use of ephedra.

Caffeine is present in sodas, chocolate, various teas, and coffee; at higher doses, caffeine is reported to alleviate fatigue, especially in endurance events. Because caffeine is a central nervous system stimulant, increased heart rate, anxiety, tremor, insomnia, and stomach upsets are common side effects. It is estimated that a minimum of six cups of coffee, tea, or cola would be necessary to produce a questionable benefit. In addition, the use of excessive caffeine or ephedra can result in a risk of cardiovascular arrhythmias, which can be life threatening. In addition to being aware of the side effects, remember that there is no FDA oversight on these products, which can result in tainting with other substances, including steroids, or other toxins that can kill you.

Author comment: Don't risk your health. Stay away from programs where there may be direct or indirect pressure from coaches, players, or staff to use steroids or other banned or illicit performance-enhancing substances.

Putting It Together: Assessing a Program's Medical Services, Facilities, and Attitudes

You now have a wealth of medical information to work with as you narrow down your lists. Many athletes have suffered chronic or career-ending injuries that dampened their enjoyment regarding their athletic choice. If you are not physically or mentally healthy, it is difficult to put your best game forward. So, consider your personal history of injury, compare that with those typical of your sport, and see how this matches up with your prospective colleges.

Next, talk with the trainer about access to medical staff. Ask about the referral process and access to other medical specialists, including mental health professionals. You should also ask who makes decisions about medically clearing an athlete. This should be done by the medical staff and not the coaching staff. Very simply, this includes issues such as clearance for practicing and competing. It is easy for an athlete to feel pressure to continue training while injured.

It is important that medical staff personnel are comfortable treating athletes. They should have the integrity to stand up to the coaching staff if necessary and do what is medically appropriate. A competent medical staff is viewed with respect by the coaching staff and will not allow itself to be bullied or allow the coach to override medical decisions. It is also important to look for a good prevention program that begins with a yearly checkup to ensure that you are ready to participate.

Next, take a look at the injury-prevention program. No injury is completely preventable, but prevention programs do minimize this risk. Good technique and safe progression of exercises as previously discussed cannot be underestimated. Part of a good prevention program is the protection aspects.

Protection

Good protection is multifaceted. This includes making use of protective equipment as well as playing on properly maintained surfaces. The following table lists some protective equipment options. Included is equipment that is not typically used such as ear protectors in wrestling, headgear in the pole vault, and chest protectors in high-velocity ball sports such as baseball or softball, in addition to more common items like dental guards. High-quality dental guards are important to protect your teeth. Mark Duncan, D.D.S., routinely sees dental problems related to old sports injuries. He explains that "the newer custom-fitted mouth guards spread the impact of the force across the dental arch, which protects your teeth much better than many of the generic mouth pieces."

As part of the recruiting visit, look at the training equipment, as well as the practice fields and training venues. If you will spend a lot of time in the weight room, ensure that the weight room is safely designed to tolerate a high volume of athletes. Plyometrics, or jumping drills, although very effective as a training technique, also can result in lower body injuries. High-quality gymnastics mats, grass, or another soft surface should be a requirement. If you know you will be doing a lot of running,

Table 9.2 Protective Equipment

Headgear or helmets—baseball, fencing, football, hockey, lacrosse, pole vaulting, wrestling
Dental guards—baseball, basketball, football, lacrosse, softball
Body gear—fencing, football, hockey, lacrosse
Chest protector—baseball, softball

especially if you have a propensity to get injured, find out if you will be training on grass, trails, or dirt roads versus concrete.

Finally, check out the training venues and grounds. For ice hockey, basketball, volleyball, football, field hockey, golf, lacrosse, or soccer, ensure that both the indoor and outdoor facilities are to your liking. Specifically, are the fields natural grass or artificial, and in either case, are they well maintained?

Medical disclaimer: The medical information in this book is designed to help you during the recruiting process but is in no way intended to be used to diagnose or treat any of the above conditions. If you have any medical concerns, please consult your physician.

Summary

- Asthma, heart conditions, and sickle cell trait are among the leading causes of death among college athletes.
- Athletes are at higher risk for use of alcohol and illicit substances.
- Athletes do suffer from mental health disorders; ensure that treatment is available.
- Is the staff knowledgeable about injuries, prevention, and *do they care?*
- The medical staff should make medical decisions, independent of the coaching staff or importance of the upcoming competition.

SECTION III

From the Field House: Interviews with College Coaches

1

Insiders' Perspectives

When we came up with the idea for this book, we realized that some prospective student-athletes might not be interested in hearing what a handful of academicians have to say about the recruiting process. When we were teenagers, we might have felt the same way. And while the information in the first two sections of this book is vital to your understanding of the various aspects of recruiting and college life, we knew it would be equally important to include a section that offers opinions and observations of the kind of people who will be in your living rooms or sitting across a desk from you in a campus visit.

The coaches we interviewed were selected because of their reputations for maintaining the highest of ethical standards while building outstanding programs and graduating outstanding young men and women. We chose mostly recently retired coaches, not only because we didn't want to appear to advocate for any one program over another, but also because their experience in the field remains fresh and their viewpoints relevant. The opinions expressed are solely those of the coaches.

The interviews generally follow a similar format. They open with some sport-specific questions, then transition into a discussion of the recruiting process and academics that student-athletes should find applicable across all sports. You'll note some repetition in some of the responses—this is intentional. We wanted each interview to stand alone as a thorough examination of the whole recruiting process, in case a student-athlete should choose to read only one or two interviews. But we also found it interesting—and instructive—to see how this diverse panel of expert coaches shared many opinions about specific aspects of the recruiting process. When you read these interviews and discover that time and again, coaches say they watch how you act off the court or field, they observe how you treat your parents, and they want you to show a genuine interest in your academic pursuits, you should probably take those messages to heart.

2

Brooks Johnson, Track and Field Coach

Brooks Johnson is an American track and field legend. He coached his first Olympian in 1960, 110-meter silver medalist Willie May, and has coached an athlete at every summer Olympics since 1968, including the relay teams in the 2008 Beijing Games. He was Team USA's head coach for women's track and field at the 1984 Summer Games in Los Angeles, where his athletes won 17 medals. Johnson was the head coach at Stanford University (1979–1992) and Cal-Poly San Luis Obispo (1993–1996), and is currently the director of the Elite Feats Track and Field Skills and Speed Camp, Lake Buena Vista, Florida.

What can a high school track athlete do to gain a higher profile or to get more exposure to elite programs if he or she is not drawing their interest?

I think the biggest thing is to create a DVD or a tape and send it to them, or send them a letter with their athletic or academic credentials. Chances are if you run fast or jump far or throw far, you're going to hit somebody's radar screen, and that information is going to be mulled over by coaches who are really on the ball. But if you're not getting the response from the program you want to get a response from, you've got to take the initiative.

Specifically, what attributes did you look for in a prospective student-athlete? Beyond their times or other statistics, what intangibles did you consider?

The first thing I did was say, "How did this kid do in the most important meet of the year?" rather than looking at their best time or their worst time. To me, that meant that they were doing well when they were under the greatest amount of stress and/or pressure.

The only personality trait I was really concerned about other than their academics was the fact that they were very competitive. Our other indicator was if a kid ran well at the Millrose Games [an annual indoor track and field invitational], we knew they were able to do well in front of big crowds, and the same with the Penn Relays. So those are the kinds of things you look for—in meets with great expectations or great anticipation, how well did the kid do?

What are some of the negative types of recruiting practices that you have witnessed, or what practices have been used to recruit against you?

Any number of things were used, from race to my personality. But in my experience, negative recruiting [actually] helps the person against whom the negative recruiting takes place. Because if a kid can get turned off because somebody was negatively recruiting or being hyper-critical of [another] program, then that isn't the kind of character we really needed [on our team] anyway.

In what sense was race used against you? How did that arise?

They started out saying that because I was a black coach at Stanford, I could only coach sprinters. Then when we started having disproportionate success in distances and middle distances, they said, "Well, he can't coach sprinters." And then they'd say, "Well, he only got the job because he's black." And there are all sorts of subtleties in between. Plus you're dealing with a racist, sexist country in the first place, so often times it didn't even have to be articulated.

How did you confront those issues and attitudes?

I simply forged ahead as best I could. There is no doubt that my recruiting was less successful because of it.

How was your school unique, or how did the prestige of your institution affect your recruiting?

Stanford is, in a sense, different, particularly to West Coast kids, who really don't care so much about the coach—they want to go to Stanford. The same as there are a lot of kids who probably don't ask who the coach is at Harvard—they want to go to Harvard. So it's not the norm—you can't use Stanford or Harvard as a measuring stick against the norm.

How best do athletes assess the true day-to-day practices and attitudes of the coaching staff—i.e., how can they get an accurate assessment of the program, rather than the best-case scenarios that they'll see during a recruiting visit?

It's difficult to say, because you may be there on a good day, on a campus visit, when things are going well. And you may be there on an exceptional day when things are going badly. So it's really difficult to say.

But I think it's a mistake to take it to that level. For example, I think I had the best success with athletes that came to the track and field program at Stanford because they wanted to be coached by myself or somebody else on my staff—that they had a specific affinity for someone's personality or persona. People who came to Stanford because they wanted to be at Stanford *per se* did not do as well as people who came to Stanford because they wanted to be coached by somebody on our staff.

I had the same conversation with Bobby Kersee (long-time track coach at UCLA). I said, "Bobby, the people that come to UCLA because it's in Brentwood, next to Hollywood, and Bill Cosby or somebody else might be jogging around the track, you have absolutely no chance at making those kids better. Now, the kids who come to UCLA because they want to be coached by Bobby Kersee, you have about a 50 percent chance of making them better." And that's about the hit rate, if they make their decision for the right reasons, and base it upon what that coach is really all about.

Do the weekly phone calls, unofficial and official visits, and other contact with coaches help athletes to best determine their potential fit?

I think it's all pretty influential, but it's probably influential for all the wrong reasons, because everybody's basically on their best behavior, and that's not real life. And usually athletes who are going to be extremely good have extreme needs—for recognition, for love, for whatever. So a program that's going to bend over backward and spend an inordinate amount of time with that kid is more likely to get that kid, whether it's a good match or not.

Do prep athletes usually have access to athletes currently in the program, and can they use them as a resource?

Yes, but that's distorted as well. If they ask a kid who's having a good year and is eminently successful, then that's going to be a distorted view. If they ask a kid who's having a bad year or coming off an injury, they may get another perspective.

What kinds of questions do kids ask you about your program when you are recruiting them?

There would be several questions, and there would be several questions that I would ask them as well. One would be, for example, "How many miles do I have to run? Or how many meets do you go to?" Or questions about the holidays. "Do I have to stay on campus over the holidays? Are you interested in hearing from my high school coach?" You'd hear any number of questions that would give you an indication as to whether they're ready to buy in full-bore to your program.

I would ask them, "What was the most important race of the year, and how did you approach it and what were the results? Other than your parents, who is the most important person in your life? Or the most influential person in your life? Why?" I would ask them, "Do you consider yourself a racer or do you consider yourself a runner? In other words, do you do track and field because you just like competing and seeing how you stand up against other people, or do you do track and field because you enjoy the sheer physical exercise or physical activity involved in it, and that's its own greatest reward?" I want racers. I want people who like seeing how they compare against other people and take a disproportionate amount of joy out of kicking someone else's ass.

What do you consider a deal-breaker when you are meeting with a recruit? That is, what might happen in an interview or a visit that would raise too many red flags?

There was a kid who was basically the number one high school runner in the country when I was at Stanford. She had straight A's and had been using our [training] program and was running very well and training very well, and had committed to Stanford. During the recruiting process, she made it known that no matter what would happen, she was never going to go to a cold-weather school. Then in one of our conversations, she pointed out that she was going to take her five visits, and one of them was going to be to Villanova.

I advised her that—and she already knew—Villanova was in a cold-climate area. And she said, "Well, I don't see anything wrong with going there, since they're going to pay for my visit and they're recruiting me." At that point I realized that our value systems were on a different plane and it wasn't going to work out, so I just said, "Hey, this concludes the recruiting process and I wish you well."

How do you view the role of the parent in the recruiting process?

That's tough, because I think it depends on the nature of the kid. There are some 18-year-olds who understand the value of athletics and academics, and there are some kids that don't. At that point, I think the parent has to get involved. Too often, I heard parents say, "Well, it's so-and-so's decision, and I'm leaving it up to them." I think that's the dumbest thing in the world, because there's no way an 18-year-old knows the difference, for example, between Harvard and Haverford.

How do you view the relationship between athletics and academics at the college or university level?

Everybody needs to understand that there's no inherent contradiction between superior athletics and superior academics. I've had an athlete on every Olympic team since 1968, and there were a couple things they all had in common. One is that they all . . . had a need to succeed or a need to overcome a perceived or real deficiency. And the other thing is that they were all inherently intelligent. That doesn't mean they had great grades or were great students, but that they all had a basic intelligence. You cannot do what an elite athlete does and be dumb.

The idea of the dumb super-jock is a stereotypical myth. For example, you cannot drop back in a passing formation, account for 21 other people, throw the pass gauging the speed at which the person is running and gauging the proper angle, and crank your body up to do that. Do you know how much you're processing, how many billions of cells and muscles and fibers you have firing to have to do that? You can't come down the basketball court as a point guard and account for the movement of nine other people and put the ball up for an alley-oop pass—you can't be stupid and do that stuff. Now, you can be undereducated, you can be under-sophisticated, and you can be under-motivated, but you simply cannot be stupid, because you're making a judgment under a disproportionate amount of stress in a fraction of a second, and that judgment has to be an intelligent one with all those respective moving parts.

How can students be sure they're picking an institution that will respect their schedules and allow them to focus on both academics and athletics?

I'm not sure, because it's not the school that will allow them to strike that balance. A lot of that has to do with their own needs and the needs of their coaches. Training is nothing but stress management and stress adaptation, so assuming there's 100 units of stress that you want to get accomplished on any given day, if the kid has been stressed 65 percent because either their roommate is a jerk or they have mid-terms or they have a lot of homework to do, that means that off-track activities have taken 65 percent of their stress. So, at the maximum, they have 35 units left to dedicate to track activities. Whereas with other athletes, their off-track stress may be 30 or 40 percent, in which case you have 60 to 70 percent of stress that you can apply on the track.

So, it really doesn't make a whole lot of sense, the idea that athletes at Harvard or Stanford or MIT cannot train to do as well as kids elsewhere—that's basically a myth that athletes and coaches themselves buy into.

What are some injuries or health disorders specific to your sport that athletes need to be aware of?

Eating disorders—and not just among distance runners. And people have this anorexic and bulimic stuff all mixed up. There are guys who are doing the same thing that women do—they get too thin and they become anemic, so it's not gender-specific.

Also, in some instances you get overuse issues—and the thing that most people don't understand is the overuse issue as it relates to the mind and the spirit, over and above what it does to the body. The most dangerous thing that happens in track and field is the malaise of the mind and the pulled muscle of the spirit. It can be a burnout factor and sometimes it goes beyond burnout—it can be a mild or extreme form of depression.

3

Bob Frederick, Athletics Director

Bob Frederick is the former athletics director at Illinois State University and the University of Kansas. Under Frederick's leadership, Kansas ranked sixth among all universities and colleges in Academic All-Americans during the 1990s. He's also the past chair of the NCAA Division I Men's Basketball Committee and served on NCAA committees dedicated to women's athletics and sportsmanship and ethical conduct. Frederick retired in 2001 after 14 years as the athletics director at Kansas, but he continues to teach classes at the university's Sport Management program and is a senior associate with Sports Management Resources, a consulting group that helps collegiate athletic directors in the areas of integrity, equity, growth, and development.

When you were hiring coaches, what criteria did you use?

I've always told my students here that the most important thing in this business is that you shouldn't get into it unless you really care about young people, so that was really a high priority for me. Coaches who cared about their student-athletes, their academics, and their personal pursuits as well as their athletics is key. If you spend time with the coaching candidates and let them talk about what's important to them, I think it's easy to determine which of them are in it primarily because of their ego or the money they could earn. That's really a concern, because there's an opportunity to make some big dollars these days if you hit it big.

For example, when I hired [former Kansas basketball coach] Roy Williams, it was fairly obvious to me that at North Carolina [where Williams was an assistant coach] they had a real family atmosphere within their basketball program, and I could tell that's how he was going to run things at Kansas, which he did. It's just so important that head coaches have academic success and student-athlete welfare at the top of their list. To do otherwise is to cheat the system and not be a legitimate part of the academic mission at the university.

You mentioned the opportunity to hit it big financially. Especially in basketball, mid-level programs are often being used as stepping-stones to bigger jobs. That's a natural part of the evolution of the position in a sense, but how does it affect the institution if it constantly has to replace its coaches?

The basketball coaching job at Illinois State University is very much a stepping-stone position, and I remember talking with the president of the university shortly after I came onto the scene. He indicated to me that he thought we should hire coaches who we thought would be around here for a long time. I immediately disagreed with him, and I told him I didn't view that as the best thing we could be doing for the institution, the young people, and the program. I said that we needed to hire people who are good enough that someday someone else is going to hire them away from us because they're doing such a good job here. I know that at times creates some difficulties for student-athletes who are left in the wake, but I think coaches need to be totally honest with their student-athletes when they recruit them. If they ask, "Coach, are you going to be here for my full four years?" I think they need to be honest and say, "I really can't guarantee that's going to happen, but it's my plan to be here."

It's [coach turnover] tougher in the short term for the student-athletes, and it can be tougher in the long term for the institution, but that's just the system that we have, and I don't see any way around that. I told our head coaches when I hired them at Kansas, "I'm going to do everything I can to help you be successful." There are sports at Kansas—just like at any institution—where achieving a better job than the one at Kansas may be a goal. Kansas basketball may be the best job there is, but when I hired [former Kansas football coach] Glen Mason and he had the opportunity to go to the Big Ten [when he was hired by Minnesota] . . . I supported that.

The hallmark of an institution of higher learning should be integrity, so we just have to be honest with the student-athletes, with the coaches, and with each other. It's not a perfect system, but when it's all said and done, we couldn't have athletics programs without the student-athletes. We could do it without the coaches, but we couldn't do it without the student-athletes.

How do you best strike the balance between academic integrity and winning when, especially at the Division I level, success is most often defined by wins and losses?

It's a difficult issue for college athletics and it's getting tougher all the time. Some people say it starts with the chancellor, who has to make academics a priority in the athletic programs, but even if the president or chancellor says it has to be a priority, and even if the athletics director says it has to be a priority, it's not going to be a priority unless the head coaches say it's a priority. If the head coach talks about the importance of going to class, achieving in class, being a good citizen on campus, and representing the institution well, it's going to be a priority for the student-athletes. Quite frankly, there are a lot of student-athletes in the Division I level in football and basketball who are only thinking about playing professionally. The tragedy is that the odds are staggeringly against them. But the coach can make it [academics] a priority.

However, if you take a vote among the alumni, they don't care about all that stuff. [*laughs*] They just care about winning games, going to bowl games, going to the Final Four and championships. Until news of a bad academic record or a scandal embarrasses them, of course. So, it's a tough balance.

What are the difficulties of an athletics director overseeing a large department and making sure you're clearly communicating your standards to all of the coaches you employ?

There are a couple of things involved. One is accountability—you have to define people's responsibilities and hold them accountable to them. And two, equally important is that the mission of the athletics department is well defined and that you preach it on a daily basis. In my case, our mission statement at Kansas was to provide student-athletes an opportunity to achieve excellence in academics, athletics, and personal pursuits while treating them with dignity and respect. So, we talked about dignity and respect at every meeting, and talked about the importance of following the rules of the NCAA and the Big 12 Conference. You have to talk about it every time so the coaches realize that it's important to you and that you're going to hold them accountable to it.

The bigger athletics departments get—and they're getting bigger and bigger and involve more and more money—[the more] you have to hire people who you can trust will do their very best to represent you and the program the way you want them to.

Some schools have tried to separate the men's and women's athletics departments. What is the danger of that approach, and what is the advantage of keeping them together, which the vast majority of universities do?

I think the advantage of having them combined is simply to avoid duplication of some efforts that can be easily combined. The issue in my mind clearly becomes treating everybody the same in your athletics program. You just can't treat the women any differently than you treat the men, and you need to be assessing all the time whether there is any differential treatment. And if there is, you have to eliminate it. If you have people who are committed to doing it right, then it's going to happen and a combined athletics program is going to be fine. It's only when one gender—and that's usually the women—are discriminated against when it's not right.

If you had a chance to sit down with a prospective student-athlete who's just entering the recruiting process, what advice would you give him or her about the decision they're about to make?

The number one thing I would say is that they need to think about their entire life in the decision-making process, and not just the following year, and try to make a decision that's based on what's best for them in the long haul. They need to be sure that when they visit a campus, they talk as much as they can—away from the coaches—with the student-athletes about their experience at that institution. If they go to a place where they don't see many student-athletes, that's a warning that there may be some issues there. They need to talk to the people who are actually playing for that coaching staff, and they need to talk to as many people as they can in the academic departments as well. If they keep you away from academics when you're on a campus visit, then you should question what their institution's priorities are regarding your education.

The head coach obviously is going to be the person who's going to determine the environment for you as a student-athlete, so if you see just the assistant coaches and don't see the head coach at all, that should be a concern for you as well. You just need to go into it with eyes wide open, with no preconceived notions about it, and don't make an emotional decision while you're there. I know the coaches will want to get you emotionally involved and make a decision, but you need to take some time and step back from it, rather than making an emotional decision on campus.

4

Dennis Denning, Baseball Coach

Dennis Denning is the head baseball coach at the University of St. Thomas, a Division III university in St. Paul, Minnesota. In his 14 years at the school, Denning's teams have won more than 77 percent of their games, and in 2001 the Tommies won the NCAA Division III national championship. Before his stint at St. Thomas, Denning spent 17 years at St. Paul's Cretin-Derham Hall High School, where his teams won six Minnesota state championships.

Baseball is one of the few sports where a young player has some professional options coming out of high school if he's good enough. What are the most important factors a player should consider when he's trying to decide between going pro or going to college?

You've got to look a few years ahead and think about where you might be. If you're a high draft choice and they're offering you a few million dollars, of course you're going to take it. And maybe you can use that to pay for some schooling to further your education. So, the main reason to turn pro would be the money. The other factor is if you're a very poor student, because then you can't get into a good college. If someone offers you a $200,000 bonus and you're a poor student, maybe you ought to take that. But even $200,000 isn't that much money after the government takes its share, and you buy a car or a house, and pretty soon you're down in the minor leagues making $800 a month. So, you have to balance all those factors when you're making your decision.

Do you think young pitchers should be allowed to throw curve balls and throw an unlimited number of pitches in a game, or does that put too much stress on their arms?

I've always thought that youth leagues come up with too many rules banning curve balls and limiting the number of innings a kid can pitch. When I grew up, we played ball all day, every day. We'd play stickball in the street from morning until night, and we were throwing tennis balls, Wiffle balls, baseballs, and softballs—which are worse for your arm than if you were just throwing baseballs. But we turned out OK. When I played Little League, midgets, juniors, VFW, and American Legion ball, we never had players with bad arms or who needed surgeries like they do now. I have observed over the years how kids' throwing arms overall have taken a huge step backward. Too many players have poor throwing mechanics and general lack of arm strength. Why would arm strength and natural throwing mechanics go backward? Is it because they didn't throw enough?

I just don't believe in a limit for a number of reasons. If you do too much of anything, it'll be bad for you. You can throw too many fastballs just like you can throw too many curveballs. So, it takes come common sense to figure it out. Sometimes you'll have one of those kids who's the biggest kid in the class when he's in sixth grade, and by the time he's in twelfth grade he's one of the smallest. So when he's 11 or 12 years old, that might be the best he's ever going to be. What are they saving this kid for, so he can play high school or college or professional baseball? Just let the little kids enjoy life and enjoy the game. If a little kid can pitch and he's got a curve ball, let him throw it. Just use some common sense. We're getting to be a nation of rules, and I guess they're made because somebody screwed something up by using poor judgment somewhere along the way. But you can tell when a kid's got a sore arm. Anticipate that and take care of him.

Do you encourage younger kids to play multiple sports, or should they concentrate on baseball year-round? What is the advantage to that approach?

Playing multiple sports is just so much better for you. Kids who play the same sport year-round, unless you're a professional, it will hurt you. When a kid spends all year playing on traveling all-star teams that have tournaments all over the country, first of all it's very expensive, and those kids just get worn out [both physically and mentally]. I always encourage kids to play all the sports they can. You have a chance to make some new friends, and it's better for your body because you're using different muscles.

Where do you stand on the aluminum-vs.-wood bat debate?

I'm a big wood-bat guy. The reason they went to aluminum bats so many years ago was that they were durable, so you'd end up saving money. Now, aluminum bats go for about $300 apiece. Well, here at St. Thomas we bought 10 aluminum bats this year, so that's $3,000. Six of the 10 broke. They don't last forever—they dent, and they break. Meanwhile, we can get wood bats for about $35 apiece, so for $3,000, we could buy about 80 of them. Would we break 80 in a year? Not likely. When I played Legion ball, I can distinctly remember that we broke about seven or eight a year. And now you can get a composite bat for about $140 and it won't break. So for my JV team, I'll get six composites every other year and we use those.

So, wood bats can last longer and they're a lot cheaper. But about 10 years ago, the NCAA was looking at switching back to wooden bats, but the aluminum bat manufacturers sued the NCAA and they backed off. They've made a few changes—now the aluminum bats have to be tested and certified. The ball can't come off the bat any faster than 97 mph. The differential can't be more than minus-3 [ounces-to-inches – i.e., a 34-inch bat cannot be lighter than 31 ounces]. So they're trying to make it safer. But some places like New York City are saying that all Little League and high school leagues have to use wooden bats. But overall, I don't think it's going to change because the bat companies are making too much money, and they subsidize the Division I programs through sponsorships and payments to the coaches. A lot of high school teams have stopped buying bats—the kids have to buy their own. And if they come out with a new bat and tell the kids it's the greatest bat ever, their dads will buy it for them because some people will do anything if they think it will help them get an edge.

When you were a high school coach, what role did you like to play in the recruiting process?

I usually stayed in a neutral position, to help the kids clarify whether whom they were talking to was legitimate. You'll run into a lot of college coaches who aren't up front with kids. That shouldn't happen, but it does happen. Coaches will run into an ethical situation where they want these kids so they'll over-recruit. If they want a kid and really do their job scouting, and they're sure the kid can play, that's one thing. But some coaches will go out and recruit too many kids and make all kinds of promises, and they don't keep the kids' needs in mind.

There are certain programs that have a reputation of playing without any integrity—they get into beanball wars and lots of fights. There are rules against that of course, but some schools still have that reputation. Or they'll bring in 50 kids in the fall, and make them all kinds of promises, then cut most of them. If I knew about that, I'd let my kids know about it.

I'd always tell the kids, wherever you go to school, make sure you ask about their graduation rate. I think Division III would be first in that area. So, I like to recruit Division I caliber athletes who really care about their education. I saw a kid recently who was a great player and got a 27 on his ACT. I asked his coach where he was going to school in the fall, and he said he was going to a junior college. When I asked why, he said the kid could play 100 baseball games a year. But how could an educator ever advocate that a great student go to a two-year college just so he can play 100 baseball games a year? So, sometimes the kids are getting advice like that from their own coaches.

So as a high school coach, I tried to give my kids some perspective and help make sure they were making their decision based on the best information available to them.

As a college coach, what attributes do you look for in a prospective student-athlete?

It all comes down to the individual. Has he got it inside him to put all his potential together and succeed? He needs concentration, dedication, a good work ethic, and he has to be coachable. And he has to love to play baseball. But of course, that's not the most important thing. If a kid comes here and tells me his number one thing is baseball, I quickly change that, so they know where I stand. And all the parents love that.

I always tell kids to make a list when they're looking at schools to determine what their priorities are. When they leave here after a visit, I always give them my own personal list, which includes questions that help clarify what they want in a school. Which school will give you the best start on a career? Which one will give you the best education? Which one has small class sizes and lets you have contact with your professors? You have to decide whether you want a small or large campus, and at Division III, you have to see what kind of financial aid is available. If you make that list, and put your list of colleges on the other end and see how they all grade out, in the end when you're making your decision, you can refer back to that, and it'll help you make an educated decision.

What might you see from a prospective student-athlete that would raise too many red flags and cause you to cool on recruiting him?

I always watch their presence on the field. I saw one kid recently who was a great player, but I saw him get into a fight in his dugout twice in five innings. This kid was so out of whack he was fighting with his teammates. I always watch to see how kids act after things go wrong, like when a pitcher gets knocked out of a game early. If he's up on the top step of the dugout and high-fiving his teammates after each inning, even when they make a few errors, that's the kind of guy I want. If a kid's always complaining about the umpire or hanging his head and whining when he doesn't get a call, that's a bad sign.

How do you want to see the parent participate in the recruiting process?

I like to see parents demonstrate an interest in the school and in academics and other things besides baseball. Academics have to come first or else you can't even play baseball. I've had parents come in here and the father or mother would answer all the questions while the poor kid is just sitting there. That's wrong. Or some parents don't even come to campus with their kids. This is a big decision—they need to participate.

But kids don't always understand all the variables they have to consider, so that's where parents have to help them out. Parents have been through all of this, and kids should listen to them. Plus, I'll always put my foot in there and say, "Your parents are going to help you pay for this," because they have to at Division III. So, they should listen to their parents.

5

Jack Emmer, Lacrosse Coach

Jack Emmer has won more games than any other college lacrosse coach, posting 326 victories over 36 seasons before he retired in 2005. He's one of only two coaches to have guided three teams (Cortland, Washington and Lee, and The United States Military Academy at West Point) to the NCAA Tournament. He played collegiate lacrosse at Rutgers University, where he was a second-team All-America pick, and he also played football. He was inducted into the National Lacrosse Hall of Fame in 2005.

Lacrosse has been primarily an Eastern sport, but it's beginning to gain popularity throughout the United States at the prep level. How has the game's development affected the level of play at the collegiate level?

The tremendous growth of lacrosse at the youth level throughout the United States has provided more and more players at the collegiate level. However, the growth at the collegiate level has been somewhat limited for men because of the laws of the land, specifically Title IX, which has been tremendous for the women's game, but has limited the growth of the men's game. Because of that, there are more and more quality teams at the collegiate level, because there aren't any more teams, so the talent has been spread throughout many more programs. Division III lacrosse has gotten a lot better, Division II lacrosse has gotten a lot better, and there are a lot more quality teams at the Division I level.

Do lacrosse coaches ever recruit athletes from other sports who didn't play lacrosse in high school? If so, what sports seem to be the most compatible with the skills necessary to succeed at lacrosse?

Years ago, that was done routinely, but currently with more and more skilled kids coming out of high school, you don't see that done as much. It's done occasionally now, but it's just not done as much. I think basketball is probably the most compatible—the movement is similar, the foot skills are similar, and it more closely resembles the game of lacrosse from the movement standpoint more than anything else.

The "money" sports like football and basketball have been on television for years, but with the explosion of cable and satellite television, one can now find lacrosse games on channels dedicated to college sports. How has this increased exposure been beneficial to the sport?

It's really helped the growth of the game. It's created a lot more interest, which has resulted in more and more youth lacrosse. There are other types of media coverage too—there are some magazines dedicated to the game of lacrosse, which has helped. But I think the exposure that ESPN has provided year after year, as ESPN enhances its programming with more and more games, has really helped the growth of lacrosse. They aired every playoff game in Division I this year, and that's a big step forward. Part of what's held this game back has been the exposure aspect. It's not uncommon, right now, to get a call from somebody in Las Vegas, for instance, who says, "I saw Army play Duke in lacrosse on Saturday and it was a great game." That kind of thing wouldn't have happened before.

What are the health issues specific to lacrosse that young athletes need to be aware of, and what does the college lacrosse community do to address those issues?

I'd say lacrosse has its share of injuries, but nothing in comparison to the game of football, let's say. A common injury in lacrosse is a hand injury—for instance, taking a blow from a check of a stick to your hand or your thumb. Goalies have thumb injuries because if a ball shot at 90 miles per hour hits his thumb, even though it's protected by a glove, sometimes it cracks the thumb. The same with hand injuries—a hard check to the hand, even though it's got a protective glove on, can cause an injury.

But I wouldn't say knees or ankles are injured more frequently than anything else. I see football as a knee-injury game—you can't say that about lacrosse. I think with basketball you have a lot of ankle injuries because you're jumping and coming down on your foot sideways and spraining the ankle, but I don't think you can say that about lacrosse.

The artificial surfaces that we're playing on now are also much improved, so they're not as conducive to injuries as they've been in the past. At times, you might have a problem with your shoulder, if somebody makes contact with it, because although they wear thin shoulder pads and they're protected, it's not like they're the big, bulky shoulder pads you wear in football. Sometimes you get an AC injury—to your acromioclavicular joint in your shoulder—either from hitting somebody or falling down on your elbow and creating a problem with that joint. But I think most of the injuries are bruises from getting hit with the ball or hit with a check, creating hematomas.

What is the biggest impediment to student-athletes finding the institution that's the best fit for them?

I think the biggest problem in this day and age is that the process is started much earlier, so the athletes who have some prowess are being recruited so early now that they're influenced by a particular school before they're even mature enough to know what they want. They're choosing schools strictly for their athletic interests without getting a good overall picture. When a kid's in ninth grade or tenth grade and these exceptional schools are all over them, a kid is just not ready to make those decisions, but that's what it's come to.

My personal opinion is that there shouldn't be any contact with a prospect until after his junior year. They [the NCAA] do have a rule on the books that a recruiter cannot call a prospect until July 1 after his junior year, but with the electronic age that we're in and the ability to e-mail prospects, that rule is totally taken advantage of. Prospects will be e-mailed and told to call the coach, and it's OK for the prospect to call the coach, so they do that electronically, and they get unofficial visits earlier than they should be happening in my opinion. So I think the NCAA should just say there can't be any contact until after the junior year. That would really help not only the college recruiters, because it would make their jobs easier, but it would help the student-athletes who are getting overwhelmed too early.

What attributes did you look for in a prospective student-athlete?

Naturally it depends on the type of institution that you're working at, but so many schools in the world of lacrosse are pretty good academic institutions, so we always started with the academic attributes of the student-athlete—can he qualify for your institution, what do his SATs and GPA look like, his rank in his class. With a military academy, we didn't restrict it to those that had strictly an interest in the military. We went out and tried to sell our institution like anybody would sell theirs, on the attributes of our school and what it could do for the individual.

But once we limited the pool to those that could qualify, we were looking for athletes who had good speed, quickness, and agility, were very competitive, and also had the stick skills needed for the game of lacrosse. We thought we could develop those stick skills better at the higher level even after we got the kid, but we would not be able to develop his speed and quickness and agility as much.

What questions would kids ask you about your program that showed you that the student-athlete had his priorities in order?

One of the things that I wanted to hear from a kid was that he just wanted an opportunity to show what he could do. The flip side of that is that college coaches shouldn't be looking for a kid who wants a guarantee that he'll get playing time. That's kind of an unhealthy approach because you never know what the student-athlete is like until you work with him, so I don't think you ever want to get into a situation where you're making promises to a young man that you may not be able to keep, like he's going to be your starting goaltender as a freshman. I just don't think that's appropriate. So what you want to hear from the young man you're recruiting is that he's going to work hard, that he's going to compete for a spot, that he's got a good work ethic, confidence in his ability, and that he realizes that it's going to be a very competitive situation.

What do you consider a deal-breaker when you are meeting with a recruit? What might happen in an interview or a visit that would raise too many red flags?

I think you always want the student-athletes that you're recruiting to show the proper respect in a home visit. Occasionally you might come across a young man who doesn't treat his mother or father well in a home visit—there's not the respect there that there should be. Or if the kid expects to be treated in a certain way when he hasn't earned that yet. I think that's a bit of a deal-breaker. You want kids that you get the feeling from that they're going to work hard at it, they're going to be selfless, they're going to care for their teammates, and not be totally concerned with themselves, since we're dealing with team sports. I think that's a feeling you get when you visit with a kid, either at your school or in his home.

How did you approach parents in the recruiting process?

The parent is very, very important in the process—not necessarily just the mother or just the father. Each family is a little different. But on a recruiting visit we'd never hesitate to spend a little more time with the mom or with the dad in winning them over to our situation, knowing full well that they were going to influence their son in his decision. Even though we often heard, "This is little Johnny's decision," we knew there was some parental influence there, without a doubt. So you're not just recruiting the prospect, you're recruiting his parents and his family.

What are some of the negative recruiting practices that you have witnessed or that other programs used to recruit against you?

As the head coach at the United States Military Academy and before that at Washington and Lee University and Cortland State University, we were very firm in talking about the positives of our program, and we worked very hard on not going into the negatives of another program. However, in our situation we did hear that other recruiters would criticize Army, for instance, because of the five-year commitment afterward and how difficult that was going to be. Particularly with mothers, they would try to drive that home if it was a competitive recruiting situation. So we had to live with the stringent nature of the military academy and how challenging it was, and people tried to play that up with prospects that we were recruiting.

The opposite of that for us was that all the challenges you have at West Point—the busy day you're going to have, the challenging curriculum, the military requirements of your education—were all going to make you a better person. But opponents would try to use that against you, as they would in any school.

How can student-athletes get a complete and accurate assessment of the program, rather than the best-case scenarios that they'll see during a recruiting visit?

I think it's important for a recruit to spend an overnight or two at the school when he visits. You have a 48-hour restriction, but upon his visit he should stay in the dormitories, he should go to class, he should eat with the students, he should go to the locker room, observe practice, talk to as many of the student-athletes and students at large as he can to get a real feel for it. We're going to put our best foot forward when the kid comes into our office with his parents. We're going to sell our institution and we're going to try to do it as honestly as we can, but the student-athlete himself needs to get out there with the students and pick their brains as to what they like and don't like about it. I think in most cases the students will be pretty honest about how they feel.

What should prospective student-athletes look for in a program to ensure that the program will help him maintain a balance between his athletic and academic interests?

First he needs to determine, can he major in what he's interested in? Some programs, because of laboratories and late classes, he can't major in because it will conflict with the practice hours. Then I think you need to determine what kind of extra help is available, what are the sizes of the classes, what kind of a relationship do you have with your professors, is extra additional instruction available on a regular basis. Is the lacrosse program monitoring your academic progress, are they aware of problems that you might have so they can help you get extra help and deal with those? I think the players in your program will be able to talk to that and the recruit will get a feel for whether that actually exists or whether they're just paying lip service to it.

6

Sue Enquist, Softball Coach

Sue Enquist was an integral part of UCLA softball for 30 years—four years as a player, nine years as an assistant coach, and 17 years as head coach. When she retired in 2006, Enquist's 887 victories were the most of any active head coach. The Bruins won five NCAA championships under Enquist, and she produced 65 all-Americans and 12 Olympians. She's the only person to win an NCAA softball championship as a player and coach, and she has been inducted into both the National Fastpitch Coaches Association Hall of Fame and the UCLA Hall of Fame. She also was a member of the coaching staff for the 1996 U.S. Olympic softball team, which won a gold medal in Atlanta. She now works as a motivational speaker and produces softball instructional videos and equipment.

Do you encourage younger kids to play multiple sports, or should they concentrate on softball year-round? What is the advantage to that approach?

I've always believed that a multisport discipline enables the athlete to work all facets of their body so they are gaining strength in all parts of their body. On a mental level, each sport brings a whole new set of challenges for them so they get a different set of experiences from each sport. And culturally and socially, it's good to participate among all different sport cultures. Then, as the athlete gets older, they start to get a feel for where they best fit in each sport.

The biggest problem we have in the direction of sport is that parents believe the earlier you specialize, the further along you will be. Statistically, they may be able to hang onto some of that, but the reality is, in my experience, the athletes that fared the best are the ones that had a more balanced athletic experience and their parents maintained their role as parents, not as training specialists or pushing their kid too early before their kid was ready physically or mentally.

How old should a player be before she decides to focus only on pitching, if that is her main talent?

Pitchers who focus on just pitching many times may find that their skills in hitting may not be where they want them to be, so they just focus solely on pitching. If you have a pitcher that can clearly hit, those players continue to do both. So it's a personal decision. But if you're a great hitter and you continue to be able to hit and perform, continue to do it. There are very few coaches in the country that are not going to let a top hitter who happens to pitch not hit. Now, I can't emphasize enough, if you are the number four hitter [in your lineup] in high school, and you go to college and now you've become the number seven hitter, I support those coaches who say it may not be worth the injury potential to let you hit. If you make the jump from each level—youth to high school to college—and you're a number three or four or five hitter, or a leadoff hitter or a number two spot, you're going to see many coaches who will utilize that pitcher on offense and defense.

What are the major health/injury issues that softball players need to be aware of, and what can a young player do to avoid them? What should coaches do to help keep their players healthy?

The number one issue is overuse injuries. These are strains, minor tears, shin splits, rotator cuff issues—not necessarily torn, but loose capsules—lower back injuries. These are all due to overuse, and because we're now in a culture where the players are competing 12 months a year with no dead period where their body doesn't shut down like it should, the most important thing a player can do if they're already in that dangerous cycle of throwing 12 months out of the year, or even if you're playing at a high level at any time, is to ice after all of your training regimens or your game regimens, and to have a proper warm-up and stretching routine before your practices and games.

Coaches need to be sensitive to the idea that there's a time to practice for long periods of time, and there's a time to practice shorter periods of time—to understand that more is not necessarily better. There's the off-season, where you hope you've got your players resting their bodies; there's the preseason, where you work on the specialty areas of the game that they need to improve on; there's the first third of the season, where you do the most work in terms of hours per day or per week; then in-season you start to taper it, where everything is situation-based, and not volume-developing type of skill work, so at the end of the season they have a strong foundation of fundamentals but they're still enjoying the game. People need to remember that baseball and softball are failure sports —they fail more than they succeed, if you're a hitter, so you have to make sure your team stays energized and excited about the game.

What are your thoughts on the advantage of playing for a female coach in softball? Is there a level playing field for male coaches in the sport at the collegiate level?

There are no advantages, there are just differences. It's dangerous to genderize it. Our sport is at a point right now where I can benefit from what a male or a female coach brings, and I look forward to the time where we don't have to separate it out, but we're still growing so much in softball. I would love to see more women getting into coaching baseball. Why don't we do it both ways? Why don't we offer 100 percent of the opportunities to men in softball, and why don't we offer 100 percent of the opportunities to women in baseball? The similarities in the game are striking, in terms of fielding fundamentals, throwing mechanics, and our hitting. There's a lot of misinformation out there, but hitting a baseball and hitting a softball are very similar. The only huge difference is pitching. But we've got a huge contingency of men out there who have backgrounds in fast-pitch softball.

There may be advantages in terms of women understanding women, but our sport has grown to the point where we're athletes, so don't treat me like a male or a female. Treat me like an athlete. Hold me accountable every day. Make sure you shine a light on my positives, hold me accountable when I cut corners. And that's got nothing to do with gender.

There are certain pockets of the country that seem to be hot-beds for softball recruiting. What can an elite player do to draw attention if she lives in a lesser-recruited region or lives in a town where there's not a competitive youth program to help her improve her skills and exposure?

There is absolutely no excuse now for the family and the athlete to not get more exposure or be able to make the connections they needed to make as there might have been 10 years ago. The Internet is your breathing tube to exposure. Get organized, get organized, get organized! Don't sit back and wait for the phone to ring. Don't think getting on the most popular traveling team is the answer. Sit down as a family, organize the things that are important to you as a player and for your family. There are thousands of Web sites out there that can give you the mechanics of how to break down the type of school you want to go to. It's not about exposure—it's about finding the puzzle piece that's going to fit your needs and your desires as a prospective student-athlete.

Once you identify the profile of the school that fits your needs, then go get on their campus. Go to their summer camps. Go to their academies and learn more about them from the inside out. You be the one to communicate with the coaches—don't wait for some recruiting service or some agent to do that for you. Don't have 10 schools on your radar, have five—but more importantly, have five that fit your puzzle piece. Your area code or your ZIP code don't matter: there's a team out there for you.

The misinformation has to do with people thinking, "Well, I live in a small town outside of, say, Chicago, and I'm never going to get exposed." Not true. Parents and the athlete have to get organized, find out the schools that match, find out how many they're graduating, find out how many are graduating from the starting lineup and that play your position. This is a math problem that can get organized four years in advance because you have the Internet. You know who is a sophomore at that college, when you're a sophomore at your high school [and tracking programs and athletes should be something to consider when making a shortlist of schools]. This is not happening enough, and consequently schools and coaches are getting the blame [for the acceptances and scholarship offers they make to build their programs]. At the end of the day, the onus [of seeking out an appropriate program and getting seen by coaches] falls on the student-athlete and the parents.

What attributes did you look for in a prospective student-athlete?

First, her GPA. Second, her skill. Third, her ability to respect the game. Fourth, her ability to understand the value of being a part of something bigger than yourself—does she have the core potential to be a good teammate? And last, when I would be in the home, I wanted to see how that student-athlete treated her family, her parents, her grandparents, her elders. It would give me an opportunity to see how much work I had to get done outside the white lines, because that behavior outside the white lines also affects your behavior inside the white lines in respecting your teammates. I would find out a lot in the in-home visits. A lot of people think the in-home visit is about finding out more about the student-athlete. For me, it was about finding out how she treated her family.

What questions from the student-athlete showed you that she had her priorities in order?

When the first question out of her mouth had to do with academics, when the second question had to do with how many people have graduated from the institution, when the questions had to do with things involving more than just her own personal success. Individuals that honor the process of getting better every day. Athletes who were more focused on, "How do you do things?' and not "What am I going to be given if I commit to your school?'

What did you consider a deal-breaker when you were meeting with a recruit? What might happen in an interview or a visit that would raise too many red flags?

The red flags would be in the area of not respecting the academics or somebody who doesn't have social responsibility as part of her priority system. Having said that, there are times when you have two prospective athletes and they've got all of the qualities that I want. The game-breaker then would be, I'm going to go with the athlete that is in love with competing and doesn't get caught up with what the scoreboard says or what her batting average is. The individual that just loved the challenge of one-on-one against the pitcher, the player that loved the challenge of thinking the ball was going to come to them every single play on defense. That would be the game-breaker, when two athletes are doing great academically, they've got great skill, they come from great families, they respect the game. Do they have that competitive spirit, where they love being in the cooker?

How do you view the role of the parent in the recruiting process?

This is very simple. In my 27 years of coaching, there was a very common theme among all of our athletes that succeeded and had a quality experience and left college loving the game—there's one entity that I give so much credit to, and that's the parent. They allowed their child an opportunity to play a sport in order to learn life lessons. The parents that learned that their roles as a parents in sport was to be a fan.

The parent that allowed their athlete to experience college and athletics, and it was their experience—the parent that lived through the athlete hour-by-hour, day-by-day, those athletes crash and burn. Those athletes walk away from sports hating the sport. Those parents who are overly involved—their intentions are good, but it's devastating what they've done to their daughters. They suck the life out of the student-athlete in terms of loving the game, they create fear because the parents never allowed the athlete to succeed and fail on her own. So when the parent, during a recruiting visit, is answering all the questions that the student-athlete has been asked, that's a red flag for me. I'd bring Mom and Dad and daughter into the office, and the first thing I'd ask the student-athlete is, "Explain to me what a good teammate looks like." Or I'd say to a student-athlete, "What are you most proud of, and what do you regret the most, about who you are at this time in your life?" When I asked a question like that and the mom or dad piped in and started answering the question, that's when I realized this was an athlete that had to deal with parents who were stunting the student-athlete's growth. Let the student-athletes step up and articulate what they are and what they are not.

Let them articulate what they feel is important regarding being part of the team.

What are some of the unethical recruiting practices that you have witnessed or what practices did other programs use to recruit against you? How did you circumvent those practices?

I always told parents to feel comfortable always sharing with me the negative recruiting, because that would allow me to respond to it. But most importantly, to every parent in every sport, it should be a red flag when you have somebody who is negatively recruiting. I can honestly tell you, in my 27 years I never once said one bad thing about another school, whether it was accurate or not. My attitude was that I had so many great things to talk about regarding my own program that I didn't have time to look over to the left or the right and negatively recruit. So the first thing I would say to parents is red-flag the schools that negatively recruit.

The second challenge to that parent is to say, "Why are you talking about another school negatively?" Step up and ask them, "Why are you talking that way about another school? We're here to talk about your school." I'm challenging every parent in America to step up and ask that. Parents have so much control in the recruiting process and they don't even realize it.

If a student-athlete encounters negative recruiting, what's the best way for her to investigate or assess the allegations made against another program?

Go to that program and hit them square in the face with it.

How can student-athletes assess the true day-to-day practices and attitudes of the coaching staff, that is, how can they get an accurate assessment of the program, rather than the best-case scenarios that they'll see during a recruiting visit?

Go to their camps and clinics, from junior high all the way through high school. Parents will say, "We're looking at the Pac-10, but we live in the Midwest." Spend the money, parents. Spend the money. Go out there, give your kid a $600 experience, because you're going to feel the culture of that program in a three-day, overnight camp. You're going to get a feel for their philosophy. The next thing in the recruiting process when you've been chosen as one of those athletes that's being recruited, talk to the starters, talk to the rotating players, and talk to the bench. Then you've got a cross-section of attitudes.

What should a prospective student-athlete look for in a program to ensure that the program will help her maintain a balance between her athletic and academic interests?

Again, talk to the student-athletes and see how many games a year do they play, how much they're practicing, how much they practice during the most demanding times of the academic year. Do you have a coach who works with the student-athletes on their academic demands? I never turned a kid down when they had a study session during practice. I never turned a kid down when they had a study session that would interfere with warm-ups on a game day. If they were going to be 15 minutes late, take care of school. Because I knew if the kids had that flexibility to take care of school, their head was clear when they came to the ball field. So there was a payoff for us—and it also sent the message that school comes first, softball comes second.

How does one maximize educational opportunities while on an athletic scholarship or while playing collegiate sports?

One, we had a system in place where the athletes forged relationships with the professors, which allowed the athlete and the professor to create a bond of working together when the athlete is on the road. Second, we created a career network so while they were in school they were also forging relationships with corporations that could be in the area of business if they're interested in that, so in the off-season they could be playing club ball but also working an internship. College is such a training center for life. Life lessons are learned on the ball field, but your college experience is going to be the only time that you're surrounded by people who are working full time to ensure that you reach your full potential.

Once you get done with college, an employer couldn't care less about your RBIs or ERA. So we wanted to make sure they understood that before they graduated, so they were well-rounded, well-educated, and have life lessons under their belts to make them a great employee and a great individual as a rookie going into corporate America. They've already learned those lessons, that you've got to come early, you've got to stay late, you've got to be resilient, you've got to be focused, you've got to be able to be resourceful, you can't worry about the people on your left or your right. Sport is the same way—those things transcend each specific sport.

7

Jeff Sauer, Hockey Coach

Jeff Sauer is the all-time winningest coach in the Western Collegiate Hockey Association. Sauer was the head coach at Colorado College for 11 years and at the University of Wisconsin for 20 years. He led the Badgers to four 30-win seasons, three Frozen Four appearances, and two NCAA championships. He retired in 2002 with 655 career victories. Sauer is now the assistant to the commissioner of the WCHA.

Hockey is unique in that it offers other post-high school options for kids who want to pursue a career in the sport. How does a young player know whether college or junior hockey is the best option for him?

One of the major problems that college hockey has right now is the education process of a young hockey player. NCAA rules do not let the coaches get to the players early in the decision process, especially in Canada. Mostly kids up there are really naïve to what is available to them at the college level, and they're so ingrained in the process in Canada—moving up the ladder playing junior hockey to major junior hockey and then to the National Hockey League—that a lot of them don't know much about college hockey in the United States. Consequently, uneducated decisions are made early in a player's career that put him in jeopardy of being unable to return to college hockey because of eligibility rules.

One of the things we're trying to do is educate the young player entering high school about the eligibility and academic rules, but also the recruiting rules that the colleges have to live with in the United States, so they can make educated decisions.

What are the benefits of playing college hockey over playing juniors?

I think college is the best of both worlds. You're able to receive a scholarship to play, if you're good enough. You combine a hockey career with obtaining an academic degree, and in the end if injuries or ability keep you from making a living as a player, you've got something to fall back on. Major junior hockey in Canada is basically the opposite of that. You're able to continue your hockey career but academics take a back seat, mostly because of travel.

What should a high school hockey player do during the off-season to sharpen his skills?

In the United States you've got the USA Development camps, you've got select camps, you've got summer leagues that kids can participate in. There's some expense in getting involved in these things, but the bottom line is that hockey is becoming like all other sports in that it's becoming a year-round sport. But I'm not a full proponent of a kid just playing hockey—I think playing other sports certainly helps his development as a hockey player. Playing baseball helps hand-eye coordination; playing lacrosse, again hand-eye coordination, plus physical conditioning.

I think off-ice conditioning with personal trainers has become a way of life in the NHL. I don't think kids in high school have to go to that extent, but certainly continuing with their conditioning programs and developing their lower body, with a lot of running, bicycling, rollerblading in the off-season, is an excellent way to go.

In my experience, a lot of the kids who come to college from the high school level, their lower bodies are fairly well-developed because of all the skating they've done. What they have to develop is their upper bodies—their shoulder and arm strength. I'm not one who says you've got to play hockey 365 days a year, but getting into a conditioning program and nutrition program is very important. But it's also important to play different sports—you get to see how you'll react in a pressure situation in a different sport, and also learn what it's like to get along with different types of athletes.

What are the health issues specific to hockey that athletes need to be aware of, and what does the hockey community do to stay on top of those issues?

Hockey players are traditionally mentally tough when it comes to injuries. A lot of athletes over my coaching career wouldn't be fully truthful with you about an injury because they wanted to play the game so much. It's such a fun game to play that I think from an injury standpoint, unless it's a very serious injury, most hockey players just play through it and keep working. So we have to stay on top of them and make sure they're getting treatment.

As a young coach back at Colorado College, I watched an operation on a knee and on a shoulder. It helped me understand the trauma on the body when this happens and what really takes place and why a coach shouldn't put pressure on trainers and doctors to get people back quicker than they should. There's a process involved— you have to repair the injury and you have to go through the rehabilitation. You'd better leave that process to the experts.

What options are available to a hockey-loving kid who lives in a state where there's no youth hockey available?

That is not quite as prevalent today as it was 15 to 20 years ago. With the expansion of the NHL, there's more interest in other parts of the United States. But in most cases, kids will go where the hockey is being played. Either the family will move, or you've got prep schools out east and in the Minnesota area that do have hockey programs that accept kids from different parts of the country. You've also got the junior programs if kids are good enough to go, and you've also got the USA developmental program at Ann Arbor, Michigan, which involves 45 kids a year at two different age levels, and those kids are actively recruited. When you look at their roster, you'll find that a lot of the kids are from nontraditional hockey areas.

Women's hockey has taken off at the youth levels and the game is now growing at the high school and collegiate level. Do you think this is a temporary trend, or is women's hockey here to

stay? What issues do women's hockey programs face to ensure their long-term viability?

I think we're kind of in a lull right now, but I don't think women's hockey is going to go away. The one thing that has changed is that some of the better Olympic players grew up playing on boys' teams or against boys. I think their skill level really developed and was intensified through that. Now with the number of girls' teams available, players are coming to college off of girls' teams, so there's been a bit of a downward slope in terms of ability, but I think that will continue to improve. It's incredible here in the WCHA, watching from the first game through last year, the caliber of play, the coaching, and the intensity have really come a long way.

What attributes did you look for in a prospective student-athlete?

Skating is always a key—you go to games or warm-ups and watch them skate, watch their agility, watch their body language and how they handle themselves on the ice. With a goaltender, you watch the athleticism, you take a look at their hand-eye coordination and catching ability, and how they handle the puck with their stick.

I liked to watch warm-ups or watch how players react to another player on the ice, what happens when he goes back to the bench, his body language after a bad shift or after a goal. I would also call opposing coaches and ask them what they thought of the kid and what he's able to do on the ice. An opposing coach may give you a better read on the kid's attitude and abilities than his own coach.

How do you view the role of the parent in the recruiting process?

There have been players—and they've been great players— that I have not taken because I didn't want to deal with the parents. I think if you ask any coach in any sport, that coach has made a decision not to pursue a player because they didn't want to deal with the problems that come with the parent.

A lot of coaches go in and try to sell the moms, because you're taking their baby away from them and it's their first time away from home, so you talk about washing clothes and the other things moms typically worry about. The mom is usually more concerned with the personal things; the dad is more concerned with where he's going to play.

I think the coaches who are most successful just go in there and are honest. They'll say, "I'm going to give your boy an opportunity to play. He might be on the left side or the right, he might be on the power play, he may need to put on some strength but I think he's going to be able to play down the road." Just be truthful and you'll never get yourself trapped in a bad situation down the road.

What did you want to hear from a recruit that showed you he had his priorities in order?

I always liked the kid who, if you asked him if he made the team, what would his jersey number be, the kid that came back and said, "I don't care, I just want a jersey." Some kids are very naïve to their abilities. They've been told all along how great they are, especially at the high school level. The kids you're recruiting are the kids that had the puck all the time and scored all the goals, won all the awards and all that type of stuff, and you have to talk to them. "We're going to give you an opportunity to be a part of our program. You're going to have to work for everything you get. There's rules you have to follow, and if you don't follow them, you'll be reprimanded." You spend a lot of time and money recruiting a player, as a coach you want that kid to be successful, so you have a stake in trying to get him to that point. So it's a two-way street.

The kids will often ask you, "What's my role on the team going to be?" Well, first of all you have to realize that you're back at square one again. You're a freshman in the program, and you've got to come in and earn your stripes, earn the respect of your teammates and the coaching staff, and earn a spot. If a kid reacts to that in a real positive manner, those are the types of things you want to see.

I've been in situations where a kid is very straightforward about his goals and what his demands will be, and as a coach if you want to live through that type of thing, you might take a chance on him. But bottom line, the kid who is humble, the kid who asks honest questions about how much practice do we have, what do we do in practice, is there a conditioning program, do we have tutoring for academic needs—kids who really have looked into your program and have an interest and are real well-rounded kids —they're the ones who are most successful.

What negative practices did you witness or did other programs use to recruit against you?

Some schools will offer a scholarship to a young man and then give him 24 hours to make a decision. I never did that but I was in a position at Wisconsin where I really didn't have to. I'd offer a kid a scholarship and say "It's there until you make your decision." I'd also ask them, "What if you decide to go to a school, you walk on the campus and you're injured the first day playing touch football and you never play a game of hockey for that school. How do you feel about your decision? Did you go there solely for hockey or did you make the decision on where you wanted to be and what you wanted to be?"

They [other coaches] talk about you personally as a coach: "He's not a good coach, he doesn't develop players for the next level," that type of thing. "You don't want to go to Madison because all they do is drink beer and chase women." But it's not as bad in hockey as it can be in other sports, I think, because hockey is a pretty small fraternity and we have a pretty good respect for each other. If there's a recruiting violation going on or some talk going on that people hear about, normally the phone is picked up and you go one-on-one with the coach that's doing it and you settle it between the two of you. In some of the other sports —football and basketball—they take it public and then it gets really out of hand. If you're confident in your program, you don't have to deal with that kind of stuff. Ultimately you sell your own institution and your own program to the kids.

What should prospective student-athletes look for in a program to ensure that the program will help him maintain a balance between his athletic and academic interests?

The type of questions recruits should ask are, "If I have a paper due on Wednesday afternoon and we're traveling to North Dakota on Thursday, can I miss practice to get the paper done or take a test?" Little things like that should be asked of the coach, because a lot of times all the coach does is put pressure on them to be hockey players and forget about the other things that go on.

8

Joe Novak, Football Coach

Joe Novak retired in 2007 after 12 years as the head coach at Northern Illinois University. Under Novak, the Huskies won or shared four Mid-American Conference West Division championships and played in two bowl games. Novak also was an assistant coach for 22 years at the University of Illinois, Indiana University, Northern Illinois, and Miami University of Ohio, where he also played his collegiate football under future Michigan coaching legend Bo Schembechler.

You coached in both the Big Ten and the Mid-American Conference. How did your recruiting strategies and tactics differ when you worked for a school in a major conference to a school in a smaller conference?

Any time you're coaching in a league like the Big Ten or SEC or the Pac-10, you know you can go after the top-notch kids that are out there. When you're coaching in the Mid-American Conference, you have to recruit the next tier down, the players who aren't maybe as well-publicized, maybe aren't quite near the finished product. You have to be a good evaluator to be successful when you're coaching at a mid-major type of school because so much of the success you have is going to be dependent on your ability to evaluate and project where these kids may be in two or three years. Whereas, when you're recruiting in a league like the Big Ten, you're after kids that are closer to being a finished product.

The number of scholarships available for a Division I-A or Football Bowl Subdivision team has dropped from 125 to 85 over the past three decades, while Division I-AA or Football Championship Subdivision schools can offer up to 63

scholarships for football. What affect has that had on the balance of power in college football, and how has it affected the depth of your rosters?

It certainly has brought around parity in college football. Years ago, when it was unlimited, I can remember Pittsburgh, for example, when [1976 Heisman Trophy winner] Tony Dorsett was recruited, they ended up being a national champion, but they brought in 60 freshmen that last year you were allowed to. That was Tony Dorsett's class. With the limitations now, it's brought around parity, and it's brought around situations where schools like ours from the MAC were able to go out and beat some of the big-conference schools. We beat Maryland, Alabama, and Iowa State back in 2003. Kids who were sitting on Nebraska's bench 30 years ago are now playing in the Mid-American Conference, and they're pretty good players.

The one thing we've been pushing for as coaches over the last several years is a fifth year of eligibility. As they've cut the scholarships from 125 down to 85, at the same time they've been adding games on our schedule. When I started out, we played nine games. Now we're playing 12 regular-season games, a possible conference championship game, and a possible bowl game, so you're up to 14 games now, with fewer scholarships. So it really has gotten to the point where teams, at the end of the season, if they've had a particularly tough year injury-wise, without the depth available to replace those guys, they're not near the same team in November that they were in September.

So, this movement would eliminate red-shirting. It would give you five years of eligibility. What coaches have to do now is, let's say they've got a freshman who maybe could help them in the kicking game, but wouldn't be a starter. You don't put him in the kicking game, because that would use up a year of eligibility. With the fifth year, you would eliminate all the red-shirting and put everybody on the field. Right now, let's say you're red-shirting 15 kids in your freshman class. Then you're not playing with 85 kids, you're playing with 70. So, if we go to fifth-year eligibility, it would eliminate all red-shirting and you'd truly have 85 kids available to play.

Football has the largest number of assistant coaches of any college sport, and at most major colleges each position or position group has its own dedicated assistant. Given the level of delegating that must occur, how would you describe the role of the head coach?

Especially in the major conferences, you're really like a CEO of a company. You really do lose a little bit of touch with the kids because you have so many other demands, from the media to the alumni. So, in most cases you're more of an organizer. Some are able to be a little bit more involved with the football side of things, while others will completely remove themselves from the Xs and Os and oversee the program.

I remember [longtime University of Washington head coach] Don James years ago said, "As the head coach, your job is to coach the coaches." And those assistant coaches coach the players. At most schools, it's gotten to be closer to that scenario.

So if a student-athlete is trying to decide which scholarship offer to accept, if he's fortunate enough to have that choice, should he look more at his relationship with the assistant coach at his position or the head coach?

Definitely both, because the head coach is still going to influence how the program is run, the philosophy, the emphasis on academics and other issues, so the head coach still is important. But the position coach also is important because that's the guy he'll be spending most of his time with and get the closest with.

What are the health issues specific to football that athletes need to be aware of, and what does the college football community do to stay on top of those issues?

Well, what's happened over the past 40 to 50 years is that the field has stayed the same size, but the kids have gotten so much bigger, stronger, and faster that the collisions on the field are so much more violent than they used to be. It's gotten considerably more physical. I know over the last 30 years we've really backed off on hitting in practice, because you just can't take those kids out there every day in practice and go hard with them physically because the collisions are that much more violent and the number of games they play is that much more extreme.

I think the biggest change I've seen in the last 20 years is the year-round conditioning program. Right here at Northern Illinois and at every school in the country, our kids are here all summer. Years ago the kids used to go home and get away, and you wouldn't see them for two to three months. You just kept your fingers crossed when they came back that they were in shape. But nowadays the kids all stay on campus all summer, they're training all summer, and the lifting and conditioning they do all summer is probably the most important part of their training, so when they come to camp in August they are in shape. You don't play yourself into shape in August like they used to. The kids are in great shape because they have to be.

Would you ever look at a student-athlete's performance in other sports as a way of assessing his competitiveness, athletic ability, or sportsmanship?

By all means. I think watching a kid play basketball in particular is helpful. You can watch for their competitive skills, watch them move, watch their agility. Certainly, their jumping ability is a great indicator on athletic ability. I liked kids who wanted to play other sports—kids who wanted to hang out and compete. I think those kids often have a better chance to be successful because they like competition. I've seen kids who had great ability but they weren't necessarily that crazy about competing. It was just something they did at times so they could play after high school because everybody expected them to. You want kids who really love it, because the commitment we're asking of kids, being here all summer, training like they do in the off-season, they've got to really enjoy it or else they're going to have a difficult time competing with the kids who truly do love it.

What attributes did you look for in a prospective student-athlete?

We all understand as coaches that playing football or basketball or whatever certainly isn't the most important thing these kids are going to be doing when they go to college. But by the same token, as I always explained it to our kids, let's try to be as good as we can be. I was always trying to find kids who had that same passion. I certainly wanted kids who wanted to try to be as good as they can be, because I always found that if they wanted to be really good in athletics, they usually wanted to be good in academics and socially with other people, so it really goes hand-in-hand. If somebody is sloppy with their academics or their athletics, they're going to be sloppy in the other areas as well. I always thought that was a great indicator of their personal pride, and how it would emerge down the road in academics and athletics.

What kinds of questions would kids ask you about your program when you were recruiting them? What questions showed you that the student-athlete had his priorities in order?

One thing I think coaches get asked nowadays is, "Are you going to be there?" If you're a coach who's not winning, people are worried that you're going to get fired. If you are winning, unless you're at Notre Dame or Michigan, they wonder, "Are you going to go on to another place down the road?" That certainly is a very legitimate concern for any youngster and his parents, because as we all know, things change if that coach leaves. The one thing I always tried to sell them on was the fact that nobody can guarantee you they'll be there for the five years that you'll be going to school. Anybody who guarantees that he's going to be at that school five years down the road, I'd back away from right now because you just don't know in this profession.

Parents and kids want to hear about the academics, and that's certainly something that we as coaches will always cover. I don't think any schools nowadays do a bad job with the academic support that we provide. I always told parents that with the support that's given by all schools, if the youngster doesn't make it academically, the vast majority of the time it's because he's not doing his part.

What do you consider a deal-breaker when you are meeting with a recruit? What might happen in an interview or a visit that would raise too many red flags?

I decided many years ago that I was coaching because I enjoyed it, and I wanted to be around kids I enjoyed.

There [are] a lot of things I'm not good at, but I always thought I was a pretty good judge of character. When I'd get around a kid and I'd watch him or get a feel for him, if I didn't get a good feel, more often than not we wouldn't recruit him.

It's good to watch them a lot of times with their parents and how they treated their parents. How did they talk to their mother and father? That can tell you a lot, especially when they're in their home. When you've got them on campus, they're on their toes a little bit, but when you go into their home and you sit around for a couple of hours and visit with them, sometimes you'll have dinner with them, and you watch how they act around their parents in the home, I think that usually will tell you a lot about that youngster.

How do you view the role of the parent in the recruiting process?

They're extremely important—especially the mother. I think at times we did a better job of selling the parents than selling the kids. I really thought that was important, because the parents—and especially the mother—have to feel comfortable with where they're sending their youngster off to, who he's going to be with. And I know that if you can sell the parents, they're going to be in that youngster's ear when you're not, telling him where he should be going. I wanted those parents to be comfortable, because I have two boys and I know as a parent I'd want to be comfortable about where they were going.

What's the best way for student-athletes to deal with negative recruiting?

I really dislike negative recruiting. I always tried to avoid talking about other people. We tried to talk about what we had, and be as honest as we could about what we were good at, maybe what we weren't quite so good at. When you get into negative recruiting, I always believed people were telling you something about themselves. I know it's out there, I know it happens, and I think probably more often when you're going after the top kids that everybody's going after, there's a lot more of it there.

How should a school's academic profile factor into the recruiting decision?

Sometimes the kids and their parents get a little too caught up in the prestige of a school. We all know that Harvard and Yale, Stanford and Northwestern are great academic institutions, but you can get a great education at Illinois, Wisconsin, Purdue, Northern Illinois. If a youngster goes to Stanford and doesn't work at it, he's not going to get a great education. I've always thought that sometimes the reputation of a school is a little bit bigger part of that decision. We've had kids at Northern Illinois and Miami who've been extremely successful after getting an education from a school like that, too.

Did you allow student-athletes to participate in study-abroad programs or play another sport in college, or is year-round access to the player a must?

It's really hard. It really is. I'm not saying it's for the better, but in the last 25 years, that's the change that I've seen—the demand that the kids have on them now. As we all know, it's gotten that way in high school, too. But it's 12 months a year if you want to truly compete. That's why it's hard for kids to play two sports, or take a summer away, if you want to compete. Not that you can't do it, don't get me wrong. But it's harder.

9

Paul Torricelli, Tennis Coach

Paul Torricelli left Northwestern University in 2007 as the winningest men's tennis coach in the school's history. In 24 years, he led the Wildcats to nine NCAA Tournament appearances and was a three-time winner of the Big Ten Coach of the Year award. He began his coaching career in 1977 at Chico State University, his alma mater, and also coached at Lake Forest College before taking over at Northwestern in 1984. He now serves as a consultant with Scholarship For Athletes, a recruiting service for high school athletes.

Tennis is a sport where one can become a professional player well before college if he or she has the talent and desire to do so. What do you think are the key advantages to playing college tennis vs. turning pro early?

You have to qualify the idea of whether somebody has the ability to play professionally—everybody has the ability to play professionally. But can you make a living at it? And can you reach a certain standard where it's worth your while? That's very difficult. For a world-class tennis player to make a living at it, you have to be in the top 150 or 200 in the world, and that's stretching it a bit. That's a remarkable achievement. So, you have to be realistic when you look at it from that perspective.

Having said that, in our country, to have a career outside of sports, the rule of thumb is you need a college degree. And without a degree, making a living and having any kind of a meaningful career is very difficult. So college tennis is a great stepping-stone to professional tennis with the added benefit of getting a degree. If you break into college and blow them away and can move into the professional ranks within a year or two, more power to you. The very best players in the country in college are still hardly assured of making a living in professional tennis. If you look at the last 10 years, the number of collegiate players that are successful in professional tennis—you can count them on one hand. James Blake right now is the top-ranked player who played college tennis. For many years when Todd Martin and Mal Washington were out there, they were among maybe five guys in the top 100 who played in college, and it's less than that now. So you really have to make a choice, and it's become increasingly difficult.

How would you describe the ideal player-coach relationship at the college level?

I think it's one where the player trusts and believes that the coach has his or her best interests at heart, in terms of him or her developing as a player, being a team member, and also his or her personal well-being. And that would include academic support. In turn, the coach believes the kid is committed to the program as a member of a team, wants to be the very best player he or she can be, and [that] there's a level of trust there too.

I think those two answers can encompass any number of coaching styles, but it's a daunting task for a coach in today's world adapting to the different kinds of kids and fitting them into a team concept.

Given that tennis is very much an individual sport, how did you get your players to embrace the team concept and work to help each other improve, rather than compete with each other, on a daily basis?

That is the number one challenge for a college coach: creating a team environment and mentality in an individual sport. I've often said that my theory is that one in twenty kids who arrive at a college campus is a team player. The other 19 have to learn what it's really like to be a team player, and some never do. Some coaches might say that number is one in 100. Others might say it's one in five. But nobody's going to tell you it's three out of four. They don't get it, and it takes awhile to learn it.

There are a number of factors that complicate it, beyond just that it's an individual sport. But we really work all the time on developing a team concept: pulling for your team-mates. One of my pet peeves when you're playing a tough dual match is if you have a couple of guys finish early and there's four guys still out there playing, and they'll go up and sit with their buddies or their parents in the stands. I'd tell them, "Go get a drink, get stretched out with the trainer, and then I need you back out there on the court watching.' A basketball player doesn't come off the court and go sit in the stands with his friends. A football player doesn't come out of the game and go sit with his parents. Granted, it's a different situation, but at the same time, getting them to think in those terms is crucial. If you're having a bad day in practice—maybe you're tired, you have an exam, you don't feel well—you can still make a contribution. If you screw around or you're lazy or you're distracted, you're going to affect the quality of the team practice. So it's not about you anymore. It's about your contribution to the team.

In my last year at Northwestern I had a freshman who, in my 30 years of college coaching, was the best kid I had at getting the team concept from the get-go. He went through the usual fall freshman adjustment, and when he came back in January, every day at practice he was just like the Ener-gizer Bunny—motivated, energized, vocal, ran for every-thing. It was just something in his character, a drive that either you have or you don't. If you get six guys like that, you'd do the job for nothing. Every coach will tell you that. You can have a highly talented guy who's high-maintenance and he just wears you out. That's what kills coaches, the kids who undermine that team thing.

I think you'll find that in all sports, even in team sports. You'll have cliques and guys who for whatever reason just aren't team guys. For some reason in tennis we seem to talk about it more, and it's more on the surface because it's an individual sport.

Did you look for young players to begin to focus on tennis and eliminate other sports by a certain age, or did you encourage them to play other sports as well? What is the advantage to each approach?

I always encouraged kids to play other sports, even through high school, because they pick up the team part in other sports. Plus it's healthy—you can look at it like cross-train-ing. One kid I was working was heading to a Division III school to play tennis, and he asked me before his senior year if he should play high school basketball that year. I told him, "You play basketball, for sure." First of all, you don't want to play for any coach who's going to tell you no. You're talking about Division III tennis, where there's a healthy balance, and how many chances do you get to play high school bas-ketball? You don't want to give that up, unless you're just not very good at it and don't enjoy it and want to concentrate on tennis, then, fine. But most college coaches I know love that. Now, obviously if you're a nationally highly ranked player who's playing 12 months and traveling around the country, he's probably not playing another high school sport. But I think it's healthy and it's a good sign, because you want kids with some balance. You know he's not going to be burned out on tennis, that's for sure.

What are the health issues specific to tennis that young ath-letes need to be aware of, and what does the college tennis community do to stay on top of those issues?

I'm seeing more and more kids who aren't in good shape. Some of these kids don't train, and they're gassed when you start to work with them as youth. When you get to college and you're training for the first time, your body takes a real hit, and if you're not fit or don't understand how to take care of yourself and get stronger, you can start to incur some injuries. Tennis injuries are injuries of attrition, where your body breaks down due to overuse, as opposed to injuries of trauma like in football or baseball. In tennis, we're not getting the top athletes in the country. If we're lucky, we're getting like the third level of athlete. The top athletes are playing basketball or football or baseball or track and field. By the time you get down to the kids playing tennis, most kids aren't that athletic, they're not that strong, they're not real fit, their balance isn't real good, so things can snowball from that. So it's a real issue, watching bodies break down, and coaches have to be real careful with that.

It's a long year, the longest schedule in college athletics, and by the end of the year, with the length of the schedule and the intensity of the matches, it's draining. It's exciting and fun, but it's also demanding, and it takes a toll on your mind and your body. And everybody is good. They're playing guys they've never heard of, guys who stunk as juniors and are now really good, guys who are three and four years older than them, guys from all over the world, and you can take a beating. So it wears you out and you get hurt, and there's no time to get healthy because there's no off-season.

And one problem with college tennis is that you don't have enough guys, with only 4.5 scholarships available. Everybody's got to play—you don't get to sit somebody down and say, "Hey, let's get you healthy, or let's sit you down and let you watch for a bit to get your confidence back up." It's not like other sports where you've got plenty of bodies. We have a roster cap; I could only carry eight guys at Northwestern for about 10 years, and it absolutely killed us. It eventually got bumped up to nine a couple of years ago, but the pool's already small and you've got no depth.

What attributes did you look for in a prospective student-athlete?

One thing you rarely hear about, but all college coaches will tell you about it, is a kid who gets to college and they find out they don't love tennis anymore. They hit their peak a long time ago, they're really tired of it, and when they get to college, there's all kinds of other things going on. They'd achieved their goal and gotten a college scholarship. That doesn't mean they don't like the team or they're not going to try, but they're not committed to it anymore, and the light bulb goes off that they're not going to be a professional. Their priorities change. They're not as hungry. They're not playing in the summer. They start talking about internships and jobs for the first time, they get sexually active or fall in love—they become college students.

So you've got to find kids that love tennis, that really love playing and want to keep getting better. And a lot of them don't. You want kids who can win and will keep working to get better. You're projecting where they're going to be two and three years down the road: athletically, their technique, and how they compete. And the character issues: what kind of kid they are, how do they fit in with the other guys on the team. In some cases, you end up passing on a kid and a couple years down the road you realize you shouldn't have. And in some cases, you take a kid and a couple years down the road you realize you shouldn't have. It's a real crapshoot.

What kinds of questions would kids ask you about your program when you were recruiting them? What questions showed you that the student-athlete had his priorities in order?

They'd ask about academic support, "What do you do when you travel? How do you handle course conflicts? What's your practice schedule? What's the calendar during the course of the year, the off-court training? What are the opportunities for individual workouts?" Those are all legitimate questions, and those are good signs, if they want to train and get better.

What do you consider a deal-breaker when you are meeting with a recruit? What might happen in an interview or a visit that would raise too many red flags?

If you get any kind of an indication that they're lazy, that they don't want to work, that they don't like tennis. The parents can sometimes be a red flag. Character issues, like if you hear that a kid is a partier and he has that reputation already in the juniors. Appearance: Your first impressions are often extremely accurate. You can take a quick look at somebody and say, "Uh-uh. I don't want that on my team." A lot of times you're right. If you get a kid who looks bad, his hair is down to whatever and he looks like a gangster, I don't want that kid on my team. And that kid might be a great kid. Two years from now, he could cut his hair and be the best kid on the team. You just don't know. But I do think appearance does mean something.

His demeanor on the court, his competitiveness, also is important. Does he look like he's enjoying it? I remember a kid who was very interested in us when we were recruiting, and I wasn't interested in him because of his demeanor on the court. He had this very pained expression on his face all the time. He didn't look like he was happy to be out there. Look like you're fighting, you're competitive, you're enjoying the experience. If you're starting out with negative body language, who wants to deal with that?

How do you view the role of the parent in the recruiting process?

I think parents should be invested in it, supportive, and interested. And parents should guide their kids through the process and support them. But the desire to be a player and the investment has to come from the kid. This has to be the kid's activity, not the parent's activity. The parent has to make sure the kid is in a good environment and making a good choice, but tennis has to be their thing. An over-involved parent can turn a kid off to tennis, or make the kid want to go far away to get away from [his or her] parents. I've had kids who couldn't bear to have their parents watch them play. You've got the tyrant father or the over-involved mother. But you've got other kids who can't play unless their parents are watching. But parents need to be the parents, not the coaches, and let go. The greatest gift you can give your child is independence. Let it be their thing. You don't walk around with your kid's water bottle and his racket bag. You don't live vicariously through your kid. If the kid doesn't love it, it's his choice.

10

Reggie Minton, Basketball Coach

Reggie Minton coached college basketball for 32 years, including 15 years as an assistant coach and 16 years as the head coach at the Air Force Academy. He also was the head coach at Dartmouth College for one season. He retired from the Air Force Academy in 2000 and is now the deputy executive director of the National Association of Basketball Coaches. He's also a trustee for the Naismith Basketball Hall of Fame and also serves on the board of directors for USA Basketball.

Basketball offers an opportunity for an elite player to continue his career professionally, but the percentage of high school players who eventually turn pro is minuscule. How can a coach help a young student-athlete understand that and prepare for life after basketball without squashing his dreams?

I've gone into many homes and heard players and parents talk about professional careers. Whenever I heard that, I tried to get them to consider everybody they know or have known, and how many of those people have had that opportunity. Of course, you don't want to stop them from dreaming, but you want them to have a realistic dream about what could happen. They can learn an awful lot about who's recruiting them. If I'm the head coach at the Air Force Academy and I'm recruiting them, and none of the guys from any of the top schools in the country are recruiting them, that's probably the first sign that they're not among the elite of the elite. That doesn't mean they're not good players and can't have a great college career, but they need to get a little more grounded and make sure that no matter which school they pick, that they're going there to get a good, solid education.

What effect has the NBA's age-restriction rule [players are not eligible to join the NBA until one year after their high school class has graduated] had on college basketball?

It's made it clear that some young people come in with the goal of being "one-and-done," and that is unfortunate in the sense that maybe they're not even looking beyond that one year. They've already decided, or someone has convinced them, that they should be a one-and-done guy, so that's the approach they take. In so doing, it's very possible that maybe they don't get a chance to really enjoy the total college experience.

I was never in favor of the restriction, personally. I think if the NBA wants to take a kid straight out of high school, let them take him. I don't know how many we're talking about, but I bet that number's not that high. And once the kid goes to college, leave him alone for a couple of years, and let him grow and mature and experience college life. Who knows? He may come to enjoy it.

Successful coaches, especially those who succeed at the mid-major level, often use those smaller programs as stepping-stones to a larger school. What approach should student-athletes take during the recruiting process to determine if the coaches they're talking to are focused on building a program vs. building a résumé?

Whenever I talked to a young man I would tell him, "The constant is the school." You could fall in love with the style of the coach, the way he plays, etc., but at the end of the day, you don't know whether that coach is going to be there throughout your entire time on campus. The school is the constant, so you'd better look strongly at the school. Obviously the coach is one variable and it's a consideration, but you have to look at something besides the basketball aspect of the equation.

What role does an AAU coach play in the recruiting process? What issues do high school players need to be aware of in order to protect their eligibility?

I think the non-scholastic coach is playing a bigger and bigger role because most young people are playing more games with him or her than with their high school coaches. It's far less regulated—in terms of who's coaching, where they're going, and what they're doing—than it would be on the high school scene. So I think you need to find out as soon as possible what the NCAA's rules are.

You need to make yourself aware of what you're allowed as an amateur to do and to accept and receive. You don't want to start taking things that would jeopardize your amateur status. There are some folks out there who may know less about the rules than you do, and they're offering or giving you things. The student-athlete's assumption may be, "Well, the coach gave it to me, so it must be all right." But that coach may or may not know NCAA rules. So it's incumbent on the prospective student-athlete and his parents to be aware of the rules that determine the eligibility of a young person going onto college. And when in doubt, call somebody like the National Association of Basketball Coaches. You don't have to walk around blindly and hope that what you're doing is legal.

At what age do you think a prospective college basketball player should stop playing other sports and focus exclusively on basketball?

You're only young once, and if you decide to focus only on basketball once you enter high school, who's to say that it's going to work out for you? What if you might find out when you're a sophomore or junior that you can hit a curveball or you can throw hard, but you never gave yourself a chance? It's just very hard to predict someone's process of maturation, both mentally and physically. If you're the best player when you're 12 years old and you're 5-foot-8, but you never get much bigger than that, and the kid you were able to whip suddenly is 6-foot-4 and he's gotten better, it's not going to work out for you. No, I'm not made that way. I don't think you need to work on one athletic skill 24/7. I think you should get involved in other sports. It probably will recharge your battery, and you're eventually going to gravitate to where you're the best anyway.

What attributes did you look for in a prospective student-athlete?

I used to watch a young person not just when he had the ball. I'd watch him when he didn't have the ball. I'd watch him when he came out to warm up. I'd watch him over on the bench. I would watch to see if he was into the game when he wasn't playing. I would watch him when one of his teammates made an error and how he reacted or didn't react to that. I wanted to see if he was a good athlete and if he was supportive.

What you don't want is someone who is very selfish. You want good character in your people. [Former NBA coach] Jeff Van Gundy once said that what you're looking for—in a teammate or a coworker—is that he's competent, reliable, trustworthy, and sincere. And the three S's are the things you don't want in a player: soft, stupid, and selfish.

What kinds of questions would kids ask you about your program when you were recruiting them? What questions showed you that the student-athlete had his priorities in order?

Young people need to know that it's OK to ask about the social life on a college campus. That was one of the questions I rarely received. It was almost like they thought, "If I asked about the social life, the coach might think I wasn't serious about academics or basketball." But that's also part of the college experience, so it's absolutely OK to ask that question.

I always started all of my presentations and conversations with academics. I was always concerned when somebody didn't want to talk about academics to some degree. I was the head coach at Dartmouth, in the Ivy League, and I went into one home where the father said, "Hey coach, you don't need to sell us on the school. We know all about the school. Our older son went to Harvard. So let's just talk about basketball." No red flag went up there, but that was the exception. But if a coach comes into your front room and he starts talking to you and your parents and his first topic is basketball, not academics, you should be somewhat leery about his priorities. I would go as far as to suggest that you say, "Coach, we'll get to basketball, but let's talk about academics."

In an ideal situation, what is the role of the parent in the recruiting process?

I told every recruit, "Your parent loves you. I don't." Your parent should be a sounding board for you. The adults, the parents who love and care about you, should be sounding boards. They may or may not have been through this specific process, but they've been through a lot more life than the kid. The chances are, if something a coach is telling you doesn't sound right, and it doesn't smell right, and it doesn't taste right, it probably isn't right. And the adults hopefully won't have stars in their eyes. The kids might have stars in their eyes, but the parents have to be much more objective. They have to have more distance from it. They can't get caught up in it. They have to listen and if necessary follow up on anything they hear to make sure that it's reasonable and rational.

For example, I got a call from a guy whose son went to a Division I school, and in the recruiting process he was told that he was going to play X number of minutes a game. No coach should ever promise that, because if you're better than the other guy, then you'll play in front of him. If he's better, he'll play in front of you. It's not like summer camp where somebody's sitting on the sidelines with a clock telling the coach, "Player X hasn't played his 10 minutes yet so we have to get him into the game." The coach is trying to win the game. And the parent should have been the one to figure that out ahead of time.

But sometimes you go in there and you can tell the father is living this dream through his son, or he has no clue about how good his son really is. "My son averages 18 points a game, so he's got to be one of the best players in the country." You come out of there with that kind of impression, and then they want to beat up on the high school coach because he's not giving his son enough shots or whatever. No coach wants to get into that with you, because we know that very seldom are you going to be able to make everybody happy.

How about once the student-athlete becomes part of your team: What should the parents' role be then?

I had a young man who played for me who, between his father and his uncle and his high school coach, they thought

I screwed him over for four years. But I was the only one at practice every day with him. And the kid finally came to me one day and said, "Coach, I want you to know that I understand you have been more than fair with me. I've tried to explain it to my father and my uncle and my high school coach, but I know you've been fair." And I told him, "As long as you know that, that's all that matters."

That's the point you have to make with the parents. They need to know that I wouldn't recruit their son if I didn't have an affinity for him. If I didn't think we could get along, or if I had some disdain or dislike for him, I wouldn't have recruited him. So when he gets to my school, he's going to have to play hard, he's going to have to perform, and he's going to have to outplay the other guy if he's going to play in front of the other guy. I will not just give him anything.

Even coaches' families aren't immune to this issue. My son played for me. I didn't recruit him, because I knew I could talk him into coming and I didn't want him to make that decision just because I talked him into it. But when he decided he was going to come, my wife said to me, "Will he start as a freshman?" I said no, and she said, "Well, I'm not sure I'm going to like this." I told her she'd have to learn to like it, because he and I both understood that he had to earn whatever he gets. But parents look at their kid a whole lot differently than a coach does. We all have some blemishes. We all have some strengths and some weaknesses, and at some point the coach has to be satisfied that you're trying to do what he's asking you to do within your capabilities. And the parent may not see that.

How prevalent is negative recruiting in college basketball, and what should student-athletes do if they encounter it?

I don't think every coach does it, but there are some guys who probably think, "We're really close, and I can get the edge by implying that something is going on at the other school, or that they have some deficiencies that we don't have." When that happens, they should turn the tables on the coach. I had someone ask me, "Is it really true that it's seven miles from the front gate at the Air Force Academy to the field house?" And I said, "I will answer that question, but don't you feel a little bit offended that another coach would imply that the distance from the front gate to the field house would be a good enough reason for you to decide not to attend a certain school?" Anytime I was ever asked about another school, I'd say that I didn't know enough about the other schools to talk about them, so I'd talk about my school. I would encourage anybody who encounters negative recruiting to wonder why it's necessary in that situation. I'd be concerned by that approach.

How can student-athletes assess the true day-to-day practices and attitudes of the coaching staff. That is, how can they get an accurate assessment of the program rather than the best-case scenarios that they'll see during a recruiting visit?

They should try, if at all possible, to visit the campus on a normal school day, usually a Friday or a Monday. If they go on a weekend and they see all the pageantry around a football game, and if they don't go to classes or the noon meal, then all they're getting is a snapshot of something that isn't normal. You can arrive on a Thursday night, after you've gone to your high school classes, and you've got 48 hours there, so you've got Friday and Saturday to get a glimpse of a normal school day and the weekend. Also, make sure you tell the coach that on your visit, you'd like to attend a class, and you'd like an academic briefing from someone on the faculty who can talk to you about your area of interest.

How important is your high school grade point average and your academic potential to college coaches?

We've got a new guideline—the Academics Performance Rate (APR)—which is going to get everybody concerned about academics, because if you don't maintain a certain level of progress, your program is going to lose scholarships and the ability to play in the postseason. So if you're a high school athlete, you want to do as well as you possibly can in the classroom because that's going to strengthen your appeal to college programs. If the greatest player in the country is sitting on a 2.1 GPA, he won't be as attractive as a very good player who's sitting on a 3.0, because coaches are not going to be judged just on wins and losses, but also on the APR, so guys are going to have to buckle down.

What should prospective student-athletes look for in a program to ensure that the program will help him maintain a balance between his athletic and academic responsibilities?

I think you have to ask some serious questions. "What kind of academic support do we get? When we travel, do we have tutors who go along on the trip who help us? How do we deal with the rigors of playing Division I basketball with a schedule that may call for 30-plus games, half of which are on the road? How many academic days do we miss, and how do you deal with that?"

11

Istvan Javorek, Strength and Conditioning Coach

Istvan "Steve" Javorek has spent over 21 years as professor of fitness and conditioning head coach for all sports at Johnson County Community College in Overland Park, Kansas. He has a reputation of helping athletes of all levels attain their fitness goals without resorting to unethical methods. He's a member of the USA College of Strength & Conditioning and Missouri Valley Weightlifting Coaches Hall of Fame. He also is a USA Weightlifting Senior International Coach and holds the distinction of being named an Emeritus Coach of Romania. He has also written a book, *Javorek's Complex Conditioning*.

What should a prospective student athlete look for in a good strength/conditioning program?

A good program should be beneficial to the athlete's chosen sport. The goal is to improve both general and specific fitness levels that will enhance their skills. Training should be personalized to help athletes achieve their personal goals. Training should also be imaginative and varied, which prevents monotony. For example, I have found that many athletes respond better to dumbbell training, so one style or form may not work for everyone. So, the end goal is maximum performance, but each athlete may need different emphases to get there. Individual specifics may include body weight changes or improvement in quickness, dexterity, orientation in space, or reaction time. Also, good coaching requires feedback from each athlete. Ask current athletes about some of these concepts.

Studies suggest that a small percentage of sport or strength and conditioning coaches condone, silently accept, or "look the other way" regarding their athletes' use of steroids, testosterone, or human growth hormone to maximize their performance. What advice would you give a prospective student-athlete regarding the use of such or related products?

I do not get involved with coaches suspected of practicing any dubious performance-enhancing methods. I always avoid any connection with anyone who does not believe in clean athletic preparation, as drugs defeat the purpose of college athletics as well as a personal quest to be your best.

From the first minute of contact with a new athlete, I express my strict opinion against performance-enhancing drugs or miraculous pills. I let the athlete know that many products are illegal and if they test positive, they could be prosecuted and suspended. This sends two strong messages to my athletes. First, I am completely against these products and secondly, I have the ability and knowledge to help them improve naturally. I also explain the health risks and what is the healthy alternative of becoming a champion.

Are there any supplements or products for weight or strength gain or weight loss that you consider acceptable, safe, and beneficial to an athlete's strength and conditioning regimen?

I do not recommend any supplements—not creatine, chromium, or other concoctions. Period! No supplement will make you bigger, stronger, or faster. I believe in well-balanced nutrition. This revolves around the nutritionally sound intake of carbohydrates, protein including red meat, fat, water, and plenty of fruits and vegetables. Athletes often forget that many supplements and products result in undesired effects also, which you don't get with natural foods.

How can athletes best achieve good results with hard, intelligent work rather than the use of supplements?

Athletes who perform different variations of a good general fitness program as part of a yearly plan of preparation specific to their sport will improve tremendously. Here at

JCCC when I was coaching Olympic weightlifters, performance boomed and almost every three to four weeks, the US Olympic Committee requested random drug tests. I am proud to say the tests were always negative. The same can be accomplished with college athletes of all levels and sports.

Injury rates are on the rise in many sports. Common examples include ACL tears in females or elbow injuries with throwing sports. How does a good strength program incorporate prevention techniques as well as balance the risk of injury and the need for peak performance?

Athletic injuries are a part of practicing sports or any form of physical activities. However, a good, scientific conditioning program must try to prevent injuries and should be adjusted to each individual athlete's yearly plan of preparation. There are a number of different theories regarding the higher rates of ACL tears in woman athletes. These include possible physical differences, hormonal changes, and training backgrounds. Other injuries can also result from overuse.

As an athlete I recognized that not enough attention was given to the rebuilding of the musculoskeletal system. Adjusting training loads according to each individual's strengths and weaknesses is very critical to injury prevention. This may involve, for example, providing a solid strength base before implementing plyometrics. Good coaching also requires attention to detail. This includes emphasizing perfect body posture, perfect technique in execution, and utilizing a full range of motion. Simply increasing weight without focusing on the above is a recipe for disaster. Often, I begin by teaching an exercise with a broomstick, which emphasizes that form is important. The conditioning coach should evaluate every athlete's skills, flexibility, knowledge of exercise techniques, and family history of sport-related injuries, which could help prevent injuries.

In summary, an organized and continuous conditioning program, which includes appropriately sequenced whole body fitness, agility drills, and plyometrics, will minimize the chances of any injuries. However, in spite of a good and detailed conditioning program, because of unpredictable factors, even well-conditioned athletes develop injuries.

Any other comments that you would like to add from your perspective regarding helping ensure that athletes find an ethical program?

A good strength program, which includes variety; organization on a daily, weekly, monthly, and yearly plan; and a concern for the daily evolution of each individual athlete's physical and psychological condition, can be beneficial and is applicable to every sport. Be drug-free, make sure you learn good technique, and find out if there is guidance for all sports and not just the revenue ones.

THE NCAA: *WHO PROTECTS STUDENT-ATHLETES?* A *PROPOSAL FOR A STUDENT-ATHLETE'S BILL OF RIGHTS*

Legendary retired track and field coach Robert Timmons has spent more than 40 years fighting for student-athletes' rights. As surprising as it might seem, in the United States, student-athletes have very few rights. To bring more attention to this topic, in 2002, Coach Timmons produced a manual, *The NCAA: Who Protects Student-Athletes? A Proposal for a Student-Athlete's Bill of Rights.* Here are a few examples demonstrating how different you as an athlete can be treated compared to other college students who are seeking to fulfill their potential in other endeavors.

1.   If you are a musician or on a college debate or chess team and you decide to transfer to another college, would anyone ask you to sit out a year and prevent you from competing or performing? The NCAA does.

2.   Students are allowed to earn as much or receive as much financial aid allowing them to complete their educations. The NCAA has multiple stipulations on what an athlete can receive.

3.   If a college coach is involved in a breach of divisional rules, the university and athletes are punished. The coach, however, is free to get another job at another university and coach without any consequences.

From *The NCAA: Who Protects Student-Athletes? A Proposal for a Student-Athlete's Bill of Rights,* by Robert Timmons

Right No. 1
Each student-athlete shall have the right to participate in intercollegiate athletics at a member institution

provided the athlete (a) has the talent to compete at the level desired by each team, (b) is in good standing with his or her school and team, (c) follows team, institution, conference, and NCAA rules and regulations, and (d) is academically eligible and otherwise qualified to participate and compete in NCAA-sanctioned events.

Right No. 2
Each student-athlete shall have the right to be governed by a penalty system that (a) protects a student-athlete's participation opportunities if he or she is not charged with violations of NCAA rules, (b) requires every student-athlete to comply with the rules and policies of the NCAA and punishes those who violate its rules, (c) punishes guilty parties commensurate with the severity of the infractions and strives for consistency when penalties are needed, (d) does not impose institutional sanctions that deny participation opportunities for entire sport teams to participate in post-season competition when few or none of the student-athletes are charged with rules violations, and (e) is compatible where possible with the minimum due process standards of the Constitution of the United States.

Right No. 3
Each student-athlete shall have the right to be free from discrimination, including the right to receive benefits and privileges generally available to the institution's students who do not participate in intercollegiate athletics.

Right No. 4
Each student-athlete shall have the right to the establishment of national rules, regulations, and policies that protect the health and safety of the student-athlete, as well as athletic officials, athletic department personnel, and sport spectators.

Right No. 5
Each student-athlete who is otherwise qualified for NCAA competition shall have four years of eligibility

during a consecutive five-year calendar period. Student-athletes classified academically as "non-qualifiers" or "partial-qualifiers" shall be entitled to receive full reinstatement of their fourth year of eligibility if satisfactory progress toward graduation is made by the end of their fourth year of enrollment.

Right No. 6
Each student-athlete shall have the right to NCAA review on a timely and regular basis the number of athletically related financial aid scholarships for student-athletes and an equitable across-the-board award system that is fair and consistent for the student-athletes who compete in each of the sports it sponsors.

Right No. 7
Each student-athlete shall have the right to work and receive earnings up to a full grant plus a reasonable, but limited, amount above that grant for the semester or term.

Right No. 8
Each student-athlete shall have the right to NCAA rules and policies that apply fairly to every student-athlete—in all areas that concern their welfare and participation opportunities.

Right No. 9
Each student-athlete shall have the right to a system of surveillance to deal with unfair rules and policies of coaches' committees or appointed administrators controlling procedures at NCAA national championships or those of conferences affiliated with the Association as they relate to issues concerning the welfare and participation opportunities of student-athletes.

Right No. 10
Each student-athlete shall have the right to periodic reviews of all NCAA rules regarding student-athletes, and the elimination of those that would be held unfair or illegal if subjected to review under constitutional standards of the federal government.

Appendix B

REFOCUSING COLLEGE ATHLETICS: PROPOSALS FOR CHANGE**

Harvard and Yale participated in a student-organized rowing competition in what is believed to be the first intercollegiate competition in 1852. No money, few spectators, no sponsors, and no athletic scholarships. This initial experiment has mushroomed into a multibillion-dollar industry in which athletic activities and athletic departments at many large universities essentially function as independent entities from the university, administration, faculty, and student body. Exceptions include those affiliated with the NCAA Division III, where athletic scholarships are prohibited, and universities affiliated with the NAIA.

Creating an atmosphere in which intercollegiate athletics is congruent with the academic mission is the ethical and practical quandary. The hypocrisy is difficult to overlook when many of the athletes, especially in basketball and football, are of a much lower academic caliber than the rest of the student body. Since the amount of time spent on preparation, training, competition, and travel can easily exceed 30 to 40 hours per week during the season, academics is hardly a priority. Add the exorbitant coaching salaries and perks, as well as frivolous expenses such as chartered airplanes or hotels, even for home games, and it becomes increasingly clear that the "tail wags the dog." Furthermore, scandals involving graduation rates, academic fraud, illicit substances, alcohol, sexual abuse, hazing, and recruiting violations, overshadow the values of fair play and teamwork.

If the goal of sport is to promote positive values and elevate the health and well-being of all students, then recreational opportunities such as intramurals and city leagues should suf-

** Reprinted from *Phi Kappa Phi Forum*, Volume 2 (Fall 2004). Copyright by Ashley Benjamin, M.D., M.A. By permission of the publishers.

fice. The truth is that college athletics provides pre-professional sport training for an elite few, advertising and public relations for the university, and a form of vicarious living for students and community; these things often come at the expense of academic integrity. However, sports may also be the only route for some students to access a college education, which may also boost the diversity of the student body.

Based on our collective experiences, the authors believe that changes need to be made at multiple levels in order to uphold the ideal of athletics as well as promote a functional, healthy relationship between student-athletes, colleges, and athletic programs. The following multilevel interventions, which address the business of big-time college athletics, would ensure that intercollegiate sport espouses the values consistent with an academic setting.

I. **Professional Sports:** Imagine being told that you have to dunk a basketball in order to practice as a professor! Sounds ludicrous but college sports often are the only way for many high school athletes to hone their talents. All professional sports organizations should take a cue from sports such as baseball or tennis, which have incorporated minor leagues for up-and-coming players without scholastic aspirations. Other options utilized by much of the world include specialized sport schools and a vibrant club system.

II. **Governing Bodies:** These include the NCAA, NAIA, and the NJCAA. Limiting discussion to the NCAA, the connection between winning and monetary rewards needs to be severed. The NCAA is notorious for focusing on graduation rates but turns a blind eye to the business of sport, in which the NCAA has a huge interest. Since all three organizations espouse competition as an end in itself, winning schools should not be rewarded monetarily as this is partially what drives the enormous expenses, cheating, and related abuse of student-athletes. A simple solution is to divide the money based on participation in the NCAA or to create a formula based on school size or conference. Therefore, winning national titles or qualifying for tournaments would not be financially lucrative.

III. **Universities:** College presidents are in a difficult position. They may privately believe that academics come first, but they also appreciate two truisms: that universities are big businesses and that the majority of alumni are not interested in the academic mission of the university. Vanderbilt University, Northern Iowa, and Jacksonville University have made courageous changes by subsuming the athletic departments under the Department of Physical Education, which allows the university to dictate policy and control revenues. For example, under the direction of the department it may be decided that it is wiser to spend $1 million on a recreational center that will help 20,000 students get fit, than to spend the money on a specialized athletic center that will benefit only a few hundred student-athletes. Finally, if the NCAA is unwilling to change, universities of good conscience (and that have low athletic budgets or are tired of the "rat race" of spending more money for more impressive facilities and higher paid coaches) may consider forming an alternate association run by universities that ensures the academic mission is fulfilled.

IV. **Athletic Departments:** The University of California, San Marcos emphasizes "life-time" sports, or sports where student-athletes continue to be life-long participants. Examples include running, tennis, and golf. This philosophy should be a role model for all universities. Rethinking of priorities is necessary as monetary excesses as discussed above could be utilized toward non-revenue programs or other college related funding. Interestingly, students who are involved in non-revenue sports tend to have higher graduation rates than the general student population. Also, athletes should graduate with meaningful degrees and of their own choosing. This eliminates any athletic department pressures to steer student-athletes toward majors in order to simply maintain eligibility or a higher team grade point average. Finally, athletic directors with known involvement in unethical or illegal activities should be banned from college athletics for a significant period of time.

V. Coaches: Big-time coaches are essentially professional coaches as defined by their exorbitant salaries and amount of time spent toward one goal: winning. Coaches need to be a part of the teaching faculty as occurs with smaller division sports. This may also decrease some of the emphasis on recruiting violations, as their job security will not be based on winning. Also, coaches guilty of academic or ethical breaches should be barred from coaching at another university for a designated period of time, which would be infraction dependent. Under current policy, the university and the athletes suffer the consequences. Yet, another athletic program can hire the culprit without any penalty. Another approach would be to penalize any university that hires a coach who is moving simply to avoid infractions that he or she was involved with. Examples such as no post-season play or loss of future scholarships would result in the hiring university "thinking twice."

VI. Student-Athletes: First, changes need to be made at all levels to reflect that student-athletes are students first. Practice times, including all the ancillary involvement, needs to be pared down. Second, schedules need to reflect the priority of academics. Examples of this include decreasing the competitive seasons in some sports by one-third. There is no reason that a basketball team needs to play more than 30 games when a 20-game season would suffice. Along this line, eliminate competition during the school week or limit the travel distances allowed during the week. Another drastic step would be to redraw conferences based on proximity.

As discussed in Appendix A, student athletes need the same rights as any other student. For example, if a student desires to transfer and compete for another college, he or she is ineligible for the next season. Envision telling a debater or musician that they cannot participate because they decided that switching schools was in their best interest. Furthermore, the university or coach can terminate that athlete's contract on a year-to-year basis yet the expectation is that the athlete should commit for their collegiate careers. This is just one example of how student-athletes are treated differently than other students. See Appendix A for more details on this topic.

VII. **Alumni:** Unfortunately, many remain connected to the university only through athletics. Contrary to public opinion, contributors to academic facilities or the general scholarship fund do not base their decisions to donate based on athletic success. In fact, many universities with the biggest alumni donations are not athletically prominent. Alumni gifts should go to a general university fund, where a portion of this can be earmarked for athletics. The connection between alumni donations and a race to building the biggest athletic complexes is truly a recipe for financial institutional disaster.

We are sure there are multiple legal, financial, and political reasons why the status quo will be maintained. However, if we want to eliminate the hypocrisy and unethical aspects of college sports and stay true to the vision of athletics within the auspices of an academic setting, the above could go a long ways to rectifying our present unethical situation. There are many other suggestions for reform. If interested, look at suggestions made by the Drake Group as well as the Carnegie Foundation; both Web sites are listed in the reference section.

ONLINE RESOURCES FOR STUDENT-ATHLETES

With the advent of the Internet, access to information as well as the latest changes is easily obtained. Divisional rules, especially on recruiting, are in constant flux and no book can keep pace with these changes. Therefore, we include an online resources section that allows you to keep up with the most recent developments. In addition, we have included Web sites pertinent to many of the topics discussed in the book. Finally, we have added some supplemental sites to help you with your overall preparation for college.

Collegiate Associations

California Community College Athletic Association (CCCAA)
http://www.coasports.org

Canadian Interuniversity Sport (CIS)
http://www.universitysport.ca

Canadian Colleges Athletic Association (CCAA)
http://www.ccaa.ca

National Association of Intercollegiate Athletics (NAIA)
http://www.naia.org

National Christian College Athletic Association (NCCAA)
http://www.thenccaa.org

National Collegiate Athletic Association (NCAA)
http://www.ncaa.com
http://www.ncaa.org

National Junior College Athletic Association (NJCAA)
http://www.njcaa.org

College Planning Resources

The College Board
Includes information about test prep, applications, essays, and interview tips.
http://www.collegeboard.com

College Parents of America

A national association serving the parents and families of college students.

http://www.collegeparents.org/cpa/index.html

CollegeScholarships.org

http://www.collegescholarships.org

The Common Application

https://www.commonapp.org/CommonApp/default.aspx

eCampusTours.com

Take an online tour of more than 1,200 campuses!

http://www.ecampustours.com

Federal Work-Study Program

http://www.ed.gov/programs/fws/index.html

FinAid

http://www.finaid.org

Free Application for Federal Student Aid (FAFSA)

http://www.fafsa.ed.gov

NCAA Scholarships

http://www.ncaa.org/wps/ncaa?ContentID=1085

Student Aid on the Web

http://studentaid.ed.gov

U.S. Department of Education Grant Programs

http://www.ed.gov/programs/find/title/index.html?src=ov

U.S. News and World Report: America's Best Colleges

http://colleges.usnews.rankingsandreviews.com/college

Issues in College Life and Athletics/Sport Reform

Alfred University Hazing Study

http://www.alfred.edu/sports_hazing/introduction.cfm

American Academy of Neurology

http://www.aan.com

American College Health Association

http://www.acha.org

American College of Sports Medicine

http://www.acsm.org

American Council on Education
http://www.acenet.edu

American Heart Association
http://www.americanheart.org

American Indian Higher Education Consortium
http://www.aihec.org

Anabolic Steroid Abuse
http://www.steroidabuse.org

Black Coaches Association
http://bcasports.cstv.com/scholarships/bca-scholarships.html

Black Excel
http://blackexcel.org

Campus Pride
A national organization for Lesbian, Gay, Bisexual, and Transgender campus groups.
http://www.campuspride.org

Campus Safety
http://www.ope.ed.gov/security

The Carnegie Foundation
http://www.carnegiefoundation.org

The Center for the Study of Sport in Society
http://www.sportinsociety.org

Chronicle of Higher Education
http://chronicle.com

The Drake Group
http://www.thedrakegroup.org

Disabled Sports USA
http://www.dsusa.org

Equity in Athletics Data Analysis (EADA)
http://ope.ed.gov/athletics

Healthy Minds.org—College Mental Health
http://www.healthyminds.org/collegementalhealth.cfm

Higher Education Center for Alcohol and Other Drug Abuse and Violence Prevention
http://www.higheredcenter.org

The Institute for Preventative Sports Medicine (IPSM)
http://www.ipsm.org

LD Online: College and College Prep
Contains information on college preparation and adjustment for students with learning disabilities.
http://www.ldonline.org/indepth/college

Gay & Lesbian Alliance Against Defamation
http://www.glaad.org

Government Accountability Office
http://www.gao.gov

National Athletic Trainers' Association
http://www.nata.org

National Center for Lesbian Rights
http://www.nclrights.org

National Coalition Against Violent Athletes
http://www.ncava.org

The National College Players Association
http://www.cacnow.org

Native American Sports Council
http://www.nascsports.org

Student Athletes Rights
http://www.studentathletesrights.org

Stop Hazing
http://www.stophazing.org

Substance Abuse and Sport
http://www.higheredcenter.org

Test of English as a Foreign Language (TOEFL)
http://www.toeflgoanywhere.org

The Women's College Coalition
http://www.womenscollege.org

Women's Sports Foundation
http://www.womenssportsfoundation.org

INDEX

Note: Page numbers followed by *f* and *t*
indicated figures and tables, respectively.

ABOUT THE AUTHORS

Ashley B. Benjamin, M.D., M.A. holds a B.S. in journalism from the University of Kansas, an M.A. in exercise physiology/physical education from The Ohio State University, and an M.D. from Kansas University Medical School. Dr. Benjamin is a sport psychiatrist, a former graduate assistant college track and cross-country coach, a former high school assistant track coach, and an exercise physiologist. He lives in Newbury Park, California.

Michael Cauthen received his B.A. from Alfred University and his M.S. in anthropology from Purdue University. Cauthen is a former Division I assistant track and field and cross-country coach who was heavily involved in the recruiting process. He presently lectures at the University of North Carolina at Greensboro.

Patrick Donnelly holds a B.A. in English from the University of Minnesota. Donnelly is an experienced sports journalist who has covered high school, college, and professional sports. He is also a former high school baseball coach. He is currently a freelance sportswriter based in Las Vegas, Nevada.